The Prose Style of
Samuel Johnson

The Prose Style

of

Samuel Johnson

BY

W. K. WIMSATT, JR.

ARCHON BOOKS
1972

Copyright 1941 by Yale University Press
Reprinted 1972 with permission in an unaltered
and unabridged edition as an Archon Book by
The Shoe String Press, Inc.
Hamden, Connecticut 06514

[*Yale Studies in English*, Volume 94]

ISBN 0-208-01141-2
Library of Congress catalog card number 78-179568

Printed in the United States of America

TO

MY MOTHER AND FATHER

PREFACE

A STUDY of the style of Samuel Johnson, as many of these pages will betray, is by no means a novelty. Within a few years of his death his style was the subject of an able treatise by the Reverend Robert Burrowes of the Royal Irish Academy; innumerable minor voices were ready to continue the discussion, and by the end of the eighteenth century Johnson's style had become an established topic of literary history. Since then it has been noticed successively by such eminent critics as Hazlitt, Coleridge, Macaulay, Arnold, Stephen, and Raleigh. The special contribution of the twentieth century has been the scientific or investigative technique. After Heinrich Schmidt's inaugural dissertation at Marburg in 1905 come the statistical compilations of Taylor, Chandler, and others. Johnson's style, after more than a century of metaphorical treatment, both affectionate and splenetic, is at length reduced to its literalities, defined and tabulated. Probably the style of no other English prose author has received so much attention.

Chapters I to V, a greater part of this study, are not devoted to the discovery of any new facts—if indeed any study of style may be said to discover facts. Aside from an advantage in consulting the earlier critics (an honor that few of them have accorded one another) and in surveying Johnson's style more comprehensively than others have done, I find my justification a philosophic one. That is, there is no quarrel with the terms that have been used to describe Johnson's style except that often they have referred to the right things only in the most nominal way. They have been used so as to indicate with sufficient justice what parts of Johnson's writing are to be considered characteristic, but not so as to describe these characteristic parts with relevance to the general science of verbal style. Such is the purpose of my first four chapters: to attach certain critical terms to parts of Johnson's rhetoric, to carry on a discussion of this rhetoric univocally and with relevance to general conclusions about Johnson's style as a medium of expression—and so to reach a clearer notion not only of the expression but of the mind from which it proceeded.

An unavoidable result has been that some of the most frequently employed terms, while borrowed from previous criticism, have assumed new meanings. Some of the chapters may be accused of relying on a specially created technical vocabulary. It was in anticipation of this that an Introduction was written, an airing of views on the whole problem of style and an explanation of the method assumed in the argument which follows.

Chapters VI and VII employ the conceptions of Johnson's style already constructed, but are a departure in an investigative direction. While Johnson's style itself has been the topic of many previous critics, Johnson's theory of style has been somewhat slighted. The great body of Johnson's critical utterances, both in conversation and in writing, his honesty of opinion, and his persistency in pronouncement make possible a rather detailed account of some of his principles of composition. The collecting of critical utterances is of course a matter not only of investigation—reading a body of works—but of interpretation—recognizing the relation of given statements to the whole question of style and to one another. Not every available passage will contain such a tell-tale word as "style" or "composition," or any more specific term of rhetoric. I believe that I have not only made a rich collection of Johnson's statements relevant to a theory of composition but have succeeded in arranging the fragments partially into a system and in establishing a relation between this system and Johnson's actual practice. The last must be the ultimate aim in the study of a writer's theory, for his theory and his writing are but different manifestations of the same thing, a preference, and if a writer is aware of his preference and is honest, his expressed theory should somehow square with his practice.

Chapters VIII and IX venture only to touch upon a vast investigative field. A study of style need not involve historical considerations but can find its complement in them. What the antecedents of Johnson's style were, and what its effects on English writing, are questions which one may relate, more or less closely, to the question what Johnson's style *is*. There may even be some who prefer to define Johnson's style in terms of its antecedents and to judge its importance by its effects. A study such as the present may properly conclude with some gesture of respect for this other subject, the historical—a tentative indication where the history of Johnson's style may be explored.

It is a pleasure to express my thanks to Professors F. A. Pottle and C. B. Tinker, the directors of the dissertation from which this study is taken; to Professors R. J. Menner and J. M. Berdan, who read long parts of the first draft; and to Professor B. C. Nangle, who read the whole manuscript just before it went to press.

And I wish to thank especially my Johnsonian friends Allen Hazen and George Lam, by whose conversation I have been from day to day instructed and encouraged.

For assistance of various other kinds I wish to thank Mr. Harold B.

Allen, Mr. M. C. Beardsley, Mr. C. H. Bennett, Mr. C. B. Bradford, Professor J. L. Clifford, Mr. P. B. Daghlian, Mr. A. S. Daley, Mr. R. W. Daniel, Mrs. D. M. Gray, Mr. J. H. Hagstrum, Professor F. W. Hilles, Mr. L. L. Martz, Mr. J. M. Osborn, Mr. W. H. Smith, and Professor Karl Young.

The work was begun while I held a Penfield Fellowship from the Catholic University of America.

W. K. W., Jr.

Silliman College, Yale University,
   January, 1941.

Euripides
Says that he'll make a survey, word by word.

The Frogs

CONTENTS

CUE TITLES

BP *Private Papers of James Boswell from Malahide Castle,* ed. Geoffrey Scott and Frederick A. Pottle, Mount Vernon, N.Y., 1928–34. 18 vols.

Burrowes Robert Burrowes, "Essay on the Stile of Doctor Samuel Johnson," *Transactions of the Royal Irish Academy,* Vol. I, Dublin, 1787, "Polite Literature," pp. 27–56. Cf. *post* p. 59, n. 31.

Chandler Zilpha E. Chandler, *An Analysis of the Stylistic Technique of Addison, Johnson, Hazlitt, and Pater,* "University of Iowa Humanistic Studies," Vol. IV, No. 3, Iowa City, 1928.

Christie O. F. Christie, *Johnson the Essayist,* London, 1924.

Courtney William P. Courtney, *A Bibliography of Samuel Johnson,* Oxford, 1915.

Dictionary Samuel Johnson, *A Dictionary of the English Language,* 6th ed., London, 1785. 2 vols.

Howe *The Complete Works of William Hazlitt,* ed. P. P. Howe, London, 1930–34. 21 vols.

Letters *Letters of Samuel Johnson, LL.D.,* ed. George B. Hill, New York, 1892. 2 vols.

Life James Boswell, *Life of Johnson,* ed. George B. Hill and L. F. Powell, Vols. I–IV, Oxford, 1934; ed. George B. Hill, Vols. V–VI, Oxford, 1887.

Lives Samuel Johnson, *Lives of the English Poets,* ed. George B. Hill, Oxford, 1905. 3 vols.

Misc. *Johnsonian Miscellanies,* ed. George B. Hill, Oxford, 1897. 2 vols.

Morley *The Spectator,* ed. Henry Morley, London, 1891.

Schmidt Heinrich Schmidt, *Der Prosastil Samuel Johnson's,* Marburg, 1905.

Taylor Warner Taylor, "The Prose Style of Johnson," *University of Wisconsin Studies in Language and Literature,* No. 2 (*Studies by Members of the Department of English*), Madison, 1918, pp. 22–56.

Works Samuel Johnson, *Works,* Vols. I–XI, ed. John Hawkins, London, 1787; Vols. XII–XIII, London, 1787; Vol. XIV, London, 1788. Cf. *Courtney,* pp. 161–2.

Volume I contains the *Life* of Johnson by Hawkins. I have chosen this text as convenient and sufficiently accurate for my purpose. In his Cornell doctoral dissertation, *Johnson's Lives of the Poets* (1938), George L. Lam reports that the text of the *Lives of the Poets* in this edition is superior to that in all later editions of the *Lives* except that of Mrs. Alexander Napier, 1890, and superior to that in all later editions of the collected works, including that published by Pickering in 1825 (pp. 242–87). For the text of the *Rambler,* see *post* Appendix B.

INTRODUCTION

Style as Meaning

BETWIXT the formation of words and that of thought there is this difference," said Cicero, "that that of the words is destroyed if you change them, that of the thoughts remains, whatever words you think proper to use." [1] This is a clear statement of the view of style and meaning which today may be conveniently called "the ornamental." The ancient rhetoricians all seem to have something like this in mind.[2] They may stress the need of meaning, or may in their metaphysics insist on the interdependence of matter and form, but when they reach the surface of meaning, the plane of most detailed organization, they are not able to speak so as to connect this with meaning. It is as if, when all is said for meaning, there remains an irreducible something that is superficial, a kind of scum—which they call style. One may consult as representative the whole treatment of rhetorical figures in Quintilian's *Institute*.

There is the opposite theory of style, one that has been growing on us since the seventeenth century. "So many *things*, almost in an equal number of *words*," says Sprat.[3] And Pascal, "La vraie éloquence se moque de l'éloquence." [4] And somewhat later Swift, "Proper words in proper places, make the true definition of a style"; [5] and Buffon, "Style is simply the order and movement one gives to one's thoughts." [6] By the nineteenth century the doctrine is proclaimed on every hand—very explicitly, for example, by Cardinal Newman:

1. *De Oratore*, III, lii, in *Cicero on Oratory and Orators*, ed. J. S. Watson (New York, 1890), p. 252.

2. Cf. Benedetto Croce, *Aesthetic as Science of Expression and General Linguistic*, trans. Douglas Ainslee (London, 1929), pp. 422–9.

3. Thomas Sprat, *History of the Royal Society* (London, 1702), p. 113. Cf. Richard F. Jones, "Science and English Prose Style in the Third Quarter of the Seventeenth Century," *PMLA*, XLV (1930), 977–1009.

4. *Pensées*, VII, 34, ed. Ernest Havet (Paris, 1866), Vol. I, p. 106; cf. VII, 28, *op. cit.*, Vol. I, p. 105.

5. *A Letter to a Young Clergyman, Lately Entered into Holy Orders*, 1721, *Prose Works*, ed. Temple Scott (London, 1898), III, 200–01.

6. *An Address Delivered Before the French Academy* [generally known as the *Discours sur le Style*], 1753, in Lane Cooper, *Theories of Style* (New York, 1907), p. 171. This, rather than the too-often-quoted "The style is the man," is Buffon's real definition of style—a point well taken by W. C. Brownell, *The Genius of Style* (New York, 1924), p. 46.

> Thought and speech are inseparable from each other. Matter and expression are parts of one: style is a thinking out into language. . . . When we can separate light and illumination, life and motion, the convex and the concave of a curve . . . then will it be conceivable that the . . . intellect should renounce its own double.[7]

In one of the best books on style to appear in our own day, Mr. Middleton Murry has said:

> Style is not an isolable quality of writing; it is writing itself.[8]

It is hardly necessary to adduce proof that the doctrine of identity of style and meaning is today firmly established. This doctrine is, I take it, one from which a modern theorist hardly can escape, or hardly wishes to.

The chief difficulty with the modern doctrine of style lies in its application to rhetorical study. The difficulty appears in two ways: partly in the implicit abandonment of the doctrine when rhetorical study is attempted, but more largely in a wide, silent rejection of the whole system of rhetoric. "We have done with the theory of style," proclaims an eminent critic in Crocean vein, "with metaphor, simile, and all the paraphernalia of Graeco-Roman rhetoric."[9] Now it must be contended that we have not done with "metaphor" —that we still have an important use for the term.[10] But for scarcely any other term of rhetoric have we better than a shrug. We no longer are willing to take seriously a set of terms which once—for centuries—were taken seriously, and which must, no matter how unhappy their use, have stood for something. In throwing away the terms it is even possible we have thrown away all definite concept

---

7. "Literature, a Lecture in the School of Philosophy and Letters," 1858, in *The Idea of a University* (London, 1907), pp. 276–7. In Lane Cooper's *Theories of Style* one may conveniently find similar expressions by Coleridge, Wackernagel, De Quincey, Schopenhauer, Lewes, Pater, and Brunetière (esp. pp. 10, 207, 222–3, 252, 320, 391, 399, 401, 422). See also *Pensées de J. Joubert*, ed. Paul Raynal (Paris, 1888), II, 275–8, Titre XXII, paragraphs IX–XXV; August Boeckh, *Encyklopädie und Methodologie der Philologischen Wissenschaften* (Leipzig, 1886), p. 128.

For the opposite way of thinking, see William Minto, *Manual of English Prose Literature* (Edinburgh and London, 1881) (first published in 1872), Introduction, pp. 14–15; George Saintsbury, "Modern English Prose," 1876, in *Miscellaneous Essays* (London, 1892), pp. 83, 84, 99.

8. J. Middleton Murry, *The Problem of Style* (Oxford, 1922), p. 77; cf. pp. 16, 71. Cf. Walter Raleigh, *Style* (London, 1897), esp. p. 62; Herbert Read, *English Prose Style* (London, 1932), *passim*. Mr. Logan Pearsall Smith would probably admit that the rich and poetic prose for which he pleads is as much a matter of expression as the plainest (*S.P.E. Tract No. XLVI, Fine Writing* [Oxford, 1936], esp. pp. 203, 220). For a cross-section of opinion from modern professional writers, see Burges Johnson, *Good Writing* (Syracuse University, 1932).

9. J. E. Spingarn, *Creative Criticism* (New York, 1917), p. 30.

10. Cf. *post* p. 11.

of the things they once stood for. The realities of antithesis and climax, for example, are perhaps less and less a part of our consciousness. But literary history without these old realities and their old terms is impossible; without an evaluation of them it is superficial. The fact is that Cicero used "figures" of this and that sort— moreover, he wrote criticism about them. Hooker and Donne and Johnson used such figures too. And the old terms when used to describe these old writings do mean something. We cannot avoid admitting that we recognize certain things as denoted by the terms, that we know the nominal definitions. Furthermore, we are not ready to call Cicero and the rest simply bad writers. We may insist, and properly, that the accounts they give of their devices, their theories of rhetoric, are insufficient—even baneful as guides to composition; as for the living use they made of what they called "devices," their actual saying of things, in this we see that their intuition was better than their theory.

ii

ANY discourse about a definition of "style" is fruitless if it concerns itself too simply with protesting: style *is this* or *is that*. Definitions are impervious to the "lie direct," mere "intrenchant air" for the sword of evidence. The only reason a term *should* mean something is the history of its application, the fact that it *has* meant something. We may say that dubious terms have a kind of repertoire of related meanings. But the meaning of a term in a given instance is what any man decides to make it, and if I dislike what he makes it, I may not tell him he is mistaken.

Nevertheless I may dislike it, and justly. This is the problem in facing definitions—that they do often bother us as bad definitions and make us wish vehemently to reject them. The basis for our uneasiness is ultimately one of relevance, relevance of a definition to the principles of the whole science of which the term is accepted as a part. If there is not a fixed real meaning for a term, there is at least an ideal one, a something to which the term *should* refer if it is to be used in its science without producing nonsense. It is the purpose of definition to determine *what* is referred to, and the business of him who formulates a definition to determine what *should be* referred to, as most relevant to the presiding science. The first step toward forming a definition, a theory, of "style" must be taken in the science of literary esthetics, more specifically in a consideration of the nature of words as esthetic medium.

It is the nature of words to mean. To consider words only as sounds, like drum taps, or to consider written letters as patterned objects, as in alphabet soup, is the same as to consider a Stradivarius as material for kindling wood. There is, to be sure, a certain truth in the contention that it is useless to speak of the limits of each art. If a painter of abstractions succeeded in conveying a concept which he described as rhythmic, it would be pointless to contend that such a concept should properly be expressed in music. Insofar as the painting did succeed as an expression, there would simply be *that* expression. On the other hand, even Croce will admit that different artistic intuitions need different media for their "externalization." [11] Even when the various media are considered as forming a continuum, a spectrum, one point in the spectrum is not another point. Red is not green. Stone is not B flat. Stone can be used for a statue; B flat cannot. Words can be used to "mean" in a way that nothing else can. In various senses the other arts may be called expressive or communicative. But it is not in any such senses that words are expressive. When Maritain says that "music *imitates* with sound and rhythms . . . the movements of the soul," [12] and when Dewey says that architecture " 'expresses' . . . enduring values of collective human life," [13] they are speaking of the kind of representation we should speak of if we said that the images of autumn, nightfall, and a dying fire in Shakespeare's sonnet stand for his sense of mortality, or if we said that the whole poem is a symbol of his sense of mortality. While the music and the architecture *are* the symbols of what they represent, the words of a writing must *express* a meaning which *is* a symbol. "A poem should not mean But be," writes Mr. Archibald MacLeish. But a poem cannot *be* in the simple sense that a statue or a piece of Venetian glass *is*. For each thing insofar as it *is*, must *be*, have *being*, according to its nature. The nature of words is to mean, and a poem *is* through its meaning.

There are such things as the Caroline shape poems, the winged or altar shapes of Herbert or Quarles; there are the typographical oddities of E. E. Cummings. There are illuminated manuscripts or illustrated books, Gothic books of Gospels, arabesque texts of the Koran on mosque walls. And people may even have wondered

11. Benedetto Croce, *op. cit.*, pp. 114–16. Cf. C. K. Ogden *et al.*, *The Foundations of Aesthetics* (London, 1925), p. 28; David Daiches, *The Place of Meaning in Poetry* (Edinburgh, 1935), esp. pp. 30, 61–3.

12. Jacques Maritain, *Art and Scholasticism*, trans. J. F. Scanlan (London, 1930), p. 58.

13. John Dewey, *Art as Experience* (New York, 1934), p. 221. Cf. Gilbert Murray, "An Essay on the Theory of Poetry," *Yale Review*, x (1921), 484; Theodore M. Greene, *The Arts and the Art of Criticism* (Princeton, 1940), esp. p. 108.

what they ought to think of Cummings. But nobody thinks that the Gospel suffers when not read in the Book of Kells. It is clear that in the case of illuminations and illustrations of a text there is not a single art expression, but two running side by side. Words, music, costume, and stage may make one expression in an opera; the poetry of Vachel Lindsay read aloud and the accompanying dance may have made one expression; it may be possible to conceive a text so referred to and interrelated with a series of pictures that the two make one expression.[14] Yet it remains true that what we call literature, whether prose or poetry, has not been a graphic medium. It has not been possible or worth while to employ words in this way.

But language is spoken before it is written; even after it is written it is implicitly spoken; and language as sound has potentialities far beyond those of language as written or visual.[15] Sound is in some sense the medium of literature, no matter how words are considered as expressive. What is more questionable is how near this medium ever can come to being that of music. Sound in its conventional semantic value is certainly not a musical medium. Further it is not musical in its whole complex of suggestive or directly imitative values, onomatopoeia, and all the more mysteriously felt shades of sound propriety.[16]

A more difficult problem of sound in literature is that of meter and such associates as rhyme and alliteration. But it is usual to insist that these elements of verse are in some way expressive. They express the emotion of poetic experience; or, by inducing in us a pattern of expectancy and playing against that the surprise of variation, they make us realize more intensely both sense and emotion.[17] Or, the verse of a whole poem may be considered as a form, an aspect or way of being known, which gives unity and particu-

14. Mr. Archibald MacLeish's *Land of the Free* (New York, 1938) is "a book of photographs illustrated by a poem. . . . The original purpose had been to write some sort of text to which these photographs might serve as commentary. But so great was the power and the stubborn inward livingness of these vivid American documents that the result was a reversal of that plan" (p. 89).

15. Cf. Otto Jespersen, *Language, Its Nature, Development and Origin* (London, 1922), *passim;* D. W. Prall, *Aesthetic Judgment* (New York, 1929), pp. 289–90.

16. Many of these values, as a matter of fact, are not, as has been commonly thought, due to any direct expressiveness of sounds but rather to linguistic analogies as ancient as the roots of language (Leonard Bloomfield, *Language* [New York, 1933] pp. 244–5; I. A. Richards, *The Philosophy of Rhetoric* [New York, 1936], pp. 63–5). For a treatment of word sounds as suggestive of or appropriate to meaning, see Otto Jespersen, *Language* (London, 1922), pp. 396–406.

17. Cf. I. A. Richards, *Principles of Literary Criticism* (New York, 1934), "Rhythm and Metre," pp. 137–42. It may be too that meter has a hypnotic function. See Edward D. Snyder, *Hypnotic Poetry* (Philadelphia, 1930), pp. 19, 39 ff.

larity to the whole—makes it the special poetic symbol that it is.[18] It may be possible to say that this second kind of expressiveness is on the same level as that of music and architecture mentioned above, a direct symbol of experience. But in this case it will be necessary to remember that the expression of the verse coalesces with and is in effect the same as that of the words in their semantic function.

Here we might let the question of language as sound medium rest were it not for the persistent appearance of the mysterious critical term "prose rhythm." From what has been said of verse it is plain that a prose rhythm is conceivable—that is, some alternation of sounds akin to meter, though more variable. If such a succession of sounds could be detected with certainty in any body of prose, and if one had no sense that this was unconnected with the meaning or detracted from it, then it would have to be admitted that in the given case a prose rhythm as an expressive medium did exist. The general question, then, is not whether there *can* be a prose rhythm but whether there *is*. And a particular question, such as that concerning English literature, is but the general question narrowed—whether there *is*. Certain things may be asserted: I. The rhetoricians of antiquity found in Greek and Latin oratory a rhythm which they analyzed almost as definitely as verse meter, particularly in the sequence of syllables ending clauses, the cursus.[19] II. The cursus was also a part of Medieval Latin prose.[20] III. There are some who hold that variations of the cursus occur in English prose.[21] IV. There is, however, no agreement, but the widest divergence of opinion, among those who have made extended studies of the nature of rhythm in English prose. Their number is not small (and each is at odds in some respect with almost all the others): those who would scan, or make meter; those who are interested in some vaguer kind of periodicity, time measurement;

18. Cf. Lascelles Abercrombie, *Principles of English Prosody* (London, 1923), pp. 15–18, 31; *The Theory of Poetry* (New York, 1926), pp. 70, 95, 138, 140–6.

19. See, for example, John W. Sandys, *A Companion to Latin Studies* (Cambridge, 1921), p. 655. François Novotný, *État Actuel des Études sur le Rhythme de la Prose Latine* (Livów, 1929), sees "un bel avenir dans notre science," but confesses: "Ces essais et leur résultats dépendent bien souvent du sentiment esthétique subjectif de l'observateur" (p. 33).

20. See, for example, Karl Strecker, *Introduction à l'Étude du Latin Médiéval*, trad. par Paul van der Woestijne (Gand, 1933), pp. 51–3; Edouard Norden, *Die Antike Kunstprosa* (Leipzig, 1898), II, 950–1.

21. See, for example, Oliver Elton, "English Prose Numbers," *Essays and Studies by Members of the English Association*, IV (Oxford, 1913), 29–54; Morris W. Croll, "The Cadence of English Oratorical Prose," *Studies in Philology*, XVI (1919), 1–55.

those who rely on the cursus; and those who find rhythm in the movement of phrases.[22]

It would be within the province only of a very special investigation to dare say what English prose rhythm *is*. And I have admitted above that the question is not whether there *can* be a prose rhythm. Yet there are some things that can be said about the possibilities of prose rhythm. If it is a quality of sound, it is either expressive of something or not. If not (if, say, it is like the number of times the letter "t" occurs on a given page), it is not a medium of art and therefore claims no interest; it is not in fact prose rhythm at all. Secondly, if it is expressive, it expresses either the same meaning as the words do otherwise, or it does not. If it expresses the same meaning, it may, like meter, express perhaps from the same level as words do otherwise, perhaps from a level more like that of music. These possibilities are admissible.[23] But thirdly, if it expresses other than the same meaning, then it must express some meaning which is proper to nonverbal sounds—some kind of musical meaning. This is perhaps conceivable, that words should do two separate things, convey their language meaning, and at the same time be a nonlinguistic tune—perhaps even harmonious with the language meaning. This, however, seems improbable in view of the limited musical value of spoken word sounds. It is, like the pictorial value of print in typographical poems, very slight.[24] Music is not written in words, but in tones and time.

The notion of a separate music is further crippled if we consider that it is impossible for any system of sound in prose to be

22. Cf. John Hubert Scott, *Rhythmic Prose*, "University of Iowa Humanistic Studies," Vol. III, No. 1 (Iowa City, 1925), p. 11. Norton R. Tempest, a more recent writer, is a scanner and at the same time belongs to the cursus school (*The Rhythm of English Prose* [Cambridge University Press, 1930], p. 134). André Classe is a timer with a kymograph, who proposes "only . . . to investigate the question of rhythm from the phonetic point of view" (*The Rhythm of English Prose* [Oxford, 1939], pp. 1, 4, 135). Such investigation doubtless does discover physical facts, but just as phoneticians distinguish between the gross acoustic quality of words and that part of the acoustic quality which has semantic value, so literary students may distinguish between the gross discoverable physical facts about "rhythm" and that part of the facts which relates to expression. Professor Sapir has distinguished between the phonetic and the esthetic analysis of rhythm ("The Musical Foundations of Verse," *Journal of English and Germanic Philology*, XX [1921], 223–4).

23. Under this head, rather than under what follows, should be considered meter in prose, in Dickens, for example. Here there is a linguistic expressiveness, just as in poetry, but not a coalescence, as in poetry, with the rest of the meaning of the words. Cf. *post* pp. 10–11, what I call "bad style." For some flagrant examples of meter in prose, see H. W. and F. G. Fowler, *The King's English* (Oxford, 1906), p. 295.

24. Cf. D. W. Prall, *Aesthetic Judgment* (New York, 1929), pp. 289, 295; *Aesthetic Analysis* (New York, 1936), pp. 105–6.

unconnected with its meaning—that is, neither contribute to it nor detract from it. Suppose a man to be writing a double composition, both prose and music; then in the use of any given piece of language he must, consciously or unconsciously, choose for the meaning or for the music. (It is impossible that two such disconnected effects should often coincide.) Or, to change the sense of "must," he must choose for the meaning and sacrifice the music, for the meaning of words is their nature, while the music of words is negligible. "In the vast majority of those words which can be said to have an independent musical value," says Mr. Middleton Murry, "the musical suggestion is at odds with the meaning. When the musical suggestion is allowed to predominate, decadence of style has begun." [25]

Let me close this part of the discussion by indicating my own notion of what ought to be called prose rhythm—if something must be called that. The notion has been well expressed by H. W. Fowler: "A sentence or a passage is rhythmical if, when said aloud, it falls naturally into groups of words each well fitted by its length & intonation for its place in the whole & its relation to its neighbors. Rhythm is not a matter of counting syllables & measuring the distance between accents." [26] Prose rhythm is a matter of emphasis; it is putting the important words where they sound important. It is a matter of coherence; it is putting the right idea in the right place. [27]

"Rhythm" as applied to prose is a metaphor. "Rhythm," when used literally, means "measure" or "regularity," and since the movement of good prose is precisely *not* regular but varied with the sense, the union of the terms "prose" and "rhythm" has been none the happiest.

25. J. Middleton Murry, *The Problem of Style* (Oxford, 1922), p. 86. And it seems to me that this is also true of criticism: when the musical suggestion predominates, decadence has begun. The authors of books on prose rhythm are aware of their danger but they cannot save themselves. See, for example, William M. Patterson, *The Rhythm of Prose* (New York, 1916), p. 84; John Hubert Scott, *op. cit.*, pp. 24, 36–7, 127, 133.

26. *A Dictionary of Modern English Usage* (Oxford, 1927), "Rhythm," p. 504.

27. Mr. Ezra Pound says: "The attainment of a style consists in so knowing words that one will communicate the various parts of what one says with the various degrees and weights of importance which one wishes" (*Guide to Kulchur*, quoted in *Times Literary Supplement*, xxxvii [1938], p. 489).

For a detailed study of inversion of subject and predicate and position of adverbs in English according to sense, see August Western, *On Sentence-Rhythm and Word-Order in Modern English* (Christiania, 1908), esp. p. 9. Cf. *post* pp. 69–71. P. Fijn van Draat, "The Place of the Adverb, A Study in Rhythm," *Neophilologus*, vi (1921), 56–88, esp. 62, 87, admits Western's general principle but would connect certain variations not with sense but with "rhythmic formulas."

iii

A FIRST step toward a theory of style might be the reflection that one may say different things about the same topic—or different things which are very much alike.[28] A rose and a poppy are different, but both are flowers. Sidney writes, "Come, sleep! O sleep, the certain knot of peace, etc." Shakespeare writes, "O sleep, O gentle sleep, Nature's soft nurse, etc.," and again, "Sleep that knits up the ravell'd sleave of care, etc." It is not that these writers have had the same meaning and have "dressed" it, or expressed it, differently. Rather they have had the same subject, the benefits of sleep, or beneficent sleep, but have had different thoughts, different meanings, which have found expression in different language. They have expressed different, if similar, meanings. Even Betterton, when he recasts one of Shakespeare's passages on sleep, has not merely reëxpressed the same meaning; he has actually changed the meaning. Different words make different meanings.

It is true that meaning is not identical with words.[29] Meaning is the psychic entity, the something in the mind—for which material is not adequate. In the language of the scholastics: *Voces referuntur ad res significandas mediante conceptione intellectus.*[30] Nevertheless, words do determine meanings relentlessly. To come at it another way, meanings vary persistently with variations of words.[31] It may be well to recall one of Newman's figures, "the convex and the concave of a curve." The convex is not the concave, but if we conceive the curve as a line, then every change in the concave produces a corresponding change in the convex. There is that much

28. Cf. A. C. Bradley, *Poetry for Poetry's Sake* (Oxford, 1901), pp. 12–13.

29. Cf. Alfred North Whitehead, *Modes of Thought* (New York, 1938), pp. 48–9; Alan H. Gardiner, *The Theory of Speech and Language* (Oxford, 1932), p. 70; Edward Sapir, *Language* (New York, 1921), pp. 14, 238; I. A. Richards, *The Philosophy of Rhetoric* (New York, 1936), p. 13; Louis H. Gray, *Foundations of Language* (New York, 1939), pp. 88, 93–4.

30. St. Thomas Aquinas, *Summa Theologica*, I, q. 13, a. 1, quoted by Désiré Cardinal Mercier, *A Manual of Modern Scholastic Philosophy* (London, 1919), II, 154. Cf. Alan H. Gardiner, *op. cit.*, pp. 44 ff., 70 ff., 102–3.

31. The term "meaning" as I am using it may be taken to include all that Ogden and Richards have divided into different kinds of language meaning—the really referential, symbolic, intellectual meaning, and the group of emotive meanings (C. K. Ogden and I. A. Richards, *The Meaning of Meaning* [New York, 1936], pp. 11–12, 126, 186–7, 224–30). Obviously if such is the meaning to which we refer, if we are thinking of works of literature, not treatises of mathematics or philosophy, it is much easier to see how meaning depends on the very words in which it is cast. I choose not to emphasize this, however, because, as will be seen shortly, some of the effects of style in which I am interested are very slightly if at all dependent on emotive meaning.

truth in the contention of Croce: "Language is a perpetual creation. What has been linguistically expressed is not repeated. . . . Language is not an arsenal of arms already made, and it is not a *vocabulary*, a collection of abstractions, or a cemetery of corpses more or less well embalmed." [32]

We may be tempted to believe that we have at length distilled words or style away from meaning when we think of *bad* style. It might be plausible and would probably be useful to formulate some rule like this: Style occurs in isolation only when it is bad, when it fails to coincide with meaning.[33] This might be almost the truth where writing is so bad that it is meaningless—for example, in errors of expression made by one unfamiliar with a language, matters of syntax and elementary vocabulary. But poor expression in the wider sense cannot be reduced to this. The nature of words is against it—their constant tendency to mean. It is not as if we could forget or fail to put meaning in words. They persist in meaning, no matter what we intend or are conscious of. We may fail to say what we intend, but we can scarcely fail to say something.

Bad style is not a deviation of words from meaning, but a deviation of meaning from meaning. Of what meaning from what meaning? Of the actually conveyed meaning (what a reader receives) from the meaning an author intended or ought to have intended. This is true even of those cases where we might be most tempted to say that the fault of style is mere "awkwardness," since the meaning is conveyed completely. In such cases, the awkwardness consists in some absence of meaning (usually but implicit) or in some contrary or irrelevant meaning, which we disregard, inferring the writer's real meaning, at least so far as it would be explicit. We must do this so continually for most writing—seek out the meaning, put the most relevant construction on every word and phrase, disregard what tries to say the wrong thing—that we fail to sense any lack of meaning and dub the cause of our annoyance metaphorically and conveniently "awkwardness."

The question what the author ought to have said is the true difficulty in judging style. *Ut jam nunc dicat*, says Horace, *jam nunc debentia dici*. It is the only difficulty, for it is the only question, and it is one we implicitly answer every time we judge style:

32. *Op. cit.*, pp. 150–1; cf. p. 68, on translation. Cf. Leone Vivante, *Intelligence in Expression* (London, 1925), pp. 2–3.

33. Frederick Schlegel has said: "Although, in strict application and rigid expression, thought and speech always are, and always must be regarded as two things metaphysically distinct,—yet there only can we find these two elements in disunion, where one or both have been employed imperfectly or amiss" (*Lectures on the History of Literature* [New York, 1841], pp. 7–8).

We do it by our sense, more or less definite, of what the author intends to say as a whole, of his central and presiding purpose. The only consideration that can determine an author in a given detail is the adequacy of the detail to his whole purpose.[34] It does not follow that when we are sure this or that phrase or passage is bad style we shall always refer our judgment precisely to our impression of the whole.[35] The steps in subordination are too complicated. Furthermore, a fault in one whole can have something in common with a fault in another whole; whence arises the classification of faults of style and a tendency to refer individual faults only to the class definition.[36] The whole is usually forgotten.

From the foregoing one may begin to infer that a detailed study of style can be fruitful—even in the hands of those who least connect style with meaning. If faults can be classed, so to some extent can merits. That which has for centuries been called style differs from the rest of writing only in that it is one plane or level of the organization of meaning; it would not be happy to call it the outer cover or the last layer; rather it is the furthest elaboration of the one concept that is the center. As such it can be considered. The terms of rhetoric, spurned by Croce and other moderns, did have a value for the ancients, even though they failed to connect all of rhetoric with meaning. To give the terms of rhetoric a value in modern criticism it would be necessary only to determine the expressiveness of the things in language to which the terms refer. This has been done for metaphor, which used to be an ornament, but has now been made "the unique expression of a writer's individual vision" or "the result of the search for a precise epithet." [37] Mr. Empson has spoken ingeniously of that highly "artificial" figure the zeugma.[38] Mr. Bateson has praised a hypallage.[39]

34. H. B. Lathrop, in arguing that emphasis is an aspect of coherence, and coherence an aspect of unity, has shown admirably how the school-book terms may be squared with this philosophy of style ("Unity, Coherence, and Emphasis," *University of Wisconsin Studies in Language and Literature*, No. 2, *Studies by Members of the Department of English* [Madison, 1918], pp. 77–98).

35. For small faults of inconsistency and irrelevancy in a composition largely good, one would have to examine only a short section of the surrounding text. At the other extreme might be a composition by a schoolboy, where one could guess the central meaning only from the title or from what the schoolboy said when asked, or where there might not be any at all.

36. An operation essential to the economy of thinking, but one which can lead to error when the reason for considering the class as faulty is forgotten, and faults of one type of whole are referred to another—for example, when what would be a fault in a poem of heroic couplets is adduced against the verse of *Christabel*.

37. J. Middleton Murry, *The Problem of Style* (Oxford, 1922), pp. 13, 83.

38. William Empson, *Seven Types of Ambiguity* (New York, 1931), pp. 89–90.

39. F. W. Bateson, *English Poetry and the English Language* (Oxford, 1934), p. 22.

The greatest obstacle to recognizing the expressive value of rhetorical devices is the fact that they recur. One notices that Cicero uses a *litotes* or a *praeteritio* several times in a few pages, or so many hundreds of balances are counted in the *Ramblers* of Johnson. This suggests play with words, disregard of meaning. One is likely to reflect: if these devices express something, then the author must be expressing, or saying, much the same thing over and over—which is useless; therefore the author is really not trying to say anything; he is using words viciously, for an inexpressive purpose.

Such an attitude would not have been possible if the theoretical rhetoricians had not thrust forward the repertory of devices so as to throw them out of focus and conceal their nature as part of language. No one thinks, for example, that sentences because they recur are artificial, that they say the same thing over or say nothing. This is the key to what our attitude toward devices ought to be. Sentences are expressive; so also are declensions, and conjugations; they are expressive forms.[40] They express, not ideas like "grass" or "green," but relations. The so-called "devices," really no more devices than a sentence is a device, express more special forms of meaning, not so common to thinking that they cannot be avoided, like the sentence, but common enough to reappear frequently in certain types of thinking and hence to characterize the thinking, or the style. They express a kind of meaning [41] which may be discussed as legitimately as the more obvious kinds such as what a man writes about—the vanity of human wishes or the River Duddon.

It might be better if the term "device" were never used, for its use leads almost immediately to the carelessness of thinking of words as separable practicably from meaning. That is, we think of a given meaning as if it may be weakly expressed in one way but more forcefully in another. The latter is the device—the language applied, like a jack or clamp, or any dead thing, to the meaning, which itself remains static and unchanged, whether or not the device succeeds in expressing it. There is some convenience in this way of thinking, but more philosophy in steadily realizing that each change of words changes the meaning actually expressed. It

40. Cf. Alan H. Gardiner, *The Theory of Speech and Language* (Oxford, 1932), pp. 130–4, 158–61.

41. The better modern treatments of rhetoric have recognized this. See, for example, Alexander Bain, *English Composition and Rhetoric* (New York, 1886), esp. pp. 20–64, though it is hard to think the doctrine of expressiveness is an abiding principle when he says that one of the functions of metaphor is to "give an agreeable surprise" (pp. 30–1). For a treatment of figures as common elements of speech, see James B. Greenough and George L. Kittredge, *Words and Their Ways in English Speech* (New York, 1901), pp. 14–17.

is better to think of the "weak" expression and the "strong" expression as two quite different expressions, or, elliptically, two different meanings, of which one is farther from, one nearer to, what the author ought to say, or what he intends to say. The whole matter of emphasis, which is the real truth behind Herbert Spencer's wooden theory of economy in words, seems to be best considered in this light. (To keep the mind from being fatigued while receiving ideas—this is Spencer's function for style.[42] One may object that the most important thing about the mind is not that it can be fatigued—but that it can entertain splendid, though often difficult and fatiguing, conceptions.) If a word is to be placed here or there in a sentence in order to be effective, to have due weight, this ought to be thought of not as a juggling of words round a meaning to give the meaning emphatic expression, but as a choice of a more emphatic rather than a less emphatic meaning, or, strictly, the choice of the meaning needed, for meaning exists through emphasis; a change of emphasis is a change of meaning. We must preserve a notion of words, even in their most purely suggestive functions, as something transparently intellectual, not intervening between us and the meaning but luminous and full of their meaning and as if conscious of it.

The expressiveness of the rhetorical device is not always so easily analyzed as that of the sentence or declension—frequently it is a form of implicit expressiveness, one which is certainly present but not simply in virtue of meanings of words or of syntax or of morphology. For example, one of the most frequent forms of implicit expressiveness, or meaning, is that of equality or likeness—with its opposite, inequality or unlikeness. Any succession of words, phrases, or sentences must in any given degree be either like or unlike, and appropriately or inappropriately so in accordance with whether the successive explicit meanings are like or unlike. The "jingles" collected by H. W. and F. G. Fowler [43] are admirable illustrations of the fault which consists in a likeness of word sounds and hence of implicit meaning where there is no corresponding explicit meaning to be sustained. "To read his tales is a baptism of optimism," they quote from the *Times*. Here there is a nasty jingle of "ptism," "ptimism"—nasty just because the two combinations so nearly alike strive to make these words parallel, whereas they are

---

42. "The Philosophy of Style," in Lane Cooper's *Theories of Style* (New York, 1907), pp. 273–4. What if a passage were read twice or pondered at length? Would it not lose most of its force—through being relieved of the duty of preventing our misconceptions? Spencer's essay appeared first in the *Westminster Review* of 1852.

43. *The King's English* (Oxford, 1906), p. 291. Cf. H. W. Fowler, *A Dictionary of Modern English Usage* (Oxford, 1927), "Jingles," pp. 308–9.

not; one qualifies the other. The case is even plainer if we take an example of the common "ly" jingle, "He lived practically exclusively on milk," and set beside it something like this: "We are swallowed up, irreparably, irrevocably, irrecoverably, irremediably." [44] In the second we are not conscious of the repeated "ly" as a jingle, any more than of the repeated "irre." The reason is that behind each of these parallel sounds (implicit parallel meanings) there is a parallel explicit meaning. So far as we advert to the sounds as sounds at all it is with a sense of their concordance with the structure of meaning. Such is perhaps the most frequently underlying reason why expressions are approved of or objected to as "euphonious" or "cacophonous," "harmonious" or "inharmonious."

And matters of sound are not the only ones to which the principle of equality and inequality applies. Even so basically wrong a thing as parataxis, the monotony of a schoolboy's writing, consists just in that he is using the same form of meaning in successive clauses and hence fails to relate his meanings, that is, fails to express the really different meanings which lurk dimly in his mind as his real intention or are at least what he should intend. Hypotaxis, the rare-sounding opposite of parataxis, but no other than all modulated writing, consists in the use of different forms of meaning to sustain the sequence of the complex whole meaning. The author whose style is the subject of this study offers on every page emphatic demonstrations of implicit meaning through equality; and it will be one of the purposes of the study to show that what is sometimes called cumbrousness or pompousness in Johnson is but the exaggeration into more rigid lines of an expressive principle that lies in the very warp of all verbal discourse.

44. The first is from E. F. Benson, quoted in *The King's English*, p. 292; the second, from John Donne, Sermon LXVI, in *Donne's Sermons*, ed. Logan Pearsall Smith (Oxford, 1919), p. 10.

CHAPTER I

Parallelism

AMONG the qualities of Samuel Johnson's style most often noticed by critics has been something which they called "balance" or "parallelism." [1] There has been no doubt what things these terms referred to, what clauses or phrases, or at least what were the most conspicuous examples. On the other hand there is a distinction, suggested even in the two terms "parallelism" and "balance," which has been either overlooked or, if noticed, pursued with disregard for the relation between the two qualities distinguished. These two qualities are parallelism of meaning and parallelism of sound. Perhaps it is the first that a critic has been more aware of when he used the term "parallelism," and perhaps the second, when he used "balance." And it is the second by which he is carried off when he dallies with the terms "cadence" and "rhythm." We may begin to form an opinion of Johnson's parallelism when we consider that of sound as auxiliary to, and made significant by, that of meaning. Parallel meaning, or multiplied similar meaning—that is one of the basic notions to be explored for Johnson's style, and those who have used terms like "repetition" and "amplification" have been nearer the truth than those who have talked most of "balance." [2]

Any series of connected meanings is in some degree a parallel series. The least degree of parallelism is that the sentences (or clauses, or phrases, or words) are all parts of the same discourse—

1. See, for example, *Burrowes* pp. 50–3; T. B. Macaulay, "Samuel Johnson," *Encyclopedia Britannica*, 11th ed., Vol. xv (New York, 1911), p. 468, col. 2 (originally in the 8th ed. of the *Encyclopedia*, 1856); Charles Grosvenor Osgood, *Selections from the Works of Samuel Johnson* (New York, 1909), p. xxxi; *Taylor* pp. 43–7. All these writers use one or both of the words I have used. Other writers with terms like "repetition," "amplification," or "tautology," have referred to the same thing as "parallelism," or to one part of it with such terms as "triplet" or "doublet." "Triple tautology," says Walpole, "or the fault of repeating the same sense in three different phrases" (*The Letters of Horace Walpole*, ed. Mrs. Paget Toynbee [Oxford, 1904], x, 372, Letter 1922, 1 Feb. 1779). Cf. *post* p. 133, n. 2. Later he invented the term "triptology" (*The Works of Horatio Walpole* [London, 1798], iv, 362, "General Criticism of Dr. Johnson's Writings").

2. Heinrich Schmidt has distinguished the two kinds of parallel but neglected to connect them (*Schmidt* pp. 14–18, 20–4, 30–3). Professor Chandler writes: "Parallelism in our selections for study has been considered from the standpoint of *thought relation* and also, from that of *structural relation*" (*Chandler* p. 18), but this is no more than a cursory remark.

with reference to the whole meaning each has the status of member. The highest degree is some kind of immediate equality with reference to a third element, and this supported by some equality of form. Suppose three clauses, the first of which tells the cause of an act, the second the act, and the third its consequence. These three meanings are parallel if the sequence is taken as a whole and if as a whole it is referred to a fourth meaning. Yet they are nonparallel if considered in their reciprocal relations. Further, if the first and second be considered as the cause of the third, they assume a special parallel relation of their own; and if the second and third be considered as the result of the first, they too assume their own parallel. Not that in a single passage all these parallel meanings will occur simultaneously, or with equal emphasis. It is the function of syntax and other forms of meaning to show the intended relations of such members to one another and to a whole or another member of a whole in which they occur.

An opposite but equally basic element of all discourse is that of difference. If two clauses are parallel, say as illustrations of a third statement, they must yet differ between themselves in some degree however slight, or both would not be used. If the first and second members of the example used above express a cause of which the meaning of the third member is the effect, the first and second are so far parallel, yet they are different too inasmuch as they express a cause and effect relation between themselves. If beets and carrots are referred to only as examples of vegetables, they are yet different, for beets are not carrots.

If we define a parallel of two explicit meanings as an equal or approximately equal relationship to a third meaning either adjacent in the context or deducible, we have a minimum on which to build a classification. The degrees of parallelism above this can hardly be defined in terms of substance. A series of degrees, however, can be usefully defined in terms of form, explicitly and implicitly expressive. A writer having a pair (or more) of parallel meanings may employ a number of forms with greater or less regard for the parallelism. The least and worst he can do is choose forms which are explicitly nonparallel in the degree in which the substance *is* parallel, forms which therefore belie the substance. This weird phenomenon, a kind of "elegant variation," will not concern us hereafter, but may serve by antithesis to emphasize the positive side of our scale of parallels.

It is a "humane illusion" to think fascism can be dealt with and won over to the idea of peace and collective reconstruction by "understanding and loyal concessions," according to Dr. Mann, who declared that democracy and fascism inhabit different planets and live at different epochs.[3]

I refer not to several minor parallels such as "dealt with and won over," but to the parallel between two parts that make the whole passage, the two things that Dr. Mann said, one of which is made to sneak into Dr. Mann from behind with an "according to," while the other blurts out the front with a "who declared." This is using the resources of the language for confusion. It is one of the bad things of journalism.

The least a careful writer can do, and sometimes—when the degree of substantial parallel is not too great—the best, is to set down his members with no other formal expression of parallelism than a negative one—an absence of special connection.

The springs that move the human form, and make it friendly or adverse to me, lie hid within it. There is an infinity of motives, passions, and ideas contained in that narrow compass, of which I know nothing, and in which I have no share. Each individual is a world to himself, governed by a thousand contradictory and wayward impulses.[4]

Here are three sentences, each complicated and containing minor parallels within itself, but each with reference to the others a unit, one of three meanings in equal relation to a more general statement which has gone before and to a conclusion which is to follow. These meanings are left unconnected. Except for the fact that each is a declarative, noncompound sentence, there is not even any resemblance in their structure.

There are in general three explicit ways of binding groups of words, of indicating parallel: by the use of conjunctive or disjunctive words; by the syntax of words, that is, the relation of one word to two or more others; and by the repetition of identical words. These ways, especially the first two, have an affinity and frequently appear in combination. In the first sentence of the passage just quoted the verbs "move" and "make" are made parallel not only by the conjunction "and" but by their syntactic relation as predicates to the subject "that." The combination of the first and the third ways may be seen in the second sentence above, "of which . . . and in which." Here the structure of the relative clauses leaves no choice but the repetition of the word "which"; nevertheless it is of great value in enforcing the parallel. Repetition of an initial word, especially of some more emphatic or special word, is called by the

3. *The Washington Post*, Washington, D.C., 11 March 1938, p. 1.
4. William Hazlitt, *Howe* iv, 19, "On the Love of the Country."

rhetoricians "anaphora." These three explicit ways of parallel are the inevitable expressions of any writer who dwells upon, elaborates, or emphasizes any point, even for a moment.

We move nearer to the characteristically Johnsonian parallel with the next degree, that of implicitly expressive forms. I say "forms," not "form," and mean a relation between A and B and one between X and Y, as opposed to a relation of A to both X and Y which makes X and Y parallel. Thus: a subject, as in the example above, makes both its predicated verbs parallel. This is explicitly expressive. But if a subject is followed by its predicate in one clause, and another subject is followed by its predicate in a second clause, the parallel exists only by the occurrence of these two like forms side by side and is expressive only implicitly. If the clauses are joined by a conjunction, this adds explicit reference to the parallel, yet the parallel continues to exist independently and is greater or less in accordance with the resemblance in form of the clauses.

All like syntactic constructions create, of course, insofar as they are like, an implicitly expressive formal parallel. Such a parallel, however, of such unavoidable occurrence, is not what I wish to class as a parallel of implicit expression. This parallel begins only when like syntactic positions are filled by words of like substance and like weight or emphasis.

and as this practice is a commodious subject of raillery to the gay, and of declamation to the serious, it has been ridiculed, with all the pleasantry of wit, and exaggerated with all the amplifications of rhetorick [5]

Here we have not two sentences, but two predicates each of three emphatic elements, each of these elements in the one exactly paralleled in syntax, and closely paralleled in substance, by each in the other, and two of them closely paralleled in weight of sound. Further, the two halves of the predicate are matched by two halves in the introductory dependent clause, these halves themselves each consisting of two elements closely matched. So the whole construction is a quintuple parallel, broken, so that the arrangement is: a,b; v, w::c,d,e; x,y,z. This is formal parallel, implicitly expressive.[6] For the sake of brevity, let us hereafter call it "implicit parallel."

Having begun with an elaborate example, we must now return

5. *Works* v, 8, *Rambler* No. 2.
6. It should be remembered that it is not the presence of a given form in member A or B that is called implicit. These forms in themselves, like other forms, such as that of a vase or barn, should be called neither explicit nor implicit. They simply are. Nor is the resemblance of form between A and B implicit. What is implicit is the support which the resemblance of form between A and B gives to the resemblance of meaning.

to the germ of the matter. The simplest form which implicit parallel can assume is that where the emphatic elements in parallel positions consist of a single word each and are the whole of the members—that is, in simple pairings of words, whether with or without conjunctive or disjunctive words or elements of identity.

> faults and follies
> labour or hazard
> so smooth and so flowery
> to enlarge or embellish [7]
> against warning, against experience [8]

It seems to me that the parts of speech involved are of no consequence to our classification.[9]

In simple pairs of words a writer may be said to employ an unavoidable measure of implicit parallel, but it is plain that in the next degree of implicit parallel, where there are two elements in each member, he has sought something that might easily have been avoided. Two nouns, for example, each modified by an adjective in the same position, make a conspicuous parallel, especially if the adjectives are of about the same weight. A good many alternatives are obvious: that either or both of the nouns lack the adjective, or that either or both be modified in some other way. The parallel has considerable value as implicit expression. Again, what parts of speech constitute the double elements is a matter of no concern. There are a good many possibilities:

> retrenching exuberances and correcting inaccuracies
> integrity of understanding and nicety of discernment
> unnatural thoughts and rugged numbers
> shaven by the scythe, and levelled by the roller
> judgment is cold, and knowledge is inert [10]

So a writer may continue to multiply parallel elements, relating the elements within the members by any kind of syntax. For instance, three elements:

> examples of national calamities,
> and scenes of extensive misery [11]

7. *Works* v, 8–12, *Rambler* No. 2.
8. *Works* vii, 225, *Rambler* No. 178.
9. But see *Schmidt* pp. 9–14 for lists of coördinate nouns, adjectives, and verbs collected from various places in the works of Johnson.
The classification of "phrasal patterns" devised by Professors Scott and Chandler (*Chandler* pp. 9–16; John H. Scott and Zilpha E. Chandler, *Phrasal Patterns in English Prose* [New York, 1932]) is concerned precisely with groupings of parts of speech.
10. *Works* iv, 105–9, *Life of Pope.*
11. *Works* xi, 77, *Rasselas,* chap. xxviii.

Four elements:

> the various forms of connubial infelicity,
> the unexpected causes of lasting discord [12]

Or he may reach five elements, as in the example with which this series was begun.

We have classed multiplications according to the degrees of parallelism which they exhibit—that is, the elements of parallel in each member. Another classification is possible, according to the number of members. All the examples of implicit parallelism given so far have been of two members. The example of multiplication (with parallelism only of substance) taken from Hazlitt had three members. But any degree of parallelism may appear in two, three, or more members.[13] One element in three members:

> reproach, hatred, and opposition [14]

Two elements in three members:

> her physick of the mind,
> her catharticks of vice,
> or lenitives of passion [15]

The greater the number of elements, or the greater the number of members, the rarer the phenomenon, the more space it takes in its context, and the more significant it is of the style of the author.

ii

WHEN a writer employs a pair of words, two words having an equal relation to their context, it seems to me that he may have one or more of four expressive purposes, according to the relation of the words to ideas and that of the ideas to objects or facts. Suppose two words, two ideas, and two objects corresponding. This is a common and perhaps the most inconspicuous form of multiplication. The purpose of these words is to give range or scope—or one might say "definition"—it is to name the number of different objects necessary to the whole meaning of the context. And we may subdivide this purpose into that of exact or complete range, and that of illustrative range. When in *Rasselas* Johnson says "the

12. *Ibid.*, p. 78.
13. Cf. John H. Scott and Zilpha E. Chandler, *Phrasal Patterns in English Prose* (New York, 1932), pp. 231–57. It is to be noticed that their use of the terms "doublet," "triplet," and "quadruplet" (defined on p. 241) does not correspond to mine in the following pages.
14. *Works* v, 12, *Rambler* No. 2.
15. *Ibid.*, p. 11.

prince and the princess," [16] his purpose is exact range; in the context he could refer to no other objects in the same way; his meaning is particular. But when in *Rambler* No. 51, speaking of the country housewife's cares, he says "robs and gellies" or "pickles and conserves," [17] he is referring to these objects as of a certain kind, of which he might have chosen others; he wishes to illustrate; his meaning is generic. To a given pair of words it may be impossible to assign one of these kinds of range exclusively. In *Rasselas*, "they clambered with great fatigue among crags and brambles." [18] Who can say whether it was only crags and brambles that caused their fatigue, or whether boulders and logs did not contribute? For that matter who can be absolutely sure that anything besides "pickles and conserves" is implied in the sentence about the country housewife? There is an ambiguity in most of these expressions which is part of their force.

In the second place suppose now two words, two ideas, but only one object, as where Addison speaks of Aristotle as "that great Critick and Philosopher." [19] Here the purpose is to refer to the object under two ideas or aspects, both of which have relevance to the whole meaning of the context.[20] This sort of thing happens often enough with two nouns (especially with abstract nouns) but more often with adjectives. For example, Johnson ascribes to Pope "a prompt and intuitive perception." [21] Two words referring to the same object may refer to it either more or less obviously under different aspects. The less obviously there are two aspects, the less obvious will be the purpose of explicit meaning.[22] In some cases the words will seem to refer to the object under the same aspect —or almost to do so. The words, whether or not ordinarily synonymous, will seem to overlap. "The constituent and fundamental principle," says Johnson.[23] There *is* a difference between "constituent" and "fundamental." Contexts could readily be invented where one would do but not the other. But in the particular context, it may be asked what relevance one has that the other has not. The question whether two words referring to the same object really

---

16. *Works* xi, 45, *Rasselas*, chap. xv.
17. *Works* v, 327.
18. *Works* xi, 42, *Rasselas*, chap. xiii.
19. *Morley* p. 383, *Spectator* No. 267.
20. Here our previous distinction might be repeated and aspects divided into those which give exact and those which give illustrative range. But the distinction would be too precarious to be of any use.
21. *Works* iv, 104, *Life of Pope.*
22. Cf. James B. Greenough and George L. Kittredge, *Words and Their Ways in English Speech* (New York, 1901), p. 115. Cf. *post* pp. 34–6.
23. *Works* iv, 104, *Life of Pope.*

convey two ideas can be decided only by what the two words convey or suggest relevant to the context.

To combine these difficulties, that of the first type of paired words, where there are two objects, and that of the second, where there are only two ideas, and to multiply them by a doubt which type is present, we have only to conceive a pair of abstract nouns, a pair of verbs or adverbs, or a pair of adjectives if thought of apart from a noun modified. Behind every abstract or general term there is a set of objects thought of under a certain aspect. If we have two abstract words, they may be so far apart that we can say a different set of objects is behind each; or they may be so close together that we see behind them the same or nearly the same set of objects, but under different aspects; again they may be so close that we see not only the same objects but, so far as any meaning relevant to the context is concerned, the same or nearly the same aspects. "Troubles and commotions," [24] says Johnson, and "activity and sprightliness." [25]

Such overlapping of meaning, at times almost complete, leads us to recognize a fourth type of meaning for word pairs—emphasis. It is present perhaps to some extent in all the types of pairs just discussed. Least, of course, and scarcely perceptible, where exact range is meant ("the prince and princess"), easily perceptible in illustrative range ("pickles and conserves") or where different aspects of one object are clearly distinguishable ("Critick and Philosopher"), heavier and heavier the nearer the aspects come, and almost the whole purpose in extreme cases ("constituent and fundamental," "troubles and commotions"). This is a purpose which we all must feel when we double words, but which we may feel is obtained at considerable cost of meaning when the words used mean nearly the same.

iii

EVERY pairing of words, as we have seen, affirms (or denies) two notions which are alike insofar as they are paired (have the same immediate relation to a third notion) and which are different insofar as one adds anything to the other. In some, in "constituent and fundamental principle," the emphasis is so far on the harmony of these notions that little if any difference, or range, is adverted to. In others, in "Critick and Philosopher," there is stress on the equal relation of these two notions to a third, "Aristotle," and with this a clear advertence to the distinction between the two. It is but

24. *Works* VIII, 285, *Idler* No. 71.
25. *Works* VII, 224, *Rambler* No. 178.

carrying this tendency to its limit to assert the equal relation of two opposites in a scale to a third notion:

> that vehemence of desire which presses through
> right and wrong to its gratification [26]

Right and wrong are antithetical, yet here, where both are affirmed in the same respect, their expressive value is that of a pair placed at extremes of a range and so emphasizing its length. Rasselas and Imlac press over crags and brambles. Vehemence of desire presses through right and wrong.

> to find, and to keep [27]
> names for day and night [28]
> none of them would either steal or buy [29]

There is little point in arguing whether each of these involves an antithesis or only a distinction.

Antithetic parallel is of course limited to two members. But, like the other forms of multiplication, it admits multiple elements of implicit parallel and sometimes through these shows itself more clearly as antithesis. It may have two elements:

> a state too high for contempt
> and too low for envy [30]

Or three:

> partiality, by which some vices have hitherto
> escaped censure, and some virtues wanted recommendation [31]

And so on, though perfect examples are very scarce.

Antithesis of this sort I should like to call antithesis I, to distinguish it from the truer antithesis to be discussed later,[32] which we may call antithesis II. While antithesis I in pointing out opposite notions either affirms or denies both in the same respect, antithesis II makes a distinction in order to affirm one part and deny the other. Antithesis I, inasmuch as it is an antithesis, is often on the verge of becoming antithesis II. If we affirm both A and its opposite B, our affirmation frequently takes the form: Not only A but B, in which case we see more easily that what we mean implies: Not A alone but both A and B, and this is antithesis II, as we shall see later.

26. *Works* v, 10, *Rambler* No. 2.
27. *Works* vi, 372, *Rambler* No. 129.
28. *Works* viii, 173, *Idler* No. 43.
29. *Works* viii, 22, *Idler* No. 6.
30. *Works* viii, 238, *Idler* No. 71.
31. *Works* vi, 370, *Rambler* No. 129.
32. *Post* pp. 38–43.

iv

IT is beyond the scope of an analysis of style to *prove* that any qualities of style *exist* in writing. A writing cannot be proved to have more or less meaning than is understood on reading it. Where a certain quality is recognized as a part of style, statistics may give a numerical ratio between the frequency of the quality in one writing and that in another. But the process of making statistics is one of gathering items under a head, and only according to a definition may the items be gathered. Only by the definition have they any relevance. It is the formulating of the definition, not the counting after that, which is the work of studying style.[33]

When a critic is conscious of quality X in a writing, no accumulation of statistics will increase his consciousness of it. But if he simply announces that the writing has X, he may be challenged. If he says that it has X because he has found X in fifteen examples of fifteen hundred words each, he is less likely to be challenged; if he adds that the average is a hundred occurrences in each example, even less likely. This, however, is not proof, but something more like persuasion, for logically the whole matter rests on the definition with which he began, and statistical details are taken, no less than a blanket statement, on faith.

In the course of analyzing Johnson's parallelism I have, as a matter of fact, done a good deal of counting both in selected passages of Johnson and in passages of Addison and Hazlitt taken by way of contrast. But in the comparative description which follows I have assumed that general statement, illustrated, is more intelligible than statistical scrupulosity and equally entitled to credence.

Three passages from Johnson have been set against three from Addison and three from Hazlitt, but not with any intention of illustrating the history of English prose. The chronological positions of Addison and Hazlitt might be reversed. The two have simply been chosen as points recognized to be at some distance from Johnson in the field of prose style.

From Johnson I have chosen *Rambler* No. 2, *Idler* No. 10, and a section of the *Life of Pope*. For the degree to which they exemplify

33. Professor L. A. Sherman counted the number of words per sentence for the *whole* of Macaulay's *History of England* and found that the average was 23.43. "Here, then, in this 23.43," he wrote, "was the resultant of the forces which had made Macaulay's literary character" ("On Certain Facts and Principles in the Development of Form in Literature," *The University Studies of the University of Nebraska*, I [No. 4, 1892], 350–3). Such, and only such, can be the conclusion reached by counting items chosen without reference to meaning. Cf. Abraham Wolf, *Textbook of Logic* (London, 1930), pp. 231, 236.

his whole tendency, one may consult a later chapter, where the consistency of his style is considered.[34] But a study of style ought not to be primarily a study of average style; it is too likely to lead to no conclusion. The same recognition of meaning that leads us to choose certain characteristics for attention leads us to choose the places where they may be found. If it is plain that Johnson's *Idlers* are on the whole of a lighter, less philosophic cast than the *Ramblers*, and that the narrative portions of the *Lives* are less discursive than the discursive portions (for it is just as plain as that), and if we look on Johnson as most different from other writers when he is being philosophic or discursive, there is no reason why we should average the characteristics of all his ways of writing in order to see what is distinctive of the Johnsonian style. I have chosen these three passages because they display a consistent texture of the characteristics which critics for a century and a half have called Johnsonian. *Rambler* No. 2, "The necessity and danger of looking into futurity," [35] is a fair example of Johnson's abstract, moral, or philosophic essay; *Idler* No. 10, "Political credulity," [36] of his treating a didactic theme more concretely; the section from the *Life of Pope*,[37] of his later discursive style.

From Addison I have chosen a part of *Spectator* No. 177, "Good-nature as a moral virtue" [38] (which shows us Addison writing on something like a Johnsonian topic); all of *Spectator* No. 106, "Sir Roger de Coverley's country seat" [39] (which treats a more typically Addisonian, seminarrative subject); and a part of *Spectator* No. 267, "Criticism on Paradise Lost." [40] From Hazlitt I have chosen

34. *Post* pp. 74–88.

35. *Works* v, 7–13; 1,500 words. Two other *Ramblers* of the same moral tone, which on analysis may be seen to have about the same weight, are No. 129, "The folly of cowardice and inactivity"; No. 178, "Many advantages not to be enjoyed together." A somewhat different type is exemplified in *Ramblers* No. 51, "The employments of a housewife in the country," and No. 181, "The history of an adventurer in lotteries," both of which employ a specific story to convey a moral. No. 51 is heavily embroidered with moral comment, while No. 181 is more purely narrative and has the same sort of lightness as some *Idlers*. A *Rambler* of literary criticism is likely to be very light. Cf. *post* pp. 83–4, the discussion of No. 88, "A criticism on *Milton*'s versification."

36. *Works* viii, 37–41; 1,100 words. Like No. 10, a specific moral lesson and of about the same weight, is No. 71, "*Dick Shifter*'s rural excursion." An *Idler* of somewhat greater weight is No. 43, "Monitions on the flight of time." An example of the lightest type of *Idler* is the topical No. 6, "Lady's performance on horse-back."

37. *Works* iv, 104–10, "Of his intellectual character . . . . the reasonableness of my determination"; 1,700 words.

38. *Morley* pp. 258–9, as far as ". . . their Fellow Sufferers"; 1,000 words.

39. *Morley* pp. 163–4; 1,200 words.

40. *Morley* pp. 383–5, "I shall therefore examine . . . . Offence to the most scrupulous"; 1,500 words.

part of the essay "On the Love of the Country," [41] part of "My First Acquaintance with Poets," [42] and part of the lecture "On Dryden and Pope." [43]

One of the first things that may be learned from a comparison of these nine passages is that we cannot assign to the simple quality of multiplication any effect distinctive of Johnson's prose. Numerically: if one counts all the multiplications of all classes (all coordinate words, phrases, and clauses, of all degrees of explicit and implicit parallel) in each passage, it is found that Johnson far outweighs Addison, but that Johnson himself is outweighed by Hazlitt.[44] We may say of Johnson and Hazlitt that in contrast to Addison their style is marked by the tendency to multiplication.[45] But Johnson is distinguishable from Hazlitt and, more strikingly than by mere multiplication, from Addison in those two tendencies which we have seen are founded in multiplication—that toward emphasis rather than range, and that toward parallelism of forms. I resume first the discussion of parallelism.

In multiplications having only explicit parallel—syntax, conjunctions, identical words—Johnson, Addison, and Hazlitt are again about equal if their usages are merely counted. But if examples are compared (i.e., if our definitions are refined), then even in these common prose elements Johnson's inclination to parallel may be

41. *Howe* iv, 17–21; 1,700 words.
42. *Howe* xvii, 106–10, as far as ". . . the cause of civil and religious liberty"; 1,700 words.
43. *Howe* v, 69–72, "The question whether Pope was a poet . . . . It is the perfection of the mock-heroic"; 1,600 words.
This passage from Hazlitt, that from *Spectator* No. 267, "Criticism on Paradise Lost," and that from Johnson's *Life of Pope* are the passages used by Professor Chandler in her parallel study of the "Stylistic Technique" of Addison, Johnson, Hazlitt, and Pater (*Chandler*).
All my figures for numbers of words are approximate, raised or lowered to the nearest hundred. In estimating, I have omitted passages of quotation and translation. *Spectator* No. 177 is cut off because of the bulk of quotation that follows. Professor Chandler (*Chandler* p. 7) counts approximately 1,500 words each for the passage from Johnson's *Life of Pope* and that from Hazlitt's lecture "On Dryden and Pope."
44. If the numbers counted are reduced to quotients per hundred words, the result is as follows: Addison, *Spectator* No. 267, 2.80; *Spectator* No. 177, 3.30; *Spectator* No. 106, 3.08; Johnson, *Pope*, 5.65; *Rambler* No. 2, 4.40; *Idler* No. 10, 3.73; Hazlitt, "Dryden and Pope," 6.13; "Love of the Country," 5.00; "First Acquaintance with Poets," 4.29. Since these quotients represent passages of different lengths an average is not obtained by adding the three figures for each author and dividing by three. But the approximate comparison afforded by these separate figures is enough for the generalities I propose.
45. What makes up for multiplication in Addison's writing is the greater amount of what might be called "sequence," as in anecdotes, progressive and unemphatic remarks, or sorites reasoning.

seen. In general Johnson tends to greater use of identical elements,[46] to nearly identical constructions of almost equal length and weight—things which become particularly noticeable in multiplications of three or more members. Consider a long multiplication from Hazlitt:

No doubt, the sky is beautiful; the clouds sail majestically along its bosom; the sun is cheering; there is something exquisitely graceful in the manner in which a plant or tree puts forth its branches; the motion with which they bend and tremble in the evening breeze is soft and lovely; there is music in the babbling of a brook; the view from the top of a mountain is full of grandeur; nor can we behold the ocean with indifference.[47]

There is a momentary inclination to implicit parallelism here: "the clouds sail . . . the sun is." The identical element "there is" appears twice. But on the whole, for the shortness of the members and the similarity of the material, there is marked variation. Beside this see one from Addison:

You would take his Valet de Chambre for his Brother, his Butler is grey-headed, his Groom is one of the gravest men that I have ever seen, and his Coachman has the Looks of a Privy-Counsellor.[48]

"His" is a rather unobtrusive identical element in each member, and "is" appears as the main verb of two consecutive members. The four nouns, "Valet de Chambre," "Butler," "Groom," and "Coachman" tend to be elements of implicit parallel. But the first is a compound of three words and is the object of a verb, while the other three are all subjects and single words. The general variety in constructions and positions of emphasis through the four members is plain. Beside these two multiplications see one from Johnson:

He has known those who saw the bed into which the pretender was conveyed in a warming-pan. He often rejoices that the nation was not enslaved by the *Irish.* He believes that king *William* never lost a battle, and that if he had lived one year longer he would have conquered *France.* He holds that *Charles* the first was a papist. He allows there were some good men in the reign of queen *Anne,* but the peace of *Utrecht* brought a blast upon the nation, and has been the cause of all the evil that we have suffered to the present hour. He believes that the scheme of the *South Sea* was well intended, but that it miscarried by

46. Cf. *Schmidt* pp. 24–5 on Johnson's use of "anaphora."
47. *Howe* IV, 18, "On the Love of the Country."
48. *Morley* p. 163, *Spectator* No. 106. It is not easy to find quadruple multiplications in Addison.

the influence of *France*. He considers a standing army as the bulwark of liberty, thinks us secured from corruption by septennial parliaments, relates how we are enriched and strengthened by the electoral dominions, and declares that the publick debt is a blessing to the nation.[49]

Here we have seven sentences, each beginning with the element of identity "he" followed by the main verb, which in each case is a verb of mental action. "He has known," "rejoices," "believes," "holds," "allows," "believes," "considers." Four of these verbs are followed by the conjunction "that." In the third sentence "that" is repeated, so that the sentence makes a pair of members, each about equal in weight to the sentences which have preceded. The fifth sentence is divided antithetically, with two parts following "but," and each about equal to the introductory stem, and all three not much different in length and weight from the simpler sentences. The sixth sentence has two antithetical parts, the second reënforced with a "that." And in conclusion comes a quadruplet laid out on the four main verbs "considers," "thinks," "relates," "declares," to all of which the subject is the first word, "he." In the eleven words of saying and thinking which govern the constructions of this long multiplication, there is a weighty element of parallel and one which is manifestly designed.[50]

In the following multiplication of even very short members notice the great variety attained by Hazlitt.

What discrimination, what wit, what delicacy, what fancy, what lurking spleen, what elegance of thought, what pampered refinement of sentiment! [51]

Where the members are short, the length and quality of single words are of importance. The identical element "what" is joined first to a long word with the abstract ending "ion," then to the short spurt of a word "wit," then to two words ending in "y" but of different lengths, and then to members which expand climactically, first

49. *Works* VIII, 40, *Idler* No. 10. Multiplications of four members or more are not frequent even in Johnson. Yet the length of these examples when they do occur makes them of considerable importance. Three examples counted in this *Idler*, one of which is nested within another, occupy about a page and a half of the total of four pages—another suggestion of the need of definition and interpretation in statistics.

50. I insert the following as an example of greater variety in Johnson's multiplication. "Her marigolds, when they are almost cured, are often scattered by the wind, the rain sometimes falls upon fruit when it ought to be gathered dry. While her artificial wines are fermenting, her whole life is restlessness and anxiety. Her sweetmeats are not always bright, and the maid sometimes forgets the just proportions of salt and pepper, when venison is to be baked. Her conserves mould, her wines sour, and pickles mother" (*Works* V, 331, *Rambler* No. 51).

51. *Howe* V, 71, "On Dryden and Pope."

an adjective and noun, then two nouns in oblique relation, then an adjective and noun in oblique relation to another noun.[52]

The examples we have just considered have all been of four or more members. Here are some shorter ones.

If conversation offered any thing that could be improved, he committed it to paper; if a thought, or perhaps an expression more happy than was common, rose to his mind, he was careful to write it.[53]

Or, with but two members to match, Johnson often uses a pair of antitheses of type II.

He never attempted to make that better which was already good, nor often to mend what he must have known to be faulty.[54]

Contrast these from Hazlitt and Addison:

There was to me a strange wildness in his aspect, a dusky obscurity, and I thought him pitted with the small-pox.[55]

When he is pleasant upon any of them, all his Family are in good Humour, and none so much as the Person whom he diverts himself with: On the contrary, if he coughs, or betrays any Infirmity of old Age, it is easy for a Stander-by to observe a secret Concern in the Looks of all his Servants.[56]

We may proceed to multiplications with implicit parallel. The number of those with one element only (doublets, triplets, or quadruplets of single words) is actually less for Johnson than for Hazlitt,[57] an effect which may be considered only complementary

52. I stress the variety of these members of the same parallel as compared with one another. Professor Chandler has pointed out the variety of all Hazlitt's "phrases," the fact that his ways of modifying nouns or pronouns, of coördinating nouns and pronouns, and of combining coördination and modification, outnumber those of Johnson or Addison (Chandler esp. pp. 9–16, 63; and cf. John H. Scott and Zilpha E. Chandler, Phrasal Patterns in English Prose [New York, 1932], p. 351; and see ibid., pp. 234–40, some examples of variety in parallelism from different authors).
53. Works iv, 105, Life of Pope. Here the parallelism is largely through the repetition of the conditional clause and the identical element "he."
54. Works iv, 107, Life of Pope. Another example of paired antitheses: "willing rather to transmit than examine so advantageous a principle, and more inclined to pursue a track so smooth and flowery, than attentively to consider whether it leads to truth" (Works v, 8, Rambler No. 2).
55. Howe xvii, 109, "My First Acquaintance with Poets."
56. Morley p. 163, Spectator No. 106. I class this as an antithesis I. Whether the knight is under a fair aspect or not, the same thing is affirmed, the effect upon his household, and that in turn is differentiated, so that the antithesis itself is of two elements.
57. The quotients are: Addison, Spectator No. 267, 1.07; Spectator No. 177, 1.80; Spectator No. 106, .83; Johnson, Pope, 2.24; Rambler No. 2, 1.20; Idler No. 10, 1.18; Hazlitt, "Dryden and Pope," 3.00; "Love of the Country," 1.65; "First Acquaintance with Poets," 1.76.

of Johnson's opportunism in the elaboration of parallels of two or more elements. It is in such more complicated parallels that the Johnsonian tendency is manifest beyond question. Here both statistics [58] and comparison of examples speak eloquently. This is preeminently the Johnsonian province.

Even in the simpler of these constructions Hazlitt is much inclined to irregularities. He will have one member longer by a prepositional phrase: "in its simple majesty, in its immediate appeal to the senses." [59] He will separate the members by a phrase which explicitly modifies one and is understood of the other: "a strange wildness in his aspect, a dusky obscurity." [60] Or he will add another adjective to one member: "the sequestered copse and wide extended heath." [61] Johnson more regularly follows the models: "excitements of fear, and allurements of desire," "fluctuating in measures, or immersed in business." [62]

Neither Hazlitt nor Addison ever reaches Johnson's extremes. When Hazlitt writes:

the utmost grandeur to our conceptions of nature, or the utmost force to the passions of the heart [63]

it is for him an excessively heavy parallel. And so for Addison when he writes:

from some new Supply of Spirits or a more kindly Circulation of the Blood [64]

Johnson does not begin to be unusual until he writes something like a doublet of five elements, cut in half and alternated, such as that we have already quoted from *Rambler* No. 2,[65] or, if we may

58. The quotients are: Addison, *Spectator* No. 267, .53; *Spectator* No. 177, .50; *Spectator* No. 106, .58; Hazlitt, "Dryden and Pope," 1.31; "Love of the Country," .76; "First Acquaintance with Poets," .29; Johnson, *Pope,* 1.94; *Rambler* No. 2, 1.60; *Idler* No. 10, 1.09.

Another tabulator might not arrive at just these figures. One of the reasons why I seek so far as possible to suppress statistical evidence is that such classifications as I develop in the first part of this chapter can hardly be applied with rigidity. In a series of judgments where emphasis and proportion must be taken so much into consideration, no person could hope to be matched exactly by another working independently.

59. *Howe* v, 69, "On Dryden and Pope."

60. *Howe* xvii, 109, "My First Acquaintance with Poets."

61. *Howe* iv, 20, "On the Love of the Country." I count this an antithesis of class I, of two elements of implicit parallel.

62. *Works* v, 9, 13, *Rambler* No. 2.

63. *Howe* v, 69, "On Dryden and Pope."

64. *Morley* p. 258, *Spectator* No. 177.

65. *Ante* p. 18.

go afield to *Rasselas,* a triplet of doublets, the first doublet having three elements, the second, two, and the third, seven:

the various forms of connubial infelicity, the unexpected causes of lasting discord, the diversities of temper, the oppositions of opinion, the rude collisions of contrary desire where both are urged by violent impulses, the obstinate contests of disagreeable virtues, where both are supported by consciousness of good intention [66]

Or, if we go to *Rambler* No. 129, an antithesis of four elements, chopped and alternated, so that instead of the commoner A,A,A,A: B,B,B,B, we have A,A:B,B; A:B,A:B.

according to the inclinations of nature, or the impressions of precept, the daring and the cautious may move in different directions without touching upon rashness or cowardice [67]

Such constructions, though they occur but rarely, yet fill a large space and are conspicuous among the emphatic effects of the whole writing.[68]

We have seen that any member of a writing stands in a relation of equality and in one of difference to the members adjacent to it. A writer may insist, by explicit or implicit means, on the equality or on the opposite, the difference of the members within their frame

66. *Works* xi, 78, *Rasselas,* chap. xxviii.

67. *Works* vi, 372. For some other examples of extreme Johnsonian parallel see *Christie* p. 34. But Christie is wrong in thinking that the quintuplet which he quotes from *Rambler* No. 207 ("Difficulties embarrass, uncertainty perplexes, opposition retards, censure exasperates, or neglect depresses" [*Works* vii, 387]) is "the only one [i.e., only one of two or more elements] of which Johnson is guilty." Heinrich Schmidt (*Schmidt* p. 21) quotes the following from *Taxation no Tyranny:* "The laws of nature, the rights of humanity, the faith of charters, the danger of liberty, the encroachments of usurpation, have been thundered in our ears, sometimes by interested faction, and sometimes by honest stupidity" (*Works* x, 101).

68. At this point belongs what I have to say of Johnson's "prose rhythm." From the discussion *ante* pp. 6–8 it should be plain why I make no more of this. Those who wish to see samples of Johnson's prose scanned may consult, for example, George Saintsbury, *A History of English Prose Rhythm* (London, 1912), p. 269; Norton R. Tempest, *The Rhythm of English Prose* (Cambridge, England, 1930), p. 69; John H. Scott, *Rhythmic Prose,* "University of Iowa Humanistic Studies," Vol. iii, No. 1 (Iowa City, 1925), pp. 93–4. If it could be shown that the members of a parallel were composed of like or nearly like patterns of tonic accent, this likeness could of course be assigned a value of implicit parallel which would be an elaboration of the broader value of like word masses in like syntactic positions. This might be said in part for the examples analyzed by these authors. One of the conditions for "perfect isochronism," according to André Classe, is "similarity of grammatical structure of the groups, and similarity of connexion between the groups" (*The Rhythm of English Prose* [Oxford, 1939], p. 100).

Under this head belongs also the matter of alliteration, a binding effect which Johnson occasionally employs in multiplications: "faults and follies"; "envy is extinct, and faction forgotten" (*Works* v, 8, 11, *Rambler* No. 2); "pleased with

of equality or parallel. He may exploit one kind of meaning or the other. And if he does one or the other consistently, his writing must assume a surface or texture of meaning directly relatable to this. If he recurrently gives to his multiplied phrases or clauses a turn toward equality, then the relations of member to member, of premise to premise and to conclusion, will be strengthened and plain; the whole sequence of meaning will have a high degree of coherence and regularity—but this will be at the expense of modulation, of individuality of premise, of variety. In a given multiplication in a given writing there must always be a specific demand for a degree of parallel and for an inverse degree of variety. Either a greater parallel or a greater variety will be the detail of meaning that better completes the whole intended meaning of the composition, fills it out to the greater relevancy and satisfaction. When Hazlitt says of Johnson, "All his periods are cast in the same mould, are of the same size and shape, and consequently have little fitness to the variety of things he professes to treat of," [69] he accuses Johnson of preferring the meaning of parallel to a more relevant meaning of variety.

v

THE tendency toward implicit parallel cannot but be accompanied by one toward overlapping, toward emphasis rather than range. Sameness of syntax, sameness of positions of emphasis in the frame of the syntax, must produce opportunities for likeness of substantial meaning. The degree of this likeness is difficult to define for simple word pairs. It is quite impossible for extended constructions with interweaving of various degrees. Johnson's inclination to emphasis rather than range can, however, be felt as a whole and can be illustrated. [70]

prognosticks of good . . . terrified likewise with tokens of evil" (*Works* xi, 43, *Rasselas,* chap. xiii). See *Schmidt* pp. 49–51 for a list of examples culled over a wide territory. The transverse alliteration of Lyly is but implicit parallel carried to its most fantastic extreme. "Althoughe hetherto *Euphues* I have shrined thee in my heart for a trustie friende, I will shunne thee heerafter as a trothles foe" (John Lyly, *Euphues,* in *Works,* ed. R. Warwick Bond [Oxford, 1902], i, 233; cf. i, 123).

69. "The structure of his sentence . . . ," says Hazlitt further, "is a species of rhyming in prose" (*Howe* vi, 101–2, *Lectures on the English Comic Writers,* 1819, Lecture v, "On the Periodical Essayists"). Hazlitt returned to this criticism again and again. "There is a tune in it, a mechanical recurrence of the same rise and fall in the clauses of his sentences, independent of any reference to the meaning of the text, or progress or inflection of the sense . . . . his periods complete their revolutions at certain stated intervals, let the matter be longer or shorter, rough or smooth, round or square, different or the same" (*Howe* xii, 6, *The Plain Speaker,* 1826, Essay i, "On the Prose-Style of Poets"). Cf. *Howe* iv, 72; vii, 310; and *post* pp. 48–9.

70. I mean emphasis absolutely (as discussed *ante* pp. 20–2), not what might be called balance or maintenance of emphasis, an effect common to all strong

The following are fair examples of how Hazlitt and Addison, even in triple multiplications, or in those of more than one element of implicit parallel, incline to the purpose of range:

> the Bishop of St. *Asaph* in the Morning,
> and Dr. *South* in the Afternoon [71]

> offering its cool fountain or its tempting shade [72]

> Their Enemies are the fallen Angels:
> the Messiah their Friend,
> and the Almighty their Protector.[73]

> to paste, pomatum, billet-doux, and patches [74]

> First, It should be but One Action.
> Secondly, It should be an entire Action;
> and, Thirdly, It should be a great Action.[75]

Johnson's way is on the whole the reverse.

> His effusions were always voluntary,
> and his subjects chosen by himself.[76]

> a deeper search, or wider survey [77]

If a search is concentrated on one spot, it may be called deep, or if the object of the search, e.g., the name of Shakespeare's great-grandfather, be considered an undiscovered spot, then a continued search, an examination of many records, becomes, if we like, a wide survey. In short, according to the way of conceiving, a determined effort to find something becomes a deep search or a wide survey.

writing and achievable in various ways according to the tendencies of the author. Johnson, for example, having used an adjective and noun at the beginning of a sentence or clause, will often find it necessary to use another adjective and noun, or a similar weight, at the end—if there is to be any adequate conclusion: "This is one of those pleasing surprises which often happen to active resolution" (*Works* xi, 43, *Rasselas*, chap. xiii); "ascribed the soundness of his sleep to the stillness of the country" (*Works* viii, 284, *Idler* No. 71). It is to be observed that these constructions though parallel in form are not parallel in substance (not yoked in equal relation to a third notion), but are in oblique relation to each other, so that there is no implicit parallel.

Cf. August Western on *"compensation-stress"* in his *On Sentence-Rhythm and Word-Order in Modern English* (Christiania, 1908), p. 8.

71. *Morley* p. 164, *Spectator* No. 106.
72. *Howe* iv, 19, "On the Love of the Country."
73. *Morley* p. 384, *Spectator* No. 267.
74. *Howe* v, 72, "On Dryden and Pope."
75. *Morley* p. 383, *Spectator* No. 267.
76. *Works* iv, 106, *Life of Pope.*
77. *Works* v, 8, *Rambler* No. 2.

the folly of him who lives only in idea,
refuses immediate ease for distant pleasures,
and, instead of enjoying the blessings of life,
lets life glide away in preparations to enjoy them [78]

gradually to amplify, decorate, rectify, and refine them.[79]

If the difference between paste and pomatum, billet-doux and patches is clear, it is not so clear where amplification shades into decoration, or rectification into refinement—particularly when the objects of the action are "thoughts." [80]

Next, as to simple word pairs. If the examples found in our nine passages are subdivided into those in which the purpose is to a great degree emphasis and those in which range is almost the whole purpose, there is not a telling difference in character between those from one author put under range and those from another, nor even a great difference in the numerical ratios of emphasis to range. Hazlitt and Johnson each show about the same ratio in favor of emphasis, somewhat greater than that of Addison.[81] Where the chief difference may be seen is in the general character of the examples of pairs for emphasis, all of which may be conveniently classified together, but which nevertheless are emphatic to differ-

78. *Works* v, 8, *Rambler* No. 2.

79. *Works* iv, 105, *Life of Pope*.

80. W. Vaughan Reynolds has made the same distinction as mine between emphasis and range when he admits that one of Johnson's triplets is tautological but contends that most are "exhaustive." He is willing to call the following from the Preface to *Lobo's Abyssinia* tautological: "He appears, by his modest and unaffected narration, to have *described things as he saw them*, to have *copied nature from the life*, and to have *consulted his senses, not his imagination*" (Works ix, 431). "If he drew from life," admits Reynolds, "he naturally consulted his *senses* only: if he described things as he *saw* them, he must have *copied nature from life*." On the other hand, he offers the following as an example of Johnson's "exhaustive" triplet, used "to express concisely three ideas in one": "And most are good no longer than *while temptation is away*, than while *their passions are without excitements*, and *their opinions are free from the counteraction* of any other motive" (*Works* v, 443, *Rambler* No. 70). ("A Note on Johnson's Use of the Triplet," *Notes and Queries*, clxv [1933], 23–4.) I make no attempt, as I have already admitted, to distinguish sharply between multiplications for emphasis (the "tautological") and those for range (the "exhaustive"), for the two purposes almost always combine. But by the same process which Reynolds follows in admitting his first example to be tautological, it seems to me possible to say of his second that it all amounts to no more than this: that most men can resist anything but temptation.
Cf. *Christie* p. 35; *Schmidt* p. 14.

81. The quotients are as follows, that for emphasis in each case coming first: Addison, *Spectator* No. 267, .27 to .47; *Spectator* No. 177, .80 to .40; *Spectator* No. 106, .42 to .17; Johnson, *Pope*, 1.18 to .41; *Rambler* No. 2, .73 to .20; *Idler* No. 10, .64 to .27; Hazlitt, "Dryden and Pope," 1.25 to .69; "Love of the Country," .94 to .29; "First Acquaintance with Poets," 1.65 to .40. I have left out of account triplets and quadruplets and, because of the peculiar way in which they combine range and emphasis, pairs showing antithesis of type I.

ent degrees. Through the course of a number of examples, Johnson's tendency to emphasis accumulates and becomes undeniably ponderous. I present for comparison all the examples which I have collected in the passage from *Spectator* No. 267, all from the lecture "On Dryden and Pope," and all from the *Life of Pope*.

Addison, *Spectator* No. 267:

> that great Critick and Philosopher
> the Counter-parts and Copies of one another
> that just and regular Progress
> so beautifully extended and diversified [82]

Hazlitt, "On Dryden and Pope":

> stripped of prejudice and passion
> the most contemptible and insignificant point of view
> he was a wit, and a critic
> established by the forms and customs of society
> the sentiments and habitudes of human life
> the thoughts and hearts of all men
> an intuitive and mighty sympathy
> wished or wanted
> with more brilliance and effect
> the involuntary and uncalculating impulses
> with a force and vehemence
> conventional and superficial modifications
> the antithesis of strength and grandeur
> the extravagances of fancy or passion
> long ease and indulgence
> smooth and polished verse
> the tug and war of the elements
> the retired and narrow circle
> a new character and a new consequence
> apotheosis of foppery and folly [83]

Johnson, *Life of Pope:*

> the constituent and fundamental principle
> a prompt and intuitive perception
> consonance and propriety
> a sedate and quiescent quality
> always investigating, always aspiring
> great strength and exactness of memory
> incessant and unwearied diligence
> form and polish large masses
> with such faculties, and such dispositions

82. *Morley* pp. 383–5.
83. *Howe* v, 69–72.

readiness and dexterity
so selected and combined as to be ready
when occasion or necessity called
minute and punctilious observation
considered and reconsidered
images and illustrations
capricious and varied
cautious and uniform
vehement and rapid
regular and constant
meditation and enquiry [84]

None of these pairs from Johnson is composed of nouns referring to different aspects of one readily identifiable object, like Addison's "Critick and Philosopher," or Hazlitt's "wit and critic." Johnson is less likely than Hazlitt to use pairs in the form of hendiadys— where the "and" could easily be displaced by an oblique construction, or where one of two nouns might become an adjective, or one of two verbs or adjectives an adverb. "Brilliance and effect" might be "brilliant effect"; "smooth and polished verse" might be "smoothly polished verse"; "tug and war" suggests "tug of war." Some of Johnson's might be altered thus, but do not so readily invite it.[85] Johnson is less likely to pair nouns which have a clear relation of genus and species and so have the effect of showing the generic direction in which the species is intended to be thought of. If "foppery" is a species of "folly," it is not quite so clear that "images" have that relation to "illustrations." On the whole the abstract and general character of Johnson's vocabulary makes it more difficult to see the exact relation of the words which he puts in pairs. The present topic has a close relation to that more celebrated one, Johnson's "Latin" or "abstract" diction, which is to be discussed in a later chapter.[86]

84. *Works* IV, 104–10.

85. *Schmidt* p. 10 says that hendiadys is infrequent in Johnson. It is even true that Johnson frequently writes the opposite of a hendiadys, two words in oblique relation where one would rather expect them to be coördinate. "Sinnverwandte Substantive subordiniert" is one of Schmidt's headings (p. 11). Cf. *post* p. 58, n. 25.

86. It must be admitted that word pairs occur plentifully in English literature long before Johnson or Addison. Professor J. M. Hart shows that the translator of the so-called Alfredian *Bede* has "almost incessant recourse to two terms for rendering one of the Latin ("Rhetoric in the Translation of Bede," *An English Miscellany Presented to Dr. Furnivall* [Oxford, 1901], pp. 150–4). Professor Oliver F. Emerson examines "practically synonymous" pairs of words in the Canterbury *Prologue* and the *Book of Common Prayer* ("Prof. Earle's Doctrine of Bilingualism," *Modern Language Notes*, VII [1893], 406–10). Cf. F. W. Bateson, *English Poetry and the English Language* (Oxford, 1934), pp. 31–2; Otto Jespersen, *Growth and Structure of the English Language*, 4th ed. (New York, 1923), pp. 96–8, 138;

Johnson's preference for emphasis rather than range in multiplications can never be fully realized except by seeing his multiplications in their contexts, their position in whole sentences and share
in the emphasis of the whole. In "My First Acquaintance with English Poets" Hazlitt writes:

I was at that time dumb, inarticulate, helpless, like a worm by the way-
side, crushed, bleeding, lifeless; but now, bursting from the deadly
bands that
      "bound them,
   "With Styx nine times round them,"
my ideas float on winged words, and as they expand their plumes, catch
the golden light of other years.[87]

The first sentence of *Rambler* No. 51 is this:

As you have allowed a place in your paper to Euphelia's letters from the
country, and appear to think no form of life unworthy of your attention,
I have resolved, after many struggles with idleness and diffidence, to
give you some account of my entertainment in this sober season of
universal retreat, and to describe to you the employments of those who
look with contempt on the pleasures and diversions of polite life, and
employ all their powers of censure and invective upon the uselessness,
vanity, and folly, of dress, visits, and conversation.[88]

Early in Hazlitt's sentence come two triplets, one on each side of
the image of the "worm," partly sensory, asyndetic, hurried; they
provide a momentary emphasis, after which the sentence rushes
on antithetically with its plumes and golden light, leaving the
triplets back by the way, like the worm itself. Johnson does the
opposite. He begins slowly, building up through couplets, "idleness and diffidence," "to give . . . and to describe," "pleasures and
diversions," "censure and invective," until he makes a climax of his
two deliberate triplets, smashingly, one upon the other. And so
with many a doublet; where it is jammed into the rush and prepara-
tion of the early part of one of Hazlitt's sentences, or scarcely heard
in passing some swift climax, it is by Johnson saved till the end, the
weightiest motive of the whole, toward which the whole labors
up and having reached which, has accomplished its destination.[89]

William Empson, *Seven Types of Ambiguity* (New York, 1931), p. 120; *ante* p. 21,
n. 22.
 87. Howe xvii, 107.
 88. *Works* v, 325.
 89. Professor Chandler writes: "Parallel structure in Hazlitt's sentences is not
limited to the duplication of predicate elements as is generally the case in Addison,
or to the duplication of clauses such as we find in Johnson; but occurs wherever the
author wishes to be emphatic or forceful" (*Chandler* p. 71).

CHAPTER II

Antithesis

BY multiplication a writer enforces what he means, or what he affirms. By every affirmation, however, something incompatible is implicitly denied; and what is denied, or what it would be relevant to deny explicitly, varies with what it is revelant to affirm. Each thing is all that it is in virtue of not being many other things, but it is what it is in each respect in virtue of not being some other particular thing. An inkwell stands on the *table* inasmuch as it does not stand on the floor. It stands *on* the table inasmuch as it does not stand under the table. It *stands* on the table inasmuch as it does not roll off. The negative defines the positive. The more peculiar and complex the affirmation the more it may need the emphasis of negation, the more negation itself, elaborated in its own aspects, may become a relevant and parallel meaning, until which is superior and which is subordinate is hardly to be told, rather the two as a pair of reflecting, reciprocal movements are the true theme of the discourse. This is characteristic of all thoughtful writing, that the author is interested not only in what is now but in what was or will be, what is in any other respect, what might be or ought to be—what he does mean and what he does not mean—in a word, in distinctions. When these distinctions crystallize into enough formality, they may be called antitheses.[1] Either term might be extended to all examples, the most formal might be called only "distinctions," the most rudimentary, "antitheses." Since our purpose is to examine the expressive tendency that underlies the figure of rhetoric called "antithesis," we shall retain that name, though most of the examples we shall have in mind or produce are not such as in most rhetorics would be called antitheses.

Perhaps the point at which antithesis will be felt by most readers as distinctly erupting from the surface of the context is where two single words are placed close together in opposition, the one idea negated, the other affirmed:

> not the power but the will to obtain a better state [2]

---

1. "Antithesis" means a "contrast of ideas expressed by parallelism of strongly contrasted words" (H. W. Fowler, *The Concise Oxford Dictionary* [Oxford, 1929]).
2. *Works* vii, 225, *Rambler* No. 178.

Yet a number of more rudimentary types may be defined. Among these some of the most noticeable are: a negative implication through a comparative; an expression of excess as in the word "too"; a statement with an exception. "Other causes besides his industry, his learning, or his wit." [3] In other words: Not his industry, his learning, or his wit, but . . . . The antithesis is left to inference. "Too envious to promote that fame which gives them pain by its increase." [4] Not generous enough to promote fame, but envious of it. "No crime but luxury." [5] Not other crimes, but luxury. The closeness of all such expressions to explicit antithesis may be seen in the following, where the germ of the antithesis contained in "more than" is developed in the next words. "Whatever facilitates our work is more than an omen, it is a cause of success." [6] And the following sequence of antitheses shows how much may be implied in a word such as "only."

> the folly of him who lives only in idea,
> refuses immediate ease for distant pleasures,
> and, instead of enjoying the blessings of life,
> lets life glide away in preparations to enjoy them [7]

The antithesis implied in the word "only" is expanded explicitly in the doublet that follows. Of course the potentiality of any expression to be expanded makes the definition of all these subantitheses a matter for hesitation.

To return to the grade of two opposed words, it is to be noted that these words need not be related by a "not . . . but." A great many ways of antithetical joining are possible. It may be by a comparative. "More frequently require to be reminded than informed." [8] "Willing rather to transmit than examine." [9] It may be by a relative or a conditional. "Frequently presumes to attempt what he can never accomplish." [10] "Which, if obtained, you could scarcely have enjoyed." [11] It may be by a preposition. "Have long accustomed themselves to receive all that chance offered them, without examination." [12] "To conquer without a contest." [13] Sometimes it is by the special meaning of some third term, though these

3. *Works* v, 13, *Rambler* No. 2.
4. *Ibid.*, p. 13.
5. *Works* v, 331, *Rambler* No. 51.
6. *Works* xi, 43, *Rasselas*, chap. xiii.
7. *Works* v, 8, *Rambler* No. 2.
8. *Works* v, 13, *Rambler* No. 2.
9. *Ibid.*, p. 8.
10. *Works* vi, 373, *Rambler* No. 129.
11. *Works* vii, 242, *Rambler* No. 187.
12. *Works* vii, 225, *Rambler* No. 178.
13. *Works* v, 8, *Rambler* No. 2.

cases are less definite. "Such busy preparations as naturally *promised* some great event." [14] "*Exalt* possibility to certainty." [15] "Whose abilities are *adequate* to his employments." [16]

Further, an antithesis concentrated in two words need not involve at all the negative expressed variously above by "not," "never," or "scarcely," by the preposition "without," or by the comparative. Let us consider this form as symbolized by A, *not* A'.[17] A and A' are notions so compatible that they might plausibly be affirmed together, and the point of the antithesis is to assert that while one is affirmed the other is negated. Suppose, however, that the negative of the antithesis be attracted into the notion which it modifies. Then we have A, *but not-A'*, a form conveniently illustrated by the following: "however unsuccessful, it will be at last rewarded," [18] which is about equivalent to "though not successful, it will be rewarded." Suppose the negative notion *not-A'* gives way to a positive equivalent, B. Then we have A, *but B*, where the antithesis consists not in a negation of one idea and affirmation of the other, but in the opposition or incompatibility of two ideas both of which are affirmed (or perhaps both negated).[19] "Events, however illustrious, are soon obscured." [20]

In every antithesis, the two affirmations or the affirmation and negation are made with respect immediately to some third notion more or less explicit in the context. In the example last quoted "illustrious" and "obscured" refer to events. The references or connections themselves are of a wide variety, but their particular character is of no importance to the antithesis. For this reason we may adopt the convention of designating the reference by "in." So we have A *in X*, *but B in X*, which is clearer if for the moment we change adjectives to nouns: "illustriousness in events, but obscurity in events." Or, A *in X*, *not A' in X*, "will in obtaining, not power in obtaining." This third element, usually named, as in all the above examples, but once, if at all, is not of importance in so simple a form.

14. *Works* v, 326, *Rambler* No. 51.
15. *Works* vii, 242, *Rambler* No. 181.
16. *Works* xi, 76, *Rasselas*, chap. xxvii. The italics in the last three quotations are mine.
17. Though the negative member often comes first, *Not A'*, *but A*, to distinguish this order from the other is not relevant to my purpose.
18. *Works* vi, 375, *Rambler* No. 129.
19. It will be noticed that we have swung very close to what we called "antithesis I" (*ante* pp. 22–3). The difference is one of emphasis. In antithesis I it is the equal relation of opposites to a third notion that is the point. In antithesis II it is the very distinction between the two notions both affirmed with respect to a third notion.
20. *Works* viii, 23, *Idler* No. 6.

It often happens, however, that this element is given a modulation that makes it contribute to the sharpness of the antithesis. If *A in X, not A' in X*, then *X*, expressed perhaps in one member, implied in the second, is not completely the same *X*, but, if only in virtue of being related once to *A* and again to *A'*, can be viewed under different relevant aspects, and this difference can be expressed by the use of the terms *X* and *X'*. So: *A in X, not A' in X'*.

> You may deny me to accompany you,
> but cannot hinder me from following.[21]

The simpler form, *A in X, not A' in X*, would be: "You may prevent me from accompanying, but not from following you." The distinction between "deny" and "hinder" corresponds to the relations of "prevent" to "accompany" and to "follow," so that in one sense it is a modulation of "prevent" and in another it is an extension of the antithesis between "accompany" and "follow." [22] Where some generic term is not easily found, it will be rather as extension of antithesis that the distinction is thought of.

In the example just seen there is a clear relevant distinction between "hinder" and "deny," but sometimes this is not so; the difference is felt to be rather "verbal":

> refuses immediate ease for distant pleasures [23]

The negative is conveyed in "refuses." So: "the future in pleasure, not the present in ease." But perhaps not much relevant meaning has been gained over: "the future in pleasure, not the present," or "the future in ease, not the present," that is, "refuses immediate for distant pleasures," or "refuses immediate for distant ease." The principal elements of this antithesis are those of time, present and future. Difference of time and difference of place, however, more often constitute the elements of extension of antithesis, or modulation of context (*X* and *X'*), as might be the case here were there a clearer relevant difference between "ease" and "pleasure." In fact

21. *Works* xi, 44, *Rasselas*, chap. xiv.
22. This tendency, analogous to that toward two or more elements of implicit parallel in multiplications, is, however, distinct from the other in that the parallel elements of a multiplication emphasize the equal relation of the members to a third notion, while the parallel elements of an antithesis emphasize rather a reciprocal relation of the members, that of adversity. The difference between two things is only notable or definable in so far as they are also alike. The likeness is the basis of the difference, against which it is measured and on which it depends. The parallel of antithesis expresses just this.
Another type of construction in which parallel emphasizes reciprocity is analogy. Occasionally Johnson makes the members of an analogy closely parallel.
23. *Works* v, 8, *Rambler* No. 2.

if this were so, it would be difficult to distinguish between the A, A' and $\ddot{X}$, X' elements. In general the A, A' elements may be considered as those in which the antithesis is more pointed and which could be less easily eliminated from the context. But for deciding that a given example belongs to this class it is not necessary to distinguish its A, A' and X, X' elements.

Just as A, *not A'* was translatable to A, *but B*, so A in X, *not A' in X'* is translatable to A in X, *but B in Y*. Or A in X, *but B in Y* can be considered a complication of A, *but B*. But it is not easy to illustrate these four forms with a single basic antithesis. The example just considered, A in X, *not A' in X'*, "the future in pleasures, not the present in ease," will yield the form A in X, *but B in Y*, "the future in pleasures, the present in pain." But for the form A, *not A'*, we have simply "the future, not the present." And to translate this into A, *but B*, it would be necessary to find some positive equivalent of "not the present" which was yet not too nearly an equivalent of "the future." Perhaps we might say, "the future, but by waiting." The following will illustrate more clearly the form A in X, *but B in Y*:

> Many things difficult to design
> prove easy to performance.[24]
>
> the regularity of her family,
> and the inconvenience of London hours [25]
>
> some phrases which, though well understood at present,
> may be ambiguous in another century [26]

This extension into two elements makes the antithesis in its most acute form. Here we have the parallel opposition mentioned in the *Oxford Dictionary*, distinctly noticeable as parallel, just as in our multiplications those of two elements of implicit parallel were much more noticeably parallel than simple word pairs. This is the form of such often-quoted antitheses as Macaulay's: "Not because it gave pain to the bear, but because it gave pleasure to the spectators." [27] A in X, *not A' in X'*, and the parallel is enforced by alliteration. A further increase of elements usually does not much increase the antithesis. Though the elements occupy parallel positions in the members of the antithesis, they are likely not to exhibit any distinction relevant to the antithesis.

24. *Works* xi, *Rasselas*, chap. xiii.
25. *Works* v, 326, *Rambler* No. 51.
26. *Works* viii, 23, *Idler* No. 6.
27. T. B. Macaulay, *History of England* (New York, 1856), i, 121, chap. ii.

> If you are pleased with prognosticks of good,
> you will be terrified likewise with tokens of evil.[28]

The real antithesis is between "good" and "evil," "pleased" and "terrified." The two words "prognosticks" and "tokens" have no difference in meaning relevant to the difference between good and evil. Except for the alliteration of "pleased with prognosticks," "terrified with tokens," there is no reason to prefer this arrangement to "tokens of good," "prognosticks of evil." In order that there should be a real antithesis of three elements, the common notion of prediction should be modulated so as to relate in one member especially to the good, and in the other to the bad.[29]

What is even more likely in extension of antithesis is a failure of correspondence of elements, a dilution or blurring. The X, X' or X, Y elements, or even the A, A' or A, B, may be expanded so that each is a phrase, roughly antithetical in the total of substantial meaning, but having no elements exactly matched in syntax or morphology. Inasmuch as X, X' and X, Y elements are, as we have seen, assumed out of the context, assimilated to the antithesis by the process of distinction, this blurring of antithetic elements is a kind of merging with the context. The antithesis, latent in all expression, bulges but does not project; or, around some point of projection, some two words clearly antithetic, there is a gradation to the nonantithetical level of the context.

We have seen that another quality of Johnson's style, his tendency to emphasis rather than range, was relatable to something which we have yet to discuss, his general and abstract diction.[30] The same thing may be said of his antithesis. Abstraction and generality are conditions which favor antithesis. Not things but aspects of them can be contrasted in words. The more a writing deals with aspects as such, that is, with abstractions, the more plastic it is and shapable into the exact oppositions of antithesis. Generality and abstraction are concentration of meaning into the pure forms which admit sharp contrast. "Honor" and "shame" make an antithesis which would be diffused in the naming of "patriot," "gentleman," "lady," and "traitor," "scoundrel," "harlot."

ii

LIKE parallelism, antithesis is something that anyone must have perceived, however indefinitely, on reading the typical prose of

28. *Works* xi, 43, *Rasselas*, chap. xiii.
29. "Promises of good . . . threats of evil," for example, would be more antithetical.
30. *Ante* p. 36.

Johnson.[31] Again there is no need of statistics to prove the existence of the quality. But if we count the number of clear antitheses of all types in our nine passages from Addison, Johnson, and Hazlitt, two conclusions will be supported. The first, that Johnson is more given to antithetical expression than either Addison or Hazlitt. (Even with an exceedingly low *Idler* No. 10, his totals are much higher than Hazlitt's and somewhat higher than Addison's.) [32] The second, that Johnson is more given to pointing his antitheses by extension or parallel. In the two classes of pronounced parallel, *A in X, not A' in X'*, and *A in X, but B in Y*, his quotients greatly exceed those of Addison and Hazlitt.[33]

But as with Johnson's parallel in multiplication, so with his parallel in antithesis—his special tendency is not adequately revealed by the excess of his averages over those of Addison and Hazlitt. Again it may be further insisted that his examples tend more to pronouncement of parallel than do those of the other two. Johnson repeatedly comes near the complete parallel of the models already presented. For example:

> If of Dryden's fire the blaze is brighter,
> of Pope's the heat is more regular and constant.[34]

> He did not court the candour,
> but dared the judgement of his reader.[35]

In Johnson's antitheses each member and each element is emphatic; it seems special and striven for. He is saying: Mark this difference and mark this. Hazlitt and Addison are more likely to be casual, irregular, or dealing with the unavoidable antitheses of their subject (an aspect of range as opposed to emphasis).

31. Johnson's antithesis has, however, received comparatively little systematic attention from the critics. See *Schmidt* pp. 42–6 and Hazlitt *post* pp. 48–9.

32. The quotients are: Hazlitt, "Dryden and Pope," 1.94; "Love of the Country," .71; "First Acquaintance with Poets," .53; Addison, *Spectator* No. 267, 1.60; *Spectator* No. 177, 1.90; *Spectator* No. 106, .92; Johnson, *Pope*, 2.06; *Rambler* No. 2, 1.87; *Idler* No. 10, .82. I use *Idler* No. 10 here because it was the *Idler* used in our study of parallels, but for antithesis it is hardly typical. *Idler* No. 6 (900 words, *Works* VIII, 21–4) has a quotient of 1.00; No. 71 (1,400 words, *Works* VIII, 283–8) has 1.36; and No. 43 (700 words, *Works* VIII, 171–4) has 2.29! Cf. *ante* p. 25, n. 36.

33. The quotients are: Hazlitt, "Dryden and Pope," .25; "Love of the Country," .24; "First Acquaintance with Poets," .06; Addison, *Spectator* No. 267, .33; *Spectator* No. 177, .40; *Spectator* No. 106, .17; Johnson, *Pope*, 1.00; *Rambler* No. 2, .47; *Idler* No. 10, .09.

34. *Works* IV, 110, *Life of Pope*. A high average of .71 per hundred words for antithesis of this type in the passage from the *Life of Pope* is due to the opportunity which Johnson found in his contrast of Dryden and Pope, ready-made elements, A and B.

35. *Ibid.*, p. 107.

His hair (now, alas! grey) was then black and glossy.[36]

Here one whole member is a parenthesis, the tone is varied by the exclamation, and one of the elements of the other member is expanded to two words.

as much the same trees and grass, that I had always been used to, as the sun shining over my head was the same sun which I saw in England; the faces only were foreign to me [37]

The Contents of both which Books come before those of the first Book in the Thread of the Story, tho' for preserving of this Unity of Action they follow them in the Disposition of the Poem.[38]

In the latter example Addison has hardly made any effort to sharpen or insist on the distinction which he finds in his material.[39]

In the lecture "On Dryden and Pope" Hazlitt, as if in accord with his neoclassic theme, lends himself more than usually to antitheses. But even here his prevailing tendency is revealed; for, though a number of these are extended to two elements, a larger number are simple, of one element, and a majority are blurred by irregularities.

in describing a row of pins and needles,
rather than the embattled spears of Greeks and Trojans

more delighted with a patent lamp,
than with "the pale reflex of Cynthia's brow"

for earthquakes and tempests,
the breaking of a flower-pot, or the fall of a china jar [40]

An important relation of antithesis to whole meaning is the degree to which antithesis breaks or turns the direction of discourse. This of course is determined in part by the number of antitheses. The more antitheses, major or minor, the more turns, great or small. But it is mostly determined by the number of major antitheses, those rooted directly in the central meaning. If a writer wishes to enforce an antithesis by multiplication, there are two main pat-

36. *Howe* xvii, 109, "My First Acquaintance with Poets."
37. *Howe* iv, 19, "On the Love of the Country."
38. *Morley* p. 383, *Spectator* No. 267.
39. The following from *Spectator* No. 267 is the only perfectly parallel antithesis I have found in the three passages from Addison: "uniform in its Nature, tho' diversified in the Execution." This is an emendation of the originally published text (*Morley* pp. xxiii, 383). In Hazlitt's lecture "On Dryden and Pope" there are the following and one or two others with perhaps as much parallel: "with no prodigies of nature, but with miracles of wit" (*Howe* v, 71).
40. *Howe* v, 70–1.

terns he may follow. He may state his antithesis, A, *not A'*, then develop one side of it by multiplication, A———A5, then the other side, A'———A'5. Or, he may break each side into its units and set these individually one from one side against one from the other in a series of antitheses: *A, not A', A1, not A'1, A2, not A'2*, and so on. The first pattern lays more emphasis on the character of each side as a whole. The two are set against each other as masses. The second insists continually and minutely on the antithesis itself.

In the lecture "On Dryden and Pope," Hazlitt states his antithesis: "the poet, not of nature, but of art." He then develops the notion of a poet of nature in a multiplication of about three hundred words. "Such was Homer, such was Shakspeare." Then with an antithetical hinge, "Pope was not assuredly a poet of this class," he returns to the poet of art and launches into an elaboration that runs for perhaps a thousand words blending into a discussion of Pope's poetry in detail. True, in the course of this there are numerous minor antitheses, some of which we have quoted above; Pope is contrasted to Shakespeare, he is contrasted to Milton; each one of his preferences is set against some opposite. But the whole emphasis, in the rapid flood of bright examples, is on what Pope was, a poet so strange that he can be characterized only by contrast to other poets.[41]

Johnson's way is different. It is true he begins his comparison of Pope and Dryden with a paragraph on Dryden's indifference to perfection and then three on Pope's meticulosity. But the third of these ends: "Pope had perhaps the judgement of Dryden, but Dryden certainly wanted the diligence of Pope." And with this begins the most impressive and emphatic part of the comparison, four paragraphs in which the attention alternates from Dryden to Pope and back, here and there a sentence or two on one or the other, but mostly the two matched in each sentence or each coördinate part of long sentences. "Dryden knew more of man in his general nature, and Pope in his local manners." "Dryden is sometimes vehement and rapid; Pope always smooth, uniform, and gentle." "Dryden is read with frequent astonishment, and Pope with perpetual delight."[42]

To Johnson's frequent use of major antitheses, and to his incessant scoring of paragraphs with all kinds of minor and implied antitheses, is due the abrupt, sectional character of his writing. It is put together with tight logic, it is eminently coherent and articulate, but it does not flow. Or, Johnson is like a man who marches a

41. *Howe* v, 69–70.
42. *Works* iv, 107–10.

short length in one direction, hitting to right and left as he goes, hammers three times at the end, then turns at right angles or back again and repeats. Logical progression is of that sort; it moves by distinctions, which are antitheses, which may be jerks.

When the purpose of the writer is persuasive rather than ex- pository, when he must argue in favor of something, antithesis may tend to retraction, nullification, or cancellation. There was no chance for this as long as Johnson was simply putting Pope and Dryden side by side for better exhibition. But in *Rambler* No. 2 he is giving moral advice. In the first five paragraphs he states the case against neglecting the present for the future, then, discrediting those who exploit this case, he asserts the necessity of man's look- ing ahead. But in the next paragraph he veers round completely, in a major antithetic reversal:

Yet as few maxims are widely received or long retained but for some conformity with truth and nature, it must be confessed, that this cau- tion against keeping our view too intent upon remote advantages is not without its propriety or usefulness. . . .

Now he is faced the other way. Yet before going ahead, as if to deny inconsistency, he has a look back in a concessive clause—

. . . though it may have been recited with too much levity, or enforced with too little distinction.

And not long does he keep even his feet going the same way. The next paragraph begins:

There would however be few enterprizes of great labour or hazard undertaken, if we had not the power of magnifying the advantages which we persuade ourselves to expect from them.[43]

"In all Johnson's disquisitions, whether argumentative or critical," says Sir John Hawkins, "there is a certain even-handed justice that leaves the mind in a strange perplexity. . . . Thus it is that he frequently raises an edifice, which appears founded and supported to resist any attack; and then, with the next stroke, annihilates it, and leaves the vacuity he found."[44]

43. *Works* v, 9–10.
44. *Works* i, 482–3, Hawkins' *Life* of Johnson. "He was fond of discrimination," said Sir Joshua Reynolds, "which he could not show without pointing out the bad as well as the good in every character" (*Life* ii, 306). "He has given a true repre- sentation of human existence," says Boswell, "and . . . he has, at the same time, with a generous benevolence, displayed every consolation which our state affords us" (*Life* i, 213). The habit is reflected in Johnson's concern for the rule of moderation, the golden mean. Cf. *Ramblers* No. 38, *Works* v, 245, and No. 129, *Works* vi, 372.

The opposite way is to favor emphatically one side of the initial antithesis, develop the other only by concession, and dwell on each for a continuous space without looking at the other. In the second paragraph of his essay "On the Love of the Country," Hazlitt states his thesis that natural objects interest us only through "recollections habitually associated with them." Then, antithetically, he concedes something of the opposite, "No doubt the sky is beautiful, etc." This concession he develops in a multiplication occupying half the paragraph, having eight members with considerable variation, summed up or repeated by a quotation of nine lines from Beattie's *Minstrel*. Only in the body of the next paragraph, after a minor antithesis, does he return to the positive side of his major antithesis, that natural objects interest us through associated recollections, but having returned to it, he dwells on it, develops it in a multiplication of three main members, each divided, the first into six, the second into three, and the third into two minor members, with great variety, the whole occupying about two thirds of the paragraph.[45] This way of writing reduces the number of turning points, the hesitations, the retractions. It soars away more boldly on the first enthusiasm, moves on the same logic without readjustment. It is this that makes possible in the writing of Hazlitt the large planes of meaning, the variegated details, all part of the same surface, the rush and flood and profusion; it is the generous abandonment to one point of view.

The danger of the antithetic mode, like that of the other kinds of meaning we have considered, is that it may assert itself at the cost of other meaning more relevant and satisfactory. Of this Hazlitt himself has accused Johnson specifically. In the Preface to the *Characters from Shakespeare's Plays* he speaks of Johnson's own Preface to the edition of Shakespeare:

He no sooner acknowledges the merits of his author in one line than the periodical revolution of his style carries the weight of his opinion completely over to the side of objection, thus keeping up a perpetual alternation of perfections and absurdities. We do not otherwise know how to account for such assertions as the following:—
"In his tragic scenes, there is always something wanting, but his comedy often surpasses expectation or desire. His comedy pleases by the thoughts and the language, and his tragedy, for the greater part, by incident and action. His tragedy seems to be skill, his comedy to be instinct."

45. *Howe* IV, 17–18. For the sake of brevity I have not presented a similar analysis of a passage from Addison. His writing, for example in *Spectator* No. 267, resolves into more antithetic turns than that of Hazlitt and fewer than that of Johnson.

Yet after saying that "his tragedy was skill," he affirms in the next page, "His declamations or set speeches are commonly cold and weak, *for his power was the power of nature:* . . ."[46]

There would seem to be much justice in Hazlitt's accusation. If Shakespeare's comedy pleases "by the thoughts and the language," doubtless the meaning is sharpened if the opposite may be said of his tragedy, that it pleases "for the greater part, by incident and action." Doubtless too this antithesis is strengthened if one may add the parallel: "His tragedy seems to be skill, his comedy to be instinct." Yet in this kind of writing there may be a kind of irresponsibility. How if Shakespeare's tragedy is not thus sharply antithetical to his comedy? And to make matters worse, how if the critic himself, perceiving in Shakespeare a quality at variance with one side of the antithesis, on the next page asserts the existence of this quality? Shakespeare's "power was the power of nature," yet a moment ago his tragedy was but "skill." Now the writing is at variance not only with its subject but with itself. And we may call this a fault of *style*—just as Hazlitt attributes it to "the very structure of his style"—because it arises from a habit of meaning. It may be called an exploitation of medium. It is cultivating expressive forms for their own sake.

46. *Howe* IV, 177. Cf. Hazlitt's other criticisms of Johnson quoted *ante* p. 32, *post* pp. 50, 62. Of all the adverse criticisms that have been made of Johnson's style Hazlitt's seems to me the most trenchant, far more formidable, for example, than Macaulay's.

Hazlitt's opinion of Johnson's antithesis is matched by Coleridge. Johnson's "antitheses are almost always verbal only; and sentence after sentence in the Rambler may be pointed out, to which you cannot attach any definite meaning whatever" (*Specimens of Table Talk* [New York, 1835], II, 140, 1 Nov. 1833). Coleridge thought the antithesis of Junius "less merely verbal than Johnson's" (*Literary Remains*, ed. Henry N. Coleridge [London, 1836], I, 239, Lecture XIV, 13 March 1818). It should be remarked that as words can hardly escape meaning something, it is impossible for antithesis to be "verbal only." What may loosely be described as a "verbal" antithesis is one which presents no distinction of meaning relevant to the context or such a distinction as in the context ought to be taken for granted. "The idle antithetical members of the sentence," says Raleigh, "*have been compared* to those false knobs and handles which are used, for the sake of symmetry, in a debased style of furniture" (Walter Raleigh, *Six Essays on Johnson* [Oxford, 1910], p. 17). "Clauses . . . which *have been compared*," says Whately, "to the false handles and keyholes with which furniture is decorated" (Richard Whately, *Elements of Rhetoric*, 2d ed. [Oxford, 1828], p. 266, Pt. III, chap. ii, No. 14). The italics are mine; I have been unable to find the source of this figure.

CHAPTER III

Diction

IN his parallelism we have seen Johnson more interested in the alignment of reasoning, the relation of premises to conclusions, than in the individuality of the premises themselves. In his antitheses we have seen him intent on showing the respect in which he does mean something by telling the respect in which he does not mean it. Both these are ways of attaining generalization, of referring to their relevant classifications the concrete or specific objects employed as the texture, really only illustrative, of thoughtful discourse. They are ways of insisting on the formal over the material. And in yet another important way Johnson did the same —in his peculiar choice of words, the distinctively Johnsonian vocabulary.

The critics have not differed much over what words are Johnsonian. "Words of Latin and Greek origin," says Schmidt, ". . . technical terms of philosophy, medicine and law," and he gives a long list of nouns ending in "ion." [1] "Pompous and long," says Matthew Arnold.[2] "In a learned language," says Macaulay, ". . . in a language in which nobody ever quarrels, or drives bargains, or makes love, in a language in which nobody ever thinks . . . . It is well known that he made less use than any other eminent writer of those strong plain words, Anglo-Saxon or Norman-French, of which the roots lie in the inmost depths of our language; and that he felt a vicious partiality for terms which long after our own speech had been fixed, were borrowed from the Greek and Latin . . . ."[3] "None but 'tall, opaque words' taken from the 'first row of the rubric,'" says Hazlitt—"words with the greatest number of syllables, or Latin phrases with merely English terminations."[4]

Scarcely a criticism of Johnson's style has been written without the mention of "long" words or "Latin" words. And the early, more

1. *Schmidt* pp. 4–8.
2. *The Six Chief Lives from Johnson's "Lives of the Poets"* (London, 1878), p. xix.
3. T. B. Macaulay, "Essay on Johnson," in *Macaulay's and Carlyle's Essays on Samuel Johnson*, ed. William Strunk, Jr. (New York, 1895), pp. 60–2.
4. *Howe* viii, 243, *Table Talk*, 1822, Essay xxiv, "On Familiar Style." Cf. *Howe* iv, 371.

vituperative criticisms abound in epithets like "polysyllabic," "pedantic," "hard," "obscure," "bombastic," "cumbrous."[5] "The teethbreaking diction of Johnson" was Walpole's expression.[6] "This may be a bookseller's project at bottom," said Archibald Campbell; "he might write his *Ramblers* to make a dictionary necessary, and afterwards compile his dictionary to explain his *Ramblers*."[7]

But we must approach the matter somewhat more thoughtfully. In the first place, if an expressive tendency sometimes leads an author to violate idiom, his violations may be exhibited as curiosities, and in proportion to their frequency the author may be more or less censured—for idiom, currency, is one of the conditions of effectiveness in the arbitrary medium of language. Yet these violations, understood however perfectly as violations, are no account of the expressive tendency that produced them. Professor Taylor has well said: "The whole tale is never told when one merely turns his pages—as one easily may—and unearths such a list of musty curiosities as the following: *proemial, momentaneous, interstitial, supplantation, supervenient, annuitant, obtunds, pravity, divaricate, amendations, propagate, procerity,* and *operose.*"[8] And the perhaps even more exaggerated examples with which O. F. Christie amuses himself are amusing only, not seriously instructive.[9]

Nor is it a stylistic evaluation of Johnson's words to consider where he learned them. The opportunities which a man has to learn this or that kind of vocabulary are certainly a part of his literary history and an important part, but they do not affect the description of his style as expression. The question whether Johnson's vocabulary is traceable to his work on the *Dictionary* is irrelevant here. And so is the question whether it is traceable to his classical education. It is not to the purpose to call his words Latin. Their derivation may have a historical connection with their type of meaning, but for the analysis of meaning this is an accident. If Johnson had been a Roman, he would probably have used Greek words. As a matter of fact it is possible that he uses almost as many

5. Some selections may be conveniently consulted in W. Vaughan Reynolds' "Reception of Johnson's Prose Style," *Review of English Studies,* xi (1935), 145–62.

6. Horace Walpole, *Letters,* ed. Mrs. Paget Toynbee (Oxford, 1904), ix, 173, 3 April 1775.

7. *Lexiphanes,* 2d ed. (London, 1767), pp. 108–9.

8. *Taylor* p. 25.

9. *Christie* pp. 27–8. From Johnson's works: speculatist, adscititious, abscinded, officinal, indiscerptible, papilionaceous, colorifick, frigorifick, fugacity, alexipharmick, equiponderant, reposited, orbity, catharticks, argumental, equilibrations, concatenations, oraculous, subducted, intenerate, oppugner, divaricate, irremeable. From Boswell's *Life:* formular, conglobulate, anfractuosities, labefactation, peregrinity, depeditation. Christie studies Johnson's treatment of these words in the *Dictionary.*

Greek as Latin words.[10] Again, it is but little more to the purpose to appeal to Johnson's *Plan of a Dictionary* and his *Preface to the Dictionary* and deduce from these his theory of propriety in English. If we consider Johnson's objection to "Gallick structure and phrase," his belief that the cultivation of the learned languages had helped to perfect and fix our language,[11] we may understand some of the limitations of his vocabulary but hardly his way of using it. A lexicographical principle is not a stylistic, not an expressive one.

If we would philosophize on Johnson's use of words, we must go again to his meaning, we must describe his words as tending to have certain kinds of meaning. At once then we see the inadequacy of simple lists of words or statistics of the occurrence of certain kinds of words defined merely by qualities that may be observed in them when isolated. What is needed is the context. For the "same" type of word becomes a different type in a different use. An impressive list of nouns in "ion," for example, such as Schmidt presents, may warrant the presumption that some way of using these has been of extraordinary frequency. But what the way is we may miss, because words in "ion" have been used by different writers in different ways.

ii

IN talking of Johnson's words there are in general three pairs of opposed notions that must be mentioned and usually have been, either more or less explicitly: the particular and the general, the concrete and the abstract, the sensory and the non-sensory. At the risk of being obvious I enter into a short discussion of the meaning and interrelation of these terms.

Generality in writing is more a matter of whole meaning than of diction, or at any rate it is hardly to be measured in terms of the latter. General terms, as opposed to particular terms, embrace almost the whole language. Only proper nouns, personal pronouns, and demonstrative adjectives and pronouns are in themselves particular.[12] And all particulars in thoughtful writing have an illustrative value, that is to say, a class value. Particularity is often a

10. Professor Chandler reports of the first thousand words of our passage from the *Life of Pope* that the percentage of classical words is 55.8, but that of Latin words only 26.3 (*Chandler* p. 42).
11. Cf. *Christie* pp. 26–7. Cf. *post* p. 104.
12. Of course any word may be particular, or "singular," in use. "That tree" is a singular term. So is "the second oak tree on the left of the road past the white wooden gates."

mere form, as when Addison introduces Eugenius in *Spectator* No. 177, or when Johnson devotes the whole of *Idler* No. 71 to Dick Shifter. All class terms are general, and those that are less general ought to be called more specific rather than more particular. Any given class word is more general or more specific according to the generic idea with relevance to which it is used. If I mention horses in a field in an enumeration of farm animals, I have been fairly specific. If I mention only horses in describing a racing farm, I have been general. For this, to be equally specific, I should know the breeds of horses, distinguish the mares, the stallions and the geldings, the fillies and the colts. And this is only to consider genera and species according to one order. There is also the matter of intersection of species. An apple in an orchard is not an apple in a lunch basket. Any term when put in different contexts assumes by implication relations to different generic scales. Further, an adjective or an abstract noun will have a more or less specific value according to the concrete noun with which it is associated. "Green woods" are less specific than "green hat," for the woods are expected to be green.

The act of generalization is a step toward that other which is called abstraction. In order to form the class concept "animals" it is necessary to see a number of dissimilar objects under an aspect which they have in common; nevertheless the concept is still of the actual objects. It is the act of attending to this concept itself which is better called abstraction. The aspect, adjectival when considered as embodied in the object, is invested with substantiality of its own; and we have "animality." [13] As a usual thing the more general the idea by the first process, the more likely the mind is to find a use in the abstraction. "Animality" is a more common abstraction than "horsiness" or "equinity," and the latter more common than "colthood" or "coltiness." The more specific the class notion becomes, the more difficult it is to conceive it abstractly or at least to find an abstract word for it. And so abstraction depends on generalization, and an author's tendency to abstraction is likely to be in proportion to his tendency to generalization.

The foregoing may have suggested the standing of the terms "sensory" and "non-sensory" in our inquiry. They are as relative as "particular" and "general." Even an onomatopoeic word has some arbitrary, generalized value, or it is not a word. And even an ab-

13. Cf. Abraham Wolf, *Textbook of Logic* (London, 1930), pp. 118–19; Désiré Cardinal Mercier, *Cours de Philosophie*, Vol. I, *Logique* (Louvain, 1902), p. 102; Richard Whately, *Logic* (in *Encyclopaedia Metropolitana*, First Division [London, 1851]), Introduction, pp. 25–6.

stract word referring to a mental state, like "thoughtfulness," is abstracted from experiences which are partly sensory and must faintly suggest them. For thinking is done through the imagination, and the imagination draws its material from the senses. An abstract word like "greenness" has much more sensory value than a concrete word like "man." All that can be said in general is that particular or more specific words tend to be more sensory than general or abstract ones. There are more physical qualities connoted in the word "colt" than in "equine." And it may be added that verbs of thought, even the more specific ones, like "speculate," "ponder," "muse," those which are dead metaphors, have little sensory content, while adjectives denoting qualities perceptible to the senses, "green," "harsh," "fragrant," have the greatest, though even this is diluted by frequent metaphorical use, as when one speaks of "harsh manners." A writer's proportion of sensory values will correspond to his use of the specific. And as no single class word can be called absolutely specific or absolutely general, so no word can be called absolutely sensory or absolutely non-sensory. The terms are contraries rather than contradictories.

iii

IT is rather as a character of general meaning than as a detail of meaning,[14] as style, that one must be content to consider Johnson's tendency to generalization. It is possible to produce a list of words from Hazlitt like the following:

brilliance, buckles, lake, lamp, library, lustre, mariner, masquerade-dress, bosom, brow, dew-drops, garden, glass, spring, sun, pale, paste, cottage, glittering, smooth, soft, stamped, stripped, trembles, laugh, wandered, winged [15]

And to make a list from Johnson to set beside them:

objects, present, schemes, felicity, commodious, serious, ridiculed, wantoning, blessings, transmit, futurity, progressive, horizon, allurements, fear, fatigue, contemplation, harvest, maxims, caution, propriety, usefulness, levity, distinction, vehemence, inquietude, fruition [16]

14. Under this head, however, one might place Johnson's fondness for relative clauses of characteristic (i.e., classification), especially those with a completely indefinite antecedent—"he that," "that which," "what," etc. I note, for example, five of these in our passage from the *Life of Pope* and no fewer than nine in *Rambler* No. 2.

15. Professor Chandler's list chosen from the passage of the lecture "On Dryden and Pope (*Chandler* p. 62).

16. From *Rambler* No. 2, *Works* v, 7–10.

We may call Hazlitt's words sensory and specific, Johnson's non-sensory and general.[17] Yet it is only in a vague and collective sense that this is so, and only because we know the contexts too that we accept these lists as representative of any quality of meaning. Though many of Johnson's words in the above list could not by any use have much sensory value, it is only the use of a word that ever gives it any. It may be instructive to compile the following list from the same *Rambler:*

raillery, gay, wantoning, shine, glide, flowery, gradual, horizon, flights, steps, eyes, ground, harvest, blights, inundations, sweep, reaping, riot, slipped, magnifying, crown, island, squire, mirth, plants, sun, gardens, physick, catharticks, lenitives, dispel, cloud, luminaries, library, caressed, huddled, fluctuating, immersed [18]

Not even at first glance so promising as Hazlitt's bright array. Yet who without the context could guess the dryly non-sensory, intellectual use of these words, the semimetaphorical "track so smooth and so flowery," "flights of the human mind," "horizon of his prospects," or "steps to a certain point," or the flat illustrative value of "an island to bestow on his worthy squire"? And if we limit the inquiry to the matter of specific or general, it is even more hopeless to define or count. Anyone looking for general words would have to admit that in our first list from *Rambler* No. 2 "schemes" and "fear" are rather general. Yet which is more general? And where is the line to be drawn? On which side of these words? Or between the two?

On the other hand, Johnson's bent for generality cannot be denied. It is part of his moral purpose. It is derived from the very subjects of his essays and suggested in their titles. It is apparent as a character of his general meaning on almost any page.[19] And if he

17. Professor Chandler reports that in the first thousand words of the passage from the *Life of Pope* there are only three sensory adjectives out of sixty-nine, and out of 105 verbs only seven "denoting action" (*Chandler* pp. 43–4).
18. *Works* v, 7–13.
19. Only Johnson's extraordinary contentment with generality could prompt some of the criticisms that have been made of his writing. Northcote said that the character of Zachariah Mudge in the *London Chronicle*, 2 May 1769, "was like one of Kneller's portraits,—it would do for anybody" (*Life* iv, 77, n.1). Boswell's friend Dempster wrote "that a great part of what was in his 'Journey to the Western Islands of Scotland,' had been in his mind before he left London" (*Life* iii, 301). Hawkins says of the same work, "His web was spun, not from objects that presented themselves to his view, but from his own pre-existent ideas" (*Works* i, 482). John Nichols told Boswell that the *Debates in Parliament* "were frequently written from very slender materials, and often from none at all,—the mere coinage of his own imagination" (*Life* iv, 408. Cf. *Life* i, 506–7, Appendix A). Miss Talbot complained to Mrs. Carter of the *Rambler*, "Why then does he not write now and then on the living manners of the times?—The stage,—the follies and fashions"

is interested in generality, in the classes to which things belong, the aspects which unify groups of objects, he becomes at moments even more interested in these aspects as things in themselves, as metaphysical realities. Allowing the physical objects to be pressed out of sight,[20] he erects the metaphysicalities or abstractions into the substantives of his discourse. And in order to accommodate these substantives he resorts at times to certain extraordinary distortions of prose.

Some examples may be seen in the following paragraph from *Rambler* No. 2:

This quality of looking forward into futurity seems the unavoidable condition of a being, whose motions are gradual, and whose life is progressive: as his powers are limited, he must use means for the attainment of his ends, and intend first what he performs last; as by continual advances from his first stage of existence, he is perpetually varying the horizon of his prospects, he must always discover new motives of action, new excitements of fear, and allurements of desire.[21]

Johnson has gone far out of his way to bring in the two very general abstractions "quality" and "condition," where the concrete form would be simply: "To look forward into the future seems unavoidable for a being whose motions are gradual." Then "attainment" is an abstraction, and instead of "for the attainment of his ends," the verbal form "to attain his ends" would be preferred by many writers.[22] But the closing phrases of this paragraph show Johnson

(*Series of Letters between Mrs. Elizabeth Carter and Miss Catherine Talbot*, ed. Montagu Pennington [London, 1809], I, 371).

Cf. *post* pp. 93–4 for evidence of Johnson's consciousness and justification of his use of generality.

20. Professor Chandler reports that in the first thousand words of the passage from the *Life of Pope* the percentage of concrete words is only 19.7, while in the same number of words from Addison it is 38.3 and from Hazlitt, 32.3 (*Chandler* p. 43). She reports also that "Johnson uses comparatively few nouns,—fewer *in proportion to his vocabulary* than any of our other writers," 37.8 per cent to Hazlitt's 44.6 and Addison's 41.8 (p. 42). The italics are mine. He might use the same nouns a good many times each. It is also possible that her definition of abstraction includes generalization.

21. *Works* v, 9, *Rambler* No. 2.

22. Robert R. Aurner says of Addison's prose, "The unusually large number of gerunds or verbal nouns adds to the natural liveliness and resiliency of his writing, and makes it seem active, kinetic, and verbal as with Dryden's, rather than heavy, potential, and substantive as with Johnson's" ("The History of Certain Aspects of the Structure of the English Sentence," *Philological Quarterly*, II, [1923], 200).

The relation of abstraction to the parts of speech is roughly this: Abstract words are nouns, though of course not all nouns are abstract. Adjectives refer to qualities conceived as *in things;* when the things are concrete, so are the adjectives. Finite verbs are adjectives predicated. The gerund and infinitive are hence abstract substantives. "Green" is to "greenness" as the participle (adjective) "running" is to "to run." Nevertheless, we tend to conceive physical actions as separable from their

in his most abnormal employment of the abstract noun in place of another part of speech—the linking of noun to noun, or piling of noun upon noun, by the preposition "of." In "attainment of his ends" the verbal notion is so strong that this objective genitive construction is hardly noticed as containing two nouns. The meaning of such genitive constructions can, however, vary widely, according to the nature of the nouns and their relation to each other. We may have, for example, the subjective genitive, "fear of men" (for death); the objective, "fear of death" (by men); the qualitative, "house of stone," and so on, through many shades of meaning perhaps uncatalogued by grammarians.[23] What Johnson specializes in is a form of the *appositional* genitive in which one noun is abstract, or both. "He must always discover new motives of action, new excitements of fear, and allurements of desire." The last two members of this triplet are a development of the first and taken together are parallel to it. The relations of the three pairs of words connected by "of" are different. "*Motives* of action" are *motives for* action—namely, "fear" and "desire," which, though parallel to "motives," occupy the position of second noun in the last two phrases. The element of action disappears at the end of the phrase, and in its place, but at the beginning, appear the two words "excitements" and "allurements," abstract, in appositional relation to "fear" and "desire." The notion "fear" (itself perhaps abstract) has the quality of exciting pulled out of it and formed into a second abstraction; so "allurements" is pulled out of "desire"; and the pairs of abstractions float in unstable expansion, each ready to collapse into one. The use of verbs would have made the expressions more concrete: "new fears to excite him and desires to allure him," and perhaps would have created a more apparent shade of tautology (multiplication irrelevant to the context).

In the first paragraph of the same *Rambler* occurs the expression:

ridiculed, with all the pleasantry of wit, and exaggerated with all the amplifications of rhetoric [24]

But "wit" is not an agent who displays "pleasantry"; both are qualities of mind or talk displayed by some agent, or better two aspects of the same mental actions or talk. To say "the pleasantries of wit"

agents and hence concrete. We go to see a race (a running), but not to see a greenness. A more persuasive abstract suggestion is obtained from those verbs, mostly of mental action, which admit a noun form on the same root. With the words "thought" or "attention" we lose most of the idea of action for that of quality.

23. For a more elaborate treatment, see John H. Scott and Zilpha E. Chandler, *Phrasal Patterns in English Prose* (New York, 1932), pp. 125–35.

24. Works v, 8.

is to make one grow out of the other, like a hump on the hump of the camel. A more ordinary form would be "pleasantry and wit," a typical Johnsonian doublet for emphasis, but less abstract, for here the two terms are parallel, each capable of an abstract or a concrete interpretation. Much the same may be said for "amplifications of rhetoric." If rhetoric is personified into a rhetorical speaker, the construction may be interpreted as a subjective genitive, with "amplifications" referring to the amplified things said by this speaker. But one is more likely to conceive "rhetoric" as a way of speaking or writing and "amplifications" as another, if a more specific, aspect of the same way.[25]

Along with these abstractions may be noted the passive voice and the absence of concrete nouns denoting agents. The abstractions assume the responsibility of the agent and are usually in an oblique case. "It has been marked with every epithet of contempt."[26] Or the verb itself becomes an abstraction, the agent disappears, and what would be the object is connected with the abstraction of a verb by some other verb. "Which escape vulgar observation,"[27] instead of "which people do not commonly observe." Or the abstraction not only assumes the responsibility of the agent but fills his shoes as subject of the action. "That vehemence of desire which presses through right and wrong to its gratification, or that anxious inquietude which is justly chargeable with distrust of heaven."[28] An abstraction of an abstraction pressing through right and wrong to another abstraction. In the *Life of Watts*, we have "Mr. Pinhorne . . . to whom the gratitude of his scholar afterwards inscribed a Latin ode."[29] In *The False Alarm*, "Lampoon itself would disdain to speak ill."[30] Or in any part of the sentence, as subject, as

25. Schmidt groups these constructions under "Fülle des Ausdrucks," along with word pairs. "Sinnverwandte Substantive subordiniert" he calls them and gives a list, in which the following are good examples of synonymy (nearness of relevant meaning, emphasis rather than range): "the coldness of neglect" (*Works* vi, 307, *Rambler* No. 119); "the infirmities of decrepitude" (*Works* v, 379, *Rambler* No. 59); "the gloom of sorrow" (*Works* v, 334, *Rambler* No. 52). He gives a shorter list where the noun is modified not by an abstraction but by an equivalent adjective (*Schmidt* pp. 9–12). *Rambler* No. 30, from which he selects "lazy idleness" (*Works* v, 198), was written by Catherine Talbot (*Courtney* p. 25).

26. *Works* v, 8, *Rambler* No. 2.

27. *Ibid.*, p. 8. Once before, in a conspicuous place, Johnson used the abstract "observation" less fortunately:

Let observation with extensive view,
Survey mankind, from China to Peru.

"Let observation with extensive observation observe mankind extensively." (For the origin and development of this paraphrase see *Life* i, 193, n. 3, 537, App. G.)

28. *Works* v, 10, *Rambler* No. 2.

29. *Works* iv, 179.

30. *Works* x, 5.

object of verb, as object of preposition, may appear abstractions that are but the faintest shade removed from personification.[31]

The danger of constant abstraction, besides its leading to occasional violation of idiom, is, like the danger of other types of meaning we have considered, that of irrelevant meaning. A series of metaphysical substantives engrafted into a discourse, standing out like shadows from every concrete substantive or rising like ghosts in the level road of verbs and adjectives, is a series of meanings that may point in many wrong directions. Abstraction is the conjuring into substantiality of qualities which in the physical world have not this dignity. Many qualities, quite relevantly named, are nevertheless, like the paint on a bench, better for lying flat. Enough has been said by many a writer [32] on the virtue of concrete nouns and active verbs—how they touch directly what is meant, cut swiftly to the heart of matters. Although in every context some abstractions may be relevantly named, it does not follow that abstraction is a safe prescription for any of the things sometimes vaguely associated with good writing, for dignity or sublimity, force or authority.

iv

BUT the two traits of generalization and abstraction lead Johnson to a third which I consider to be preëminently the Johnsonian trait of vocabulary—the use of general or abstract words which have a scientific or philosophic flavor. "Philosophick" he called them him-

31. As early as 1787 the Reverend Robert Burrowes published his "Essay on the Stile of Doctor Samuel Johnson," which in some respects is as penetrating as anything since written (See *Burrowes*). "The instrument, the motive, or the quality therefore," he writes, "which ordinary writers would have in the oblique case, usually takes the lead in Johnson's sentences; while the person, which in connected writing is often expressed by some weak pronoun, is either intirely omitted, or thrown into a less conspicuous part. Thus, 'fruition left them nothing to ask,' and innocence left them nothing to fear,'—'trifles written by idleness and published by vanity,'—'wealth may, by hiring flattery, or laying diligence asleep, confirm error or harden stupidity' . . . . and we are teized with the repeated mention of 'ear of greatness,'—'the bosom of suspicion,'—and 'the eye of wealth, of hope, and of beauty'" (p. 45). Burrowes devotes three pages to abstractions of various kinds, closely paralleling much that I have said above. He collects some examples that I should not venture to exhibit as typical: "places of little frequentation," "circumstances of no elegant recital," "with emulation of price," "the library which is of late erection," "too much temerity of conclusion" (pp. 46–7).
   The two parts of Burrowes' essay were reprinted anonymously and as original, verbatim, in the *Port Folio* [Series V], Vol. XI (Philadelphia, 1821), pp. 300–09; Vol. XII (1821), pp. 32–42.

32. See for example the trenchant lecture "On Jargon" by Sir Arthur Quiller-Couch, *On the Art of Writing* (Cambridge, England, 1916), pp. 96–103.

self.[33] There are certain words for denoting objects which may not denote these any more generically than other words denoting the same objects, but which suggest that the objects are to be thought of as a class, rather than as individuals; they emphasize by their tone the aspect under which the class is conceived and have little or no connotation of complete appearance or the physical accidentals which clothe individuals of the class. These terms speak as having been coined by men who knew more accurately than common men the precise aspect, or complex of aspects, that constitute the class, who named classes only after studying them and with the advantage of vast preliminary erudition, men who understood the nature of things. These, in short, are scientific terms, what Schmidt recognizes as the "technical terms of philosophy, medicine and law,"[34] careful terms, and because careful, weighty, carrying authority. Such, for example, is the word "equine." As a noun it refers to no other object than a horse, but it suggests that the writer knows what a horse is: as an adjective it means "horselike," yet it is one word, established, whereas there is that of the makeshift, unready, unauthoritative, about "horselike." The difference is most apparent in terms which actually belong to science. But it appears all through the language. It is the difference between "domicile" and "home," between "cursive" and "running," between "incise" and "cut," even, by extension of the implication, between "frequently" and "often."

It happens that almost all of these terms, if not all of them, are Latin and Greek. This is the accident of their derivation, that the learned tongues were levied upon for the terminology of philosophy and then for that of the growing physical sciences, "natural philosophy," and that the learned tongues were Latin and Greek.[35] So Latin and Greek derivation becomes implicitly learned and authoritative; the character is more or less extended to all words of direct Latin or Greek derivation, whether strictly scientific or not, down to adverbs of such common occurrence as "frequently" and "subsequently." In these the character is of course very faint but can become noticeable by multiplication.

It happens too that Latin and Greek learned derivatives are long.[36] And to length of words I am ready to grant some expressive

33. *Post* p. 109.
34. *Ante* p. 50.
35. Cf. Otto Jespersen, *Growth and Structure of the English Language* (New York, 1923), pp. 115–16.
36. Professor Taylor counts the number of syllables per word of sections of Johnson's prose and finds the average high, 1.55 in exposition, 1.53 in biographical narrative. "Wordsworth's *We Are Seven* averages 1.18 syllables per word; a sec-

value—that of emphasis. The scientific authority, the deliberation and certainty, is backed up by a thump on the table. The big word is big enough to enforce its big meaning,[37] to increase the strength of the less emphatic parts of the sentence, to clinch the already more emphatic parts. If Johnson would use a doublet of nearly synonymous words mainly for emphasis, why not one big one, or a doublet of big ones?

In considering philosophic words we have of course the same problem of context as with the specific and sensory. We must proceed, not by statistics, but by examining the function of such words as may securely be called Johnsonian. When Johnson said of *The Rehearsal*, "It has not wit enough to keep it sweet," then in correction of himself, "It has not vitality enough to preserve it from putrefaction," [38] he composed in the second version what I believe everyone will admit to be a highly characteristic Johnsonian expression. Moreover, it cannot be disputed that its character depends largely on the diction. Yet one bent on listing Johnsonian words could hardly stop in manageable limits if words like "vitality," "preserve," "putrefaction," were to be included. "Such was the intense vitality of the Béarnese prince." Surely the word "vitality" itself has its innocence. And see what Carlyle could do with the plural. "He was full of bright speech and argument; radiant with arrowy vitalities." "Putrefaction" is less exonerable; its use shines through it more, and perhaps did even more in Johnson's day. Yet Marryat in 1833 was certainly not being Johnsonian when he wrote: "The body is never allowed to remain many hours unburied in the tropical climates, where putrefaction is so rapid." And even in 1756 Gray wrote to Wharton: "I maintain that one sick rich patient has more of pestilence and putrefaction about him than a whole ward of sick poor." [39] And for the word "preserve," who would care to list its humble uses? It is when "vitality" is the alternative to "wit,"

tion from James's *Psychology* that I have in mind, 2.07. Between the two styles lies the ocean. I have come to the conclusion through analyzing many passages that *normal* exposition—by which limitation I mean to exclude simple personal prose on the one hand and technical prose on the other—will fall between 1.45 and 1.50 syllables per word, and that normal descriptive or narrative prose will find its limits between 1.30 and 1.40" (*Taylor* pp. 27, 30). He finds that Macaulay has about the same word length as Johnson, and De Quincey a somewhat greater. [But of course they may not use long words in the same way as Johnson. "Philosophick" words are long words, but long words, not necessarily "philosophick" words.] Johnson's word length remains about the same throughout his career (*Taylor* pp. 29–30). Cf. *post* p. 87.

37. Cf. Herbert Spencer, "The Philosophy of Style," in Lane Cooper's *Theories of Style* (New York, 1907), pp. 276–7.

38. *Life* IV, 320.

39. *New English Dictionary*, "vitality," 3, 4; "putrefaction," 1, 1.b.

or to what would be of its own generic level, "life," that its philosophic character is seen. And "putrefaction" loses its philosophic character when applied in a matter-of-fact, gruesome way to a corpse, or disgustingly to a sick man, but shows this character in full when used in the abstract realm of literary criticism. "Preserve" in this context shows perfectly how a common word (not directly Latin in derivation, but French) becomes philosophic when it displaces a still more common word. The Old English "cēpan" might father a sturdy enough plain English word, but never a philosophic one.

As a further illustration I offer the following sentence from *Rambler* No. 2.

In agriculture, one of the most simple and necessary employments, no man turns up the ground but because he thinks of the harvest, that harvest which blights may intercept, which inundations may sweep away, or which death or calamity may hinder him from reaping.[40]

"Agriculture" is the "philosophic" term for "farming"; "intercept," for "cut off"; "inundations," for "floods." The terms "harvest," "blights," "sweep away" are non-philosophic or plain, of the same rank as the alternatives just suggested. In this sentence there would perhaps be small loss of meaning were all of the six terms plain.

The danger is once more that of irrelevant meaning. If it is remembered that a "philosophic" word has a kind of meaning, a connotation, which its plain equivalent lacks, it will be easily understood that to use "philosophic" diction constantly is to give to writing an irrelevant overtone, to emphasize or attempt to emphasize every word in a monotonous uproar. It is to Johnson's "philosophic" diction that Hazlitt refers when he says: "He always translated his ideas into the highest and most imposing form of expression," [41] and when he says again, "The fault of Dr. Johnson's style is, that it reduces all things to the same artificial and unmeaning level." [42]

40. *Works* v, 9.
41. *Howe* iv, 371, "On Manner," in the *Examiner*, 27 Aug. 1815.
42. *Howe* vi, 101–2, *Lectures on the English Comic Writers*, 1819, Lecture v, "On the Periodical Essayists."

CHAPTER IV

Other Qualities

IF we recall our definition of style as the last and most detailed elaboration of meaning,[1] we must see that only a few of the qualities that may be ascribed to a writing are properly stylistic. This precludes a complete account of a writing in a study of style. One of the characteristics of Johnson's biographical writing is his analytic disposal of material, the life of a poet in one part, and in another the literary estimate. It is this more than any other quality that distinguishes earlier biography from the Stracheyan school of synthesis and interpretative arrangement. Yet this is not one of the topics to be discussed in a study of style. It is part of a broader study of meaning; in defining style as a part of meaning we imply room for such another part.

There are other qualities of writing which may be legitimately discussed as style, but most often not as peculiar to a given writer. They are parts of detailed meaning, but are kinds of meaning shared so widely among writers that, even when appearing in combination with more peculiar qualities, they are not parts by which the style of the given writer may be defined. Such, for example, is sentence length. It is possible to study the length (and with it the structure) of the Johnsonian sentence and to compile relevant statistics. The latter Professor Taylor has done and reports for the early *Ramblers* a high average of 51.4 words per "indicated" (punctuated) sentence and even of 36.7 per "actual" (structural) sentence, but a decrease through Johnson's later career to 28.3 and 18.6 in expository sections of the *Lives*.[2] If we compare Johnson's sentences with those of other English prose masters, we find him heavy in the scale of length and complexity, but not heaviest, and not as heavy as other writers whose prose on the whole may seem less massive.[3] But there is a description of Johnson's sentence by

1. *Ante* p. 11.
2. *Taylor* p. 41. The matter of the changing length of Johnson's sentence is noticed again *post* p. 88.
Professor Taylor's well-drawn distinction between "indicated" and "actual" sentence length has a relation to what is said *post* Appendix A about punctuation.
3. Professor Aurner studies the sentences of Caxton, Lyly, Bacon, Dryden, Addison, Johnson and Macaulay, counting numbers of clauses and of words. Caxton, whose sentences are the loosest, averages 5.26 clauses and 65.07 words. Dryden, "the most powerful agent of literary history in reducing the sentence to reasonable

Professor Osgood which seems to me more relevant to the question of style than any other that has been written.

His sentences are nearly always declarative, and the normal order of statement is seldom altered. Entire sentences from capital to period are not as a rule periodic; but his sentences are often compound, and the single member or clause is generally cast into periodic form. The subordinate clauses are also unvaried and narrow in range, and are kept strictly subordinate in sense, as well as in structure; his commonest subordinate form is the relative clause restrictive.[4]

ii

IN the same category as sentence-length I should put what is called "imagery." It is a true stylistic quality (more important than sentence-length) but one that has no special relevance to the description of Johnson's style. Boswell himself several times praises Johnson's "imagery" or "fancy," [5] and recently the notion has been taken up by O. F. Christie.

proportions," averages in a passage of the *Essay of Dramatic Poesy* 6.01 clauses and 60.76 words. Johnson in a *Rambler* passage averages 4.08 clauses and 44.03 words. Cf. with the higher figure of Professor Taylor quoted above (Robert R. Aurner, "The History of Certain Aspects of the Structure of the English Sentence," *Philological Quarterly,* II [1923], 187–208).

Professor Aurner's average of 44.03 words per sentence for the *Rambler* is taken from Edwin H. Lewis, *The History of the English Paragraph* (Chicago, 1894), p. 115. The average is that of 94 paragraphs. For 58 paragraphs of *Rasselas,* Professor Lewis finds an average of 30.78.

Professor Chandler reports of the passages chosen by her for analysis, "In general, the minimum limit of Pater's sentences (65) is the maximum limit of Addison's (63) and of Johnson's (65) (*Chandler* pp. 85–6). It is alarming to compare the minimum of 65 given to Pater by Professor Chandler with the average sentence length of 36.5 given to the same author by L. A. Sherman, "Some Observations upon the Sentence-Length in English Prose," *University Studies of the University of Nebraska,* I (1892), 130.

The weight of English sentences has been further studied according to the "number of clauses saved by the substitution of present and past participles or by the use of apposition." In 500 periods from the *Life of Milton* Johnson stands about midway among English authors. Pater is high; Addison, low (G. W. Gerwig, "On the Decrease of Predication and of Sentence Weight in English Prose," *University Studies of the University of Nebraska,* II [1894], 20–1, 38. Cf. L. A. Sherman, *Analytics of Literature* [Boston, 1893], pp. 296–7.)

4. Charles G. Osgood, *Selections from the Works of Samuel Johnson* (New York, 1909), p. xxxi. Cf. *Taylor* p. 49; *Schmidt* p. 28. The general question of periodicity I avoid, believing that as much as is relevant to Johnson's style has been implied in what was said above about emphasis (*ante* pp. 32–7). Professor Taylor counts in 298 sentences of the first ten *Ramblers* four notably loose sentences of exposition and thirty-one notably periodic; in 585 sentences of exposition from the *Lives,* no loose sentences and twenty-three periodic (*Taylor* pp. 42–3).

5. *Life* II, 335; III, 317; IV, 116, 428. In *Life* I, 40, n. 3 Boswell quotes Miss Seward to the same effect.

It is in "imagery" that Johnson excels, in picturesqueness of phrase, in apt and concentrated and vivid expressions. This is Johnson's predominant quality, in which, as a prose writer, he has never since been surpassed.[6]

But "imagery" has not generally been chosen for remark by those who praised Johnson's style. And to me it seems that the term is susceptible of such wide interpretation that among the different qualities which may go by the name one at least is sure to be found in almost any good writing, and that the "imagery" of Johnson's writing is imagery only in the most diluted sense. One of the most recent and most deliberate students of imagery, Professor Spurgeon, writes: "When I say 'images' I mean every kind of picture, drawn in every kind of way, in the form of simile or metaphor—in their widest sense." [7] If one may judge from Professor Spurgeon's extended treatment of the subject,[8] she means that imagery is not only non-literal but pictorial—that it is simile or metaphor which has a strong imaginative appeal. This is probably the most useful way to define imagery, the best way to preserve a limited meaning for the term. But if imagery is to be taken in this way, the question how much imagery is to be found in a writing will have a close connection with that already discussed, how much sensory terminology is to be found, how many of the author's terms suggest sense impressions, or images. And, as we have already seen, Johnson's terms tend to be non-sensory, his meaning to be general and abstract. If Johnson's writing may be said to contain imagery, we must understand the term in another sense, that of simply nonliteral expression. If it be remembered that not all nonliteral expression, that is, not all metaphor, need be highly sensory, it can be admitted that in some sense Johnson's writing contains imagery. Since a great part of language, and almost all abstract language, is metaphor, dead, half dead, or alive, the use of metaphor,—"the unique expression of a writer's individual vision," or "the result of the search for a precise epithet"—shades imperceptibly into the use of the proper word, the word most relevant in a context. This is the merit of good diction in its most unspecified sense, a sense in which it may be attributed to every good writer. And it is only in this sense that imagery may be attributed to Johnson. The extracts

6. *Christie* p. 57.
7. Caroline F. E. Spurgeon, *Shakespeare's Iterative Imagery* (London, 1931), p. 4.
8. *Op. cit.* and *Shakespeare's Imagery* (New York, 1935). Cf. G. Wilson Knight, *The Wheel of Fire* (London, 1930); *The Imperial Theme* (London, 1931); *The Shakespearian Tempest* (London, 1932).

arrayed by Christie [9] to illustrate Johnson's style and particularly the shorter, epigrammatic ones, support this conclusion. "Time is, of all modes of existence, most obsequious to the imagination." [10] The word "obsequious" is metaphorical, relevant, expressive, a good example of Johnson's felicity of diction. There is an odor of the "philosophic" about it; nevertheless it has its more special value in the context and justifies itself eminently. This is Johnson's kind of imagery, which is founded, like all apt diction, in an imaginative concept, but in which there is little sensory value and no need of such value. We need not imagine Time as a butler bowing to his master the Imagination. This is too much; it spoils by irrelevance. Apt diction draws on all the implications of words but leaves most of them remotely implicit. Johnson refines "obsequious" of almost all sensory value, perhaps down to its etymological sense, of "following," certainly to its archaic metaphorical sense of "obedient."

Perhaps this is the thing most characteristic of Johnson's "imagery," a tendency to reverse dead metaphors, to force them back to their etymological meaning so that they assume a new metaphorical life. Professor Chandler writes:

Whatever power of suggestion terms such as *sedate* and *quiescent* . . . may have when separated from the context is lost when found in the clause, "good sense alone is a *sedate* and *quiescent* quality, which manages its possessions well but does not increase them"; . . . The diction here is not suggestive but exact. One is reminded of the primary meaning of words, not of their acquired meaning: of their denotation; not, of their connotation.[11]

And the Reverend Robert Burrowes offers a good illustration.

Ardour, which in his preface to his Dictionary, he observes, is never used to denote material heat, yet to an etymologist would naturally suggest it; and Johnson accordingly, speaking of the "*ardour* of posthumous fame," says that "some have considered it as little better than *splendid* madness; as a *flame kindled* by pride and *fanned* by folly.[12]

9. *Christie* pp. 38–57.
10. *Works* ix, 260, *Preface to Shakespeare.*
11. *Chandler* p. 44.
12. *Burrowes* p. 49. Cf. *Works* ix, 211, *Preface to the Dictionary.*
I do not mean to imply that Johnson is the only writer who uses words in this way. Even one so different from Johnson as James Joyce has been detected in the same usage (Joseph Prescott, "James Joyce: a Study in Words," *PMLA,* liv [1939], 308–9). And see Geoffrey Tillotson, *On the Poetry of Pope* (Oxford, 1938), pp. 72–3, for the use of words in their "literal Latin sense" by Sylvester, Sandys, and Pope.

iii

MISCELLANEOUS other qualities of Johnson's prose might be considered in brief and have been by other writers. Schmidt, for example, glances at asyndeton, polysyndeton, climax, oxymoron, rhetorical question, and others. This seems to me perfunctory, a mere following of a manual of rhetoric. My purpose has been to exploit those rhetorical topics which have special relevance to the Johnsonian style. There remain two others which I have reserved to this point as less important than parallelism, antithesis, and abstract and philosophic diction, but more important than those just briefly dismissed. These two are "inversion" and its special form "chiasmus."

The Reverend Robert Burrowes considered that Johnson's "endeavours to attain magnificence . . . taught him the abundant use of inversions . . . . Almost all his sentences begin with an oblique case." [13] Macaulay speaks of Johnson's "harsh inversions, so widely different from those graceful and easy inversions which give variety, spirit, and sweetness to the expression of our great old writers." [14]

W. Vaughan Reynolds, defending Johnson against the Reverend Robert Burrowes, maintains that Johnson's "use of inversions is not 'abundant' . . . . In the first ten *Ramblers* I can find only seventeen inverted constructions—not an inordinately large number in sixty-five pages of the 1792 edition of his *Works*. Johnson's critics seem to have paid too much attention to his inversions." [15]

It is perhaps true that seventeen is not an "inordinately large number" of inverted constructions for ten *Ramblers*. But what this means is not so clear. What is an inverted construction? What is an inordinately large number?

Not the number of Johnson's inversions, but their kind, must be the first critical inquiry. The meaning of the term "inversion" is not a thing to be assumed. Inversion, in general a reversal of a sequence, cannot be specifically understood until some normal sequence is defined. The application of the term "inversion" to English sentences must be based on the assumption that there is a normal order of words in the English sentence. This, it may be supposed, is roughly that of subject, then predicate, and within the predicate,

13. *Burrowes* pp. 47–8.
14. *Macaulay's and Carlyle's Essays on Samuel Johnson*, ed. William Strunk, Jr. (New York, 1895), p. 62. Schmidt and Professor Chandler have also noted Johnson's inversions (*Schmidt* pp. 36–9; *Chandler* p. 48).
15. "The Reception of Johnson's Prose Style," *Review of English Studies*, XI (1935), 150 and n. 6.

first verb, then object or predicate nominative or adverbial modifier. But if inversion means a deviation from this order, or even if it means particularly a deviation at the beginning of the sentence, we are swamped with inversions in every writer. Every time we begin a sentence with an adverbial clause of any kind, or with a prepositional phrase or an infinitive phrase, not to mention other forms less frequent, we are guilty of inversion.

To define Johnsonian inversion we must determine what forms of inversion are admitted by English idiom and what are not. Johnson's peculiar use of inversion is the use of forms that are not English.

Inversion, we may generalize, is in harmony with English usage when the subordinate clause or phrase put in the initial position modifies some word, usually a verb, which follows immediately or almost immediately, or when the clause or phrase is a loose modifier of the whole clause that follows. Even the object of a verb is acceptable at the start of a sentence when followed immediately by subject and verb, though the construction always has the tone of license, of the rhetorical or poetic. The substantive clause as object is likewise an acceptable license, though it has in prose the archaic tone. As subject in the first position it can scarcely be distinguished from a predicate, and an anticipatory "it" subject is more normal.

Johnson's peculiar inversion includes, in the first place, a number of these acceptable but licentious inversions of noun objects or of substantive clauses.

These benefits of nature he improved.[16]

That he who spends more than he receives, must in time become indigent, cannot be doubted.[17]

In the second place he verges on the unidiomatic by separating these elements too widely from the words on which they depend.

The composition of the pudding she has, however, promised Clarinda, that if she pleases her in marriage, she shall be told without reserve.[18]

Whether perfect happiness would be procured by perfect goodness, said Nekayah, this world will never afford an opportunity of deciding.[19]

In the third place, he is unidiomatic in his inversion of nouns in oblique cases. And this is his worst fault of inversion. The preposi-

16. *Works* IV, 104, *Life of Pope.*
17. *Works* VII, 224, *Rambler* No. 178.
18. *Works* V, 329, *Rambler* No. 51.
19. *Works* XI, 76, *Rasselas,* chap. xxvii.

tional phrase which we have already mentioned as acceptable at the start of a sentence is, of course, an oblique noun with its governing preposition—"in case," "for the moment," "over the mantel." These acceptable prepositional phrases, however, usually depend on verbs. Johnson's peculiarity is that he inverts phrases depending on nouns or on adjectives. Also a few of his phrases depending on verbs are for special reasons unidiomatic.

Of composition there are different methods.[20]

Of genius, that power which constitutes a poet; that quality without which judgement is cold, and knowledge is inert; that energy which collects, combines, amplifies, and animates; the superiority must, with some hesitation, be allowed to Dryden.[21]

On necessary and inevitable evils, which overwhelm kingdoms at once, all disputation is vain.[22]

From this inattention, so general and so mischievous, let it be every man's study to exempt himself.[23]

For this suspicion, every catalogue of a library will furnish sufficient reason.[24]

With the news of a lottery I was soon gratified.[25]

Of the gardener I soon learned that his lady was the greatest manager in that part of the country.[26]

As an expressive tendency inversion is not far different in Johnson from what it is in other writers. And his violation of idiom is interesting stylistically only in that it indicates the extreme of the tendency. The usual purpose of any writer in inverting is to obtain

20. *Works* IV, 105, *Life of Pope.*
21. *Works* IV, 109, *Life of Pope.*
22. *Works* XI, 77, *Rasselas,* chap. xxviii.
23. *Works* VIII, 174, *Idler* No. 43.
24. *Works* V, 12, *Rambler* No. 2.
25. *Works* VII, 239, *Rambler* No. 181.
26. *Works* V, 327, *Rambler* No. 51.

In the same category I put oblique cases at the beginning of medial or final substantive clauses. "It is not to be inferred that of this poetical vigour Pope had only a little" (*Works* IV, 109, *Life of Pope*). "He saw immediately, of his own conceptions, what was to be chosen, and what to be rejected" (*Works* IV, 104, *Life of Pope*). The inversion of nonrestrictive relative pronouns which depend on nouns is also a strain on idiom. "Our language, of which the chief defect is ruggedness and asperity" (*Works* VI, 107, *Rambler* No. 88).

It is not my contention that these constructions abound in Johnson, but that, being so odd, they occur frequently enough to make a strong impression. I count, for example, in *Rambler* No. 2 one pair of substantive clauses and one noun with preposition; in *Idler* No. 10 one noun with preposition; in our passage from the *Life of Pope* three objects of verbs, eleven nouns with prepositions.

relevance through order, and especially that kind of relevance known as coherence, which means sequence or continuity. Or, since continuity is maintained by a series of emphases, we may say that the purpose of inversion is emphasis. A sentence following another sentence in a continued discourse must in some way relate to it, either roughly to the whole, or more precisely to one of the parts, and if one of the parts of the second sentence relates particularly to a part of the first or the whole, then this meaning can be strengthened implicitly by the form of juxtaposition. It is in this regard that we all start most of our sentences. We strive to begin with that element of the new sentence which relates most clearly to the final element of the preceding sentence or to its whole sense. (For the same reason we keep the pronoun near its antecedent.) This sentence ordering, "inversion" if one likes, is even taught in school books.[27] It might be illustrated, though superfluously and tediously, by several of our Johnsonian examples if they were restored to their contexts.[28]

But there are some further reasons why a writer may maneuver a given element to the fore in a sentence. One is a more absolute reason of emphasis, at the start of a new topic, where a writer would call attention not to what has gone immediately before, but to what is to be the next immediate center of interest. Johnson has been talking of Pope's diligence and perseverance. He next wishes to say a few words about Pope's method of composition. Therefore: "Of composition there are different methods." [29] Again, there is a use that is more peculiarly Johnsonian, inversion for the purpose of clearing the way for another construction. "It is not to be inferred that of this poetical vigour Pope had only a little, because Dryden had more." [30] After the disposal of "poetical vigour" at the start of the sentence, "little" and "more" may follow in antithetic

27. See, for example, Joseph M. Thomas *et al.*, *Composition for College Students* (New York, 1932), p. 170. Cf. H. W. Fowler, *A Dictionary of Modern English Usage* (Oxford, 1927), "Inversion," esp. p. 287.

28. Schmidt notes this purpose of continuity in inversions of object and verb (*Schmidt* p. 38).

Professor Lewis would make Johnson's coherence depend not on the ordering of words so that "the mind shall pass from one sentence to another without check" but on "the directness of the thought and the skill of the balance." But as he offers little illustration, it is difficult to contend with him. He says more specifically: "Few men have used initial connectives less than Johnson did, and none has depended less upon them. Of 300 sentences in *Rasselas* 25 only are joined by formal conjunctives, whether initially or internally" (Edwin H. Lewis, *The History of the English Paragraph* [Chicago, 1894], pp. 116–17, 176).

29. *Works* iv, 105, *Life of Pope*. The same expressive purpose is to be observed in the pair of substantive clauses with which *Rambler* No. 2 opens (*Works* v, 7–8).

30. *Works* iv, 109, *Life of Pope*.

balance at the ends of their respective clauses. Finally, an inverted element itself may be put in antithetic position.

If of Dryden's fire the blaze is brighter, of Pope's the heat is more regular and constant. Dryden often surpasses expectation, and Pope never falls below it. Dryden is read with frequent astonishment, and Pope with perpetual delight.[31]

The unidiomatic inversions in the first sentence of this passage are a contribution to the balanced antithesis of the whole.

Johnson's inversion is intrinsically an expressive word order. It is part of his inclination to logic, his interest in the pattern of premises and conclusion, which sometimes sacrifices the quality of his premises. It happens not to be idiomatic in English; it is idiomatic in some other languages. Forms of expressiveness available in one language need not be available in another. The mastery of a language consists in accommodating the needs of intrinsic formal expressiveness to the limitations of idiom. This Johnson at moments fails to do because his idiom is fused with another idiom, the Latin. Where the demands of expressive form are more easily or more economically answered by the Latin idiom, he adopts the Latin, when another writer would preserve English idiom by recasting his meaning. And very often what he gains in coherence is more than offset by the intrusion of irrelevant meaning which is concomitant with the unidiomatic. There is an insurgence and agony of language; the emphasis shouts too loud.

iv

A CONSTRUCTION which occurs occasionally in Johnson and which may be called an inversion perhaps more accurately than those just considered is the rhetorical figure of "chiasmus." Chiasmus is reversed order in a pair of expressions: 1—2:2′—1′. 2′ and 1′ may be analogous to 1 and 2 and hence form an inverted parallel.

Her marigolds(1), when they are almost cured, are often scattered by the wind(2), the rain(2′) sometimes falls upon fruit(1′) when it ought to be gathered dry.[32]

Or the relation may be antithetic:

a life in which pleasures(1) are to be refused for fear of invisible punishments(2), and calamities(2′) sometimes to be sought, and always endured, in hope of rewards(1′) that shall be obtained in another state.[33]

31. *Works* iv, 110, *Life of Pope.*
32. *Works* v, 331, *Rambler* No. 51.
33. *Works* vii, 223, *Rambler* No. 178. This is chiasmic on a scheme of pleasure—pain:pain—pleasure.

A third possibility is that 2' and 1' should stand in some functional relation to 1 and 2, for example, that of result to cause.

They have never contemplated the difference between good(1) and evil(2) sufficiently to quicken aversion(2'), or invigorate desire(1').[34]

It will be observed that in the first two of these examples the context contains other more or less isolable elements parallel in the two chiasmic halves. If these come between 1 and 2 and between 2' and 1', they make a pair of pivots on which the chiasmic elements turn; so they add somewhat to the chiasmic effect. In the first example "scattered" and "falls" are of this sort, and in the second, "refused" and "sought." [35]

The expressive value of chiasmus is more complex than that of inversion. First there is a value of continuity in the juxtaposition of 2 and 2', but since these are not identical terms, or referentially equivalent, as often in inversion, but are usually alike only in that they are analogous parts of parallel constructions, there comes with the expression of continuity one of movement, of passage from idea to idea. At times, especially in verse, when 2 and 2' can be interpreted as having the same relation to 1, there occurs a moment of suspension while the reader need not decide whether he is completing one clause or entering on another, a suspension which is expressive in that it suggests for 2' a double relevance, both to 1 and to 1'. This is one of Mr. Empson's kinds of poetic ambiguity.[36]

A second value of expression in chiasmus is that of the elements 1 and 1', which are the extremes, the second bringing us back to the first, where we started. There is an unbroken sense of movement in the chiasmus, 1 introducing 2 by an explicit logical connection, 2 introducing 2' by an implication of juxtaposition and analogy, 2' introducing 1' by another explicit connection and 1' reminding us by analogy of 1. Hence a sense of completeness and of reciprocal relation, which is relevant especially to antithesis,

34. *Works* VII, 225, *Rambler* No. 178.

35. See *Schmidt* p. 36 for some other examples, among which the following is quite clear-cut, as the halves consist of simple enumerations of three words each: "whose ancestors have, by their virtue, their industry, or their parsimony, given them the power of living in extravagance, idleness, and vice" (*Works* V, 95, *Rambler* No. 15).

The greatest concentration of chiasmus which I have noted in Johnson's works is in *Rambler* No. 129 (*Works* VI, 370–5), seven occurrences in the 1,400 words. But occurrences are usually few, and I dwell on this figure only because of its highly special and neoclassic character, which makes even a sprinkling perceptible, and because of its relation to the forms of "inversion" more common in Johnson's prose.

36. William Empson, *Seven Types of Ambiguity* (New York, 1931), p. 67.

whether in prose, or in the heroic couplet,[37] where combined with the closure of rhyme chiasmus is at its best.[38]

37. See *post* pp. 125–8 for a discussion of the couplet as an antecedent of Johnson's prose.

38. For shorter accounts of Johnson's style which I have not had occasion to quote in the course of these chapters see Charles Wells Moulton, *Library of Literary Criticism* (Buffalo, 1902), iii, 753–68.

CHAPTER V

Consistency of Johnson's Style

MORE perhaps than any other English prose writer Johnson is said to have changed his style as he grew older, to have bettered it. Macaulay says:

Since Johnson had been at ease in his circumstances he had written little and had talked much. When therefore he, after the lapse of years, resumed his pen, the mannerism which he had contracted while he was in the constant habit of elaborate composition was less perceptible than formerly, and his diction frequently had a colloquial ease which it had formerly wanted. The improvement may be discerned by a skilful critic in the *Journey to the Hebrides*, and in the *Lives of the Poets* is so obvious that it cannot escape the notice of the most careless reader.[1]

And within the era of tabulation Professor Taylor has offered corroboratory evidence in one respect, that of sentence length.[2] The only voice raised in emphatic dissent has been that of Dr. Birkbeck Hill.[3] It must be apparent that in some sense Macaulay is right, that in some way Johnson's writing is "lighter" in the *Lives of the Poets* than in the *Rambler*. The question to be decided, then, is one of classification or definition. Is the greater "lightness" of the *Lives* of a sort that should be referred to Johnson's style? It is just this that Dr. Hill denies, and his denial is what I wish to sustain and elaborate.

As a preliminary, something may be said of Johnson's conversation itself, which Macaulay praises highly before making it the source of Johnson's improvement in writing. "When he talked, he clothed his wit and his sense in forcible and natural expressions." [4] "As respected style, he spoke far better than he wrote. Every sentence which dropped from his lips was as correct in structure as the most nicely balanced period of the *Rambler*. But in his talk there were no pompous triads, and little more than a fair proportion of

1. "Samuel Johnson," *Encyclopedia Britannica*, 11th ed., Vol. xv (Cambridge, England, 1911), p. 470, col. 2. Cf. *Misc.* ii, 351–2, Tyers' *Sketch*; Leslie Stephen, *Samuel Johnson* (New York, n.d.), pp. 168, 186.
2. *Post* p. 88.
3. "Dr. Johnson's Style," *Macmillan's Magazine*, lvii (1888), 190–4. Cf. the opinion of Alexander Chalmers *post* p. 84, n. 44; and Allen T. Hazen, *Samuel Johnson's Prefaces & Dedications* (New Haven, 1937), p. xxii, n. 19.
4. *Macaulay's and Carlyle's Essays on Samuel Johnson*, ed. William Strunk, Jr. (New York, 1895), p. 60.

words in -*osity* and -*ation*. All was simplicity, ease and vigour." [5]
Macaulay's description fits a good deal of the recorded conversation of Johnson. There are many shorter conversational passages in
the *Life* in the same style as the sustained monologue of 20 July
1763:

In civilized society, personal merit will not serve you so much as money
will. Sir, you may make the experiment. Go into the street, and give one
man a lecture on morality, and another a shilling, and see which will
respect you most. If you wish only to support nature, Sir William Petty
fixes your allowance at three pounds a year; but as times are much altered, let us call it six pounds. This sum will fill your belly, shelter you
from the weather, and even get you a strong lasting coat, supposing it
to be made of good bull's hide. Now, Sir, all beyond this is artificial, and
is desired in order to obtain a greater degree of respect from our fellow-
creatures. And, Sir, if six hundred pounds a year procure a man more
consequence, and, of course, more happiness than six pounds a year,
the same proportion will hold as to six thousand, and so on as far as
opulence can be carried.[6]

In this extraordinary piece of reporting, if we may believe it is not
an assemblage of pieces, but represents Johnson's unbroken discourse,[7] we have something like a spoken essay, and it must be
admitted it is something quite unlike a *Rambler*. Here is the
method by example rather than generality, the swift tide of un-
elaborated short statement, the deft insertion of subordinate matter
without recourse to periodicity. The style of Johnson the writer
appears in a few philosophic words, "procure," "opulence"; but
most of the words are plain and blunt, the outcrop of the underlying specific vein of meaning. The tone is the dogmatic cynicism
of the conversational Johnson (when he talked to be contradictory), like the dogmatism of his essays, but not like their more
hopeful castigation of vice and folly. Emphasis is secured, not by
balanced antithetic words (though there is antithesis) or by
weighty groups of big words, but by conversational methods,
by short independent clauses, syntactic isolation, by "Sir," "Now,
Sir," "And, Sir." [8]

5. *Loc. cit.*, p. 468, col. 2.
6. *Life* I, 440. The above is less than a third of the whole passage.
7. Mr. Geoffrey Scott, after a study of Boswell's Journals and "papers apart,"
came to the conclusion "that, whenever the *Life* contains a long and closely rea-
soned chain of discussion between a group of speakers, the source did not consist
of a number of brief notes, subsequently enlarged at leisure, but in an immediate
feat of memory where the entire argument was swiftly preserved in condensed language and remained in that form until Boswell came to write the *Life*" (*BP* VI, 144).
8. This conversational device of Johnson's, by which he so often raises himself
to a height from which to descend emphatically into his sentence, is the mark
of a man who must find other strong means of emphasis in his writing.

Grant, then, that Macaulay's description of Johnson's talk is a fair statement of some of the truth. There is on the other hand the fact that Johnson frequently did speak just such philosophic words as appear in his writing. "There is a good deal of Spain that has not been perambulated." "In the description of night in Macbeth, the beetle and the bat detract from the general idea of darkness,— inspissated gloom." "A speech on the stage, let it flatter ever so extravagantly, is formular." "There is in it such a *labefactation* of all principles, as may be injurious to morality." "It has been maintained that this superfoetation, this teeming of the press in modern times, is prejudicial to good literature." "Sir, among the anfractuosities of the human mind, I know not if it may not be one, that there is a superstitious reluctance to sit for a picture." "He might have *exuberated* into an Atheist." [9] Mr. S. C. Roberts has made what seems a just observation, "that while long words and laboured phrases may well be a source of weariness or irritation in a familiar essay, they may nevertheless provide entertainment in conversation." Phrases which in the *Rambler* would be "quoted as illustrating the verbal elaboration of Johnson's literary style . . . . are typical of the kind of sentence that readers of Boswell delight to quote." [10] But it may be added that we read such utterances with delight in Boswell only because we hear the great moral essayist speaking as he writes; it is intimate, revealing, surprising, and funny. There is a shade of self-parody that Johnson himself seems to feel and exploit. [11]

Between these extreme examples and the other sort, which best support Macaulay's estimate, there is the average, a kind of grave, carefully shaped conversation which is much more like a moral essay than that of any other man who ever talked. Examples may be found at random in the *Life*.

JOHNSON. 'Every society has a right to preserve publick peace and order, and therefore has a good right to prohibit the propagation of

9. *Life* I, 410; II, 90, 234, 367 (Cf. *BP* VI, 45); III, 332; IV, 4, 98. It will be seen that these are not confined to the middle part of Johnson's career.

10. *Doctor Johnson* (New York, 1935), p. 49.

11. We have already (*ante* p. 61) had occasion to quote perhaps the best example, Johnson's correction of himself in pronouncing judgment on *The Rehearsal*. "He seemed," says Boswell of this occasion, "to take a pleasure in speaking in his own style" (*Life* IV, 320). Sir Walter Raleigh explains that "Johnson's talk was free from self-consciousness; but Boswell, when he was in the room, was conscious of one person only, so that a kind of self-consciousness by proxy is the impression conveyed" (*Johnson on Shakespeare* [London, 1929], p. xxxi). It appears to me rather that Johnson's "complacency," his consciousness and amused acceptance of his own worth, included a certain study of himself and intention to be what he was. See, for example, *Life* I, 204, 443; II, 15, 66, 362; III, 7, 260; IV, 166, 179, 183–4; *Letters* II, 313–14, No. 860.

opinions which have a dangerous tendency. To say the *magistrate* has this right, is using an inadequate word: it is the *society* for which the magistrate is agent. He may be morally or theologically wrong in restraining the propagation of opinions which he thinks dangerous, but he is politically right.' [12]

Johnson admitted that "he made it a constant rule to talk as well as he could both as to sentiment and expression," "to impart whatever he knew in the most forcible language he could put it in." [13] And we have clear evidence that to his contemporaries his conversation did seem like his essays. Sir John Hawkins wrote that Johnson talked "in such language, that whoever could have heard and not seen him, would have thought him reading." [14] "Johnson spoke as he wrote," recollected Sir Brooke Boothby. "He would take up a topic, and utter upon it a number of the *Rambler*." [15] "His conversation is the same as his writing," wrote Mrs. Harris of Salisbury in 1775.[16] The young lady from America, Miss Beresford, who was fortunate enough to hear Johnson in the coach to Oxford in 1784, said to Boswell aside, "How he does talk! Every sentence is an essay." [17]

Miss Burney had just been reading the *Life of Cowley* when she reflected:

how very like Dr. Johnson is to his writing; and how much the same thing it was to hear or to read him; but that nobody could tell that without coming to Streatham, for his language was generally imagined to be laboured and studied, instead of the mere common flow of his thoughts. "Very true," said Mrs. Thrale, "he writes and talks with the same ease, and in the same manner." [18]

If we suppose that Miss Burney's notion of Johnson's writing was at this moment formed chiefly from reading the *Life of Cowley*, then this passage supports Macaulay's contention that there is a connection between Johnson's conversation and his later style. But one may wonder whether her recent reading of this work was sufficient to alter a notion of Johnson's writing that must have been formed over a number of years by the reading of the *Ramblers* and other works of his middle period. And the same may be said of Mrs. Thrale. Both these ladies, while praising Johnson's talk as

12. *Life* ii, 249.
13. *Life* i, 204; iv, 183–4; cf. ii, 323.
14. *Works* i, 164.
15. Robert Anderson, *Life of Johnson* (1815), p. 322, quoted in *Misc.* ii, 391.
16. *Letters of the 1st Earl of Malmesbury* (1870), i, 302, quoted in *Life* ii, 520, App. B.
17. *Life* iv, 284. For further illustration see *Works* i, 385; *Life* v, 12; *Misc.* ii, 237–48, Reynolds' imitation of Johnson's conversation.
18. C. B. Tinker, *Dr. Johnson & Fanny Burney* (New York, 1911), p. 71. Cf. Bowles's description of Johnson's conversation, *Life* iv, 236–7.

natural and easy, are struck with the resemblance between his talk and his writing. What they seem to mean is that Johnson's writing itself is easy, not only the *Lives,* which they are just reading, but the *Ramblers* and *Rasselas,* the works which they would think of as characteristic. *"The Rambler,"* Mrs. Thrale was to say in the *Anecdotes,* ". . . expressed in a style so natural to him, and so much like his common mode of conversing." [19] And: "We used to say to one another familiarly at Streatham Park, Come, let us go into the library, and make Johnson speak *Ramblers.*" [20]

It appears to me unlikely that Johnson's conversation was a source of whatever lightness appears in his later writings, that as he grew older and wrote and talked more he talked himself into a simpler way of writing. What is more tenable is that all his life Johnson exhibited different degrees of his own peculiar style both in his talk and in his writing, and that especially in his writing this is to be referred to differences of subject matter.

ii

WE may begin to illustrate this from a body of Johnson's writing which lies closest to his conversation, his letters. Macaulay noticed the lightness of some of the letters, particularly those from the Hebrides. "His letters from the Hebrides to Mrs. Thrale are the original of that work of which the Journey to the Hebrides is the translation." [21] And Macaulay compares a sentence from the *Journey:*

Out of one of the beds, on which we were to repose, started up, at our entrance, a man black as a *Cyclops* from the forge.[22]

and what Johnson had written to Mrs. Thrale:

When we were taken upstairs a dirty fellow bounced out of the bed where one of us was to lie.[23]

Macaulay could have cited a number of other passages of this kind.[24] Where the letters to Mrs. Thrale and the *Journey* touch on

19. *Misc.* I, 348.
20. Hayward's *Piozzi,* I, 297, quoted in *Misc.* I, 347, n. 3.
21. *Macaulay's and Carlyle's Essays on Samuel Johnson,* ed. William Strunk, Jr. (New York, 1895), p. 61.
22. *Works* x, 371.
23. *Letters* I, 251, No. 326.
24. For example, Johnson wrote in the *Journey:* "To make this way, the rock has been hewn to a level with labour that might have broken the perseverance of a *Roman* Legion" (*Works* x, 353), while to Mrs. Thrale he had written, "These roads have all been made by hewing the rock away with pickaxes, or bursting it with

the same subjects, it is true that the *Journey* is cast in more emphatic patterns and is more serious or philosophic—that is, the "style" is heavier. The purpose of the *Journey* is certainly not that of the letters to Mrs. Thrale; its whole intended meaning is not the same. What is of more importance to note in Johnson's collected *Letters* is the clean cleavage between his essay style and at least two other styles, the factual and the playful, all three of which occur side by side almost from the beginning to the end.[25] Dr. Hill says, "In his letters little change in his diction can be traced from the first one to the last."[26] Little change from first to last, but abrupt changes within the space of a single letter at any time from first to last. In December 1755 we find him writing to Miss Boothby:

Of the fallaciousness of hope, and the uncertainty of schemes, every day gives some new proof; but it is seldom heeded, till something rather felt than seen, awakens attention. This illness, in which I have suffered something and feared much more, has depressed my confidence and elation; and made me consider all that I have promised myself, as less certain to be attained or enjoyed. I have endeavoured to form resolutions of a better life; but I form them weakly, under the consciousness of external motive. Not that I conceive a time of sickness time improper for recollection and good purposes, which I believe diseases and calamities often sent to produce, but because no man can know how little his performance will answer to his promises; and designs are nothing in human eyes till they are realized by execution.

But in the same letter:

Mr. Fitzherbert sent to-day to offer me some wine; the people about me say I ought to accept it, I shall therefore be obliged to him if he will send me a bottle.[27]

What has become of the Rambler? What has affected him so suddenly? The answer is certainly not that he has lost his style. Rather he has lost his subject. Even the Rambler cannot make antitheses and parallels out of Mr. Fitzherbert and his bottle of wine, or at least does not try.

gunpowder" (*Letters* I, 243, No. 323). Cf. Johnson's descriptions of the Buller of Buchan, *Letters* I, 237, No. 322 and *Works* x, 335. Cf. Boswell's different way of treating the subject with emphasis, *Life* v, 100.

25. Cf. the opinion of Dr. Hill, *Letters* I, xiii. Mr. Augustine Birrell says of the letters, "They are in every style, from the monumental to the utterly frivolous" ("The Transmission of Johnson's Personality," *Johnson Club Papers* [New York, 1899], p. 14). Cf. his *Obiter Dicta, Second Series* (London, 1887), "Dr. Johnson," pp. 143–4.

26. "Dr. Johnson's Style," *Macmillan's Magazine*, LVII (1888), 193.

27. *Letters* I, 47–8, No. 78.

Twenty-eight years later the same contrast appears. In November 1783 he writes to Mrs. Thrale:

Those that have loved longest love best. A sudden blaze of kindness may by a single blast of coldness be extinguished, but that fondness which length of time has connected with many circumstances and occasions, though it may for a while [be] suppressed by disgust or resentment, with or without a cause, is hourly revived by accidental recollection. To those that have lived long together, every thing heard and every thing seen recals some pleasure communicated, or some benefit conferred, some petty quarrel, or some slight endearment. Esteem of great powers, or amiable qualities newly discovered, may embroider a day or a week, but a friendship of twenty years is interwoven with the texture of life.[28]

His next letter to the Thrale household, one to Susanna, begins:

Here is a whole week, and nothing heard from your house. Baretti said what a wicked house it would be, and a wicked house it is. Of you however I have no complaint to make, for I owe you a letter. Still I live here by my own self, and have had of late very bad nights; but then I have had a pig to dinner, which Mr. Perkins gave me. Thus life is chequered.[29]

The whole collection of Johnson's letters is a patchwork of this sort. The pieces of Ramblerism are usually short, sometimes no more than a phrase or sentence containing an inversion, a philosophic term, or a balance. "That I have answered neither of your letters you must not impute to any declension of good will, but merely to the want of something to say." [30] "Some supervenient cause of discord may overpower this original amity." [31] "He had raised money and squandered it, by every artifice of acquisition, and folly of expence." [32] The longest, as long as a *Rambler,* is the carefully written letter on books to Dr. Barnard, the King's librarian.[33] Passages of factual simplicity are to be found in almost all the letters and toward the end of even the most discursive ones. Playful or antic passages are most typical of the letters to Mrs. Thrale or her daughters, though giving way to a strain of melancholy after Mr. Thrale's death in the spring of 1781.[34] Johnson's

28. *Letters* II, 350, No. 900.
29. *Letters* II, 351–2, No. 901.
30. *Letters* I, 118, No. 170.
31. *Life* I, 324.
32. *Life* II, 281.
33. *Letters* I, 142–7, No. 206.
34. In his frivolous style I find Johnson not at his happiest. His resources are too limited; he seems too much to descend as the great lexicographer to a few simple tricks of naiveté that would not be thought funny in another man. There is, for example, his way of harping on a word, an over-plain kind of repetitious bumptious-

letters, with their abrupt changes in topic, mood, and style, their juxtaposition of paragraphs of wholly different consistency, exhibit in miniature the differences which are to be found in his writing career.

iii

THE passages which are to follow, illustrating the consistency of Johnson's style from the Preface to *Lobo* to the *Lives of the Poets,* have not been selected at random. I have argued above [35] that the analysis of elements of style cannot be a blind experiment by which we discover some quality in the writing which we could not discover by reading. Analysis can be only a corroboration and detailed appraisal of some quality perceived by the reader as part of meaning. Some passages from Johnson's early and some from his late prose have been culled with great care as examples of *Ramblerism;* others have been chosen for their lightness. The purpose has not been to show averages in the different periods. One must admit that there are more *Ramblers* in the *Rambler* period, that in the late period there is more of the opposite kind of writing.

We have an early forecast of the *Rambler* in the Preface to *Lobo,* 1735.[36] The narrative translation itself of course offered not much

ness. "I enquired of my barber after another barber; that barber, says he, is dead, and his son has left off, to turn maltster. Maltsters, I believe, do not get much money" (*Letters* I, 174). "Here is a rout and bustle; and a bustle and a rout" (*Letters* I, 366, No. 432). Cf. *Letters* I, 166, No. 237; I, 175, No. 254. Johnson's best frivolity is his gentle teasing of females; e.g., *Letters* II, 136–7. But on the whole the Rambler is out of place, elephantine among the fragilities of prattle and gossip. Also he has too charitable a nature. It is possible to admire his playful letters in that it is wonderful he could write them at all, as he himself thought of a woman who could preach, but it is impossible to call them fine and mean what we mean when we refer, let us say, to Madame de Sévigné's "lanternes" or to the dainty nastiness of Horace Walpole. See Walter B. C. Watkins, *Perilous Balance* (Princeton, 1939), pp. 38–9 for a comparison of the letters to Mrs. Thrale and the *Journal to Stella.*

35. *Ante* p. 24.

36. The earliest available—unless one will study Johnson's Pembroke College Latin prose exercises, one of which has been printed by Dr. Hill (*Life* I, 60, n. 7). It seems to me that the germs are there. "Quaedam minus attentè spectata," begins the young Johnson, "absurda videntur, quae tamen penitus perspecta rationi sunt consentanea."

It might be illuminating to see some of the periodical essays which Johnson is said to have contributed to the *Birmingham Journal* in 1733. See *Life* I, 85 and *Courtney* p. 2.

For the opinion that Johnson's characteristic manner does not appear in his early works, see *Misc.* I, 466, Murphy's *Essay; Works* I, 22; Robert Anderson, *Life of Johnson* (London, 1795), p. 229. For the opposite opinion, that which I am advancing, see, besides *Life* I, 87–9, Alexander Chalmers, *British Essayists* (London, 1817), XIX, xliii; Edmund Gosse, *Leaves and Fruit* (New York, 1927), pp. 360–1.

It is perhaps true that after the *Rambler* Johnson showed less inclination to devi-

opportunity for Johnson to exercise himself.[37] But the Preface, or at least part of it, was an original, discursive composition, an essay.[38] If a count is made of parallels and antitheses, it will be found to have about the weight of a moderately heavy *Rambler*. The very second sentence contains a chiasmic antithesis of type II with two parallel elements: "his attempt stands in need of no apology, whatever censures may fall on the performance." Boswell quotes three paragraphs which gave Edmund Burke particular delight, the last of which is as follows:

The reader will here find no regions cursed with irremediable barrenness, or blest with spontaneous fecundity; no perpetual gloom or unceasing sunshine; nor are the nations here described either devoid of all sense of humanity, or consummate in all private and social virtues: here are no *Hottentots* without religion, polity, or articulate language; no *Chinese* perfectly polite, and completely skilled in all sciences: he will discover what will always be discovered by a diligent and impartial enquirer, that wherever human nature is to be found, there is a mixture of vice and virtue, a contest of passion and reason; and that the Creator doth not appear partial in his distributions, but has balanced in most countries their particular inconveniencies by particular favours.[39]

The *Debates in Parliament*, 1740–1743, again exhibit the Johnsonian style, this time almost unmixed. Here there was no hindrance of facts or narrative; he might luxuriate in abstract emphasis. "They are commonly formed," says Dr. Hill, "of general statements which suit any one speaker just as well as any other. The scantier were the notes that were given him by those who had

ate from his characteristic style. There are, for example, in his early writing some excursions in irony that must surprise the reader who has known only the major works. In "A Compleat Vindication of the Licensers of the Stage," 1739, Johnson approaches the plain, bitter statement of Swift. "There are scattered over this kingdom several little seminaries, in which the lower ranks of people, and the younger sons of our nobility and gentry are taught from their earliest infancy the pernicious arts of spelling and reading, which they afterwards continue to practise, very much to the disturbance of their own quiet, and the interruption of ministerial measures. These seminaries may, by an act of parliament, be at once suppressed, and that our posterity be deprived of all means of reviving this corrupt method of education, it may be made felony to teach to read without a license from the Lord Chamberlain" (*Works* xiv, 57). Passages of the same "modest proposal" technique may be found in *Marmor Norfolciense*, 1739 (*Works* xiv, 25, 32), and in "A Project for the Employment of Authors," in the *Universal Visiter*, April 1756 (*Works* xiv, 206).

37. Cf. *Life*, i, 87.

38. The first 800 words (*Works* ix, 431–4 "... many agreeing in the same account"). The quotient for multiplications of two or more elements of implicit parallel is 1.75; for antithesis II of all types, 2.00. Cf. *ante* p. 30, n. 58; p. 44, n. 32. The last part of this Preface is matter of fact, explanatory of the writer's policy in translation.

39. *Works* ix, 432. Cf. *Life* i, 88–9. And Boswell points out Johnson's hand in the Dedication to Warren the bookseller.

heard the debate, the more he had to draw on his imagination. But his was an imagination which supplied him with what was general much more readily than with what was particular."[40] Here one may pick almost at random. The following passage from the "Debate on Addressing His Majesty for Removing Sir Robert Walpole" is written in a style that is sustained with little variation through the whole of the two volumes. It is an uninteresting puffy prose, that of Johnson expressing other men's opinions, without the moral conviction and spirit of the *Ramblers*.

To endeavour, my Lords, to remove from places of publick trust all those who appear to want either the virtues or abilities necessary for executing their offices, is the interest of every member of a community. And it is not only the interest but the duty of all those who are either by the choice of the people, or by the right of birth, invested with the power of inspecting publick affairs, and intrusted with the general happiness of their country. That therefore every motive combines to make it the duty, and every argument concurs to prove it the privilege of your Lordships, is too evident to be doubted.[41]

If Johnson could be heavy before the *Ramblers*, he could also be (and it is equally relevant to our purpose to note it) light during the period of the *Ramblers*.[42] Dr. Hill has maintained that this is evident in Johnson's miscellaneous writings. "The Preface to the Dictionary, the Life of Sir Thomas Browne, the Review of Jonas Hanway's Journal, and of Soame Jenyns's Nature and Origin of Evil . . . are free from any excess of mannerisms."[43] But one may find the principle better illustrated even within the *Ramblers*. A topic on which Johnson was always forced to employ his lightest style was specific literary criticism. The reference to this poem and that, the quotation of passages and reference to them, the use of technical terms, "verse," "foot," "syllable," "long" and "short," all conspired to prevent Johnson's logic from taking hold of the theme and carrying it to the realm of elaborate generality. This sort of subject matter in a great measure accounts for the lightness of the *Lives*. Johnson has no sooner done with the recital of biographical

40. *Life* i, 506, App. A.
41. A passage of 1,500 words from which this is taken (*Works* xii, 139, "Lord Carteret began . . ."–142, ". . . it cannot continue") has for implicit parallels of two or more elements a quotient of 1.47; for all types of antithesis II, 2.00.
42. The question whether Johnson's extensive revisions for the fourth edition of the *Rambler*, 1756, should be considered evidence of a reform in style is rather involved, and since I believe they should not, I have removed my discussion of the matter to Appendix C, *post* pp. 152–4.
43. "Dr. Johnson's Style," *Macmillan's Magazine*, lvii (1888), 190. He refers to the fact that Boswell found only one instance of "*Brownism*" in the papers which Johnson wrote for the *Literary Magazine* in 1756. Cf. *Life* i, 308.

events than comment on particular works claims his attention. He manages to insert only interludes of essay, of general appraisal of literary character. And if we look at such a *Rambler* as No. 88, on Milton's versification, we see the complete anticipation of many sections of the *Lives*.[44] How could Johnson be most Johnsonian when he had such as the following to write?

The great peculiarity of *Milton's* versification, compared with that of later poets, is the elision of one vowel before another, or the suppression of the last syllable of a word ending with a vowel, when a vowel begins the following word. As

Knowledge——
Oppresses else with surfeit, and soon turns
Wisdom to folly, as nourishment to wind.

This license, though now disused in *English* poetry, was practised by our older writers, and is allowed in many other languages ancient and modern, and therefore the cricks on *Paradise Lost* have, without much deliberation, commended *Milton* for continuing it.[45]

Passages of the same lightness are to be found in *Rasselas*, except that here the occasion is not literary criticism but narrative. Such a passage as that running through Chapters xiii–xv, a continuum of rather pure narrative, has a marked difference in weight from philosophic conversation such as that of Chapters xxvii–xxviii. The following is from Chapter xiii.

As they were walking on the side of the mountain, they observed that the conies, which the rain had driven from their burrows, had taken shelter among the bushes, and formed holes behind them, tending upwards in an oblique line. "It has been the opinion of antiquity, said Imlac, that human reason borrowed many arts from the instinct of animals; let us, therefore, not think ourselves degraded by learning from the coney. We may escape by piercing the mountain in the same direction. We will begin where the summit hangs over the middle part, and labour upward till we shall issue up beyond the prominence."

The eyes of the prince, when he heard this proposal, sparkled with joy. The execution was easy, and the success certain.[46]

44. "If the 'Lives of the Poets' be thought an exception to Dr. JOHNSON'S general habit of writing, let it be remembered that he was for the most part confined to dates and facts, to illustrations and criticisms, and quotations; but when he indulged himself in moral reflections, to which he delighted to recur, we have again the rigour and loftiness of the RAMBLER, and only miss some of what have been termed his *hard words*" (Alexander Chalmers, *British Essayists* [London, 1817], xix, xliii).

45. This *Rambler* of 1,000 words (*Works* vi, 103–9) has for implicit parallel of two or more elements a quotient of only .70; though for all types of antithesis II a quotient of 1.30, much nearer to that of more abstract *Ramblers*.

46. Chapters xiii–xv, a passage of 1,600 words (*Works* xi, 41–7), have for implicit parallel of two or more elements a quotient of .56; for all types of antithesis

Contrast it with the following from Chapter xxvii.

The highest stations cannot therefore hope to be the abodes of happiness, which I would willingly believe to have fled from thrones and palaces to seats of humble privacy and placid obscurity. For what can hinder the satisfaction, or intercept the expectations, of him whose abilities are adequate to his employments, who sees with his own eyes the whole circuit of his influence, who chooses by his own knowledge all whom he trusts, and whom none are tempted to deceive by hope or fear? Surely he has nothing to do but to love and to be loved, to be virtuous and to be happy.[47]

Sixteen years later the same mixture of styles is to be observed. The *Journey to the Western Islands* consists for the most part of paragraphs of narrative or description alternate with paragraphs of discussion. We find on one page a passage like the following:

But it must be remembered, that life consists not of a series of illustrious actions, or elegant enjoyments; the great part of our time passes in compliance with necessities, in the performance of daily duties, in the removal of small inconveniencies, in the procurement of petty pleasures; and we are well or ill at ease, as the main stream of life glides on smoothly, or is ruffled by small obstacles and frequent interruptions. The true state of every nation is the state of common life. The manners of a people are not to be found in the schools of learning, or the palaces of greatness, where the national character is obscured or obliterated by travel or instruction, by philosophy or vanity; nor is publick happiness to be estimated by the assemblies of the gay, or the banquets of the rich.

And on the next page:

Finding nothing to detain us at *Bamff,* we set out in the morning, and having breakfasted at *Cullen,* about noon came to *Elgin,* where, in the inn that we supposed the best, a dinner was set before us, which we could not eat. This was the first time, and except one, the last, that I found any reason to complain of a *Scottish* table; and such disappointments, I suppose, must be expected in every country where there is no great frequency of travellers.[48]

These passages are a fair sample of the *Western Islands,* though occasional phrases or sentences where the two modes blend are more striking or amusing. "Such capricious and temporary waters,"

II, 1.56. I include the second short paragraph of the quoted passage, with its doublet of two elements of implicit parallel, for the sake of showing how such elements occur even in the narrative of *Rasselas.*

47. Chapters xxvii–xxviii, a passage of 1,400 words (*Works* xi, 74–80), have for implicit parallel of two or more elements a quotient of 2.14; for all types of antithesis II, 2.43.

48. *Works* x, 338–9.

says the Rambler, "cannot be expected to produce many fish." And again he antithesizes a species of geese. "They are so tame as to own a home, and so wild as sometimes to fly quite away." [49] A reflection on the character of the Highlanders which appears to me to be the longest stretch of abstraction in the whole book is about heavy enough to be a *Rambler*.[50]

Much the same is to be said of *Taxation No Tyranny*. Here argument of a general political character—on "fundamental principles, or common axioms, which being generally received are little doubted, and being little doubted have been rarely proved" [51]— is interspersed with more specific examination of the question at issue. "Suppose it true, that any such exemption is contained in the charter of *Maryland*, it can be pleaded only by the *Marylanders*." [52] The first fifteen hundred words of the essay, a passage among the most homogeneously Johnsonian, will be found about as heavy as a moral *Rambler*.[53]

The *Life of Pope* is an exception among the *Lives*, containing more elaborate discussion than any other; in choosing a passage from it for comparison with Addison and Hazlitt I have, as I confess above,[54] followed Professor Chandler, who used great discrimination in finding a passage so specially Johnsonian. But a like passage from the *Life of Dryden*, for example, is almost as difficult to find as one from the *Western Islands*. So common throughout the *Lives* are paragraphs like the following:

> Davenant was perhaps at this time his favourite author, though Gondibert never appears to have been popular; and from Davenant he learned to please his ear with the stanza of four lines alternately rhymed.[55]

One series of paragraphs, however, on such ductile topics as Dryden's genius, his learning, his prose style, his refinement of the language,[56] offers some good examples of Johnson's essay style as it survived in the *Lives* wherever it found sustenance.

49. *Works* x, 359, 380.
50. *Works* x, 428, "It may likewise . . ."–434, ". . . perceive the benefit," a passage of 1,500 words. For implicit parallels of two or more elements the quotient is 1.00; for all types of antithesis II, 2.47.
51. *Works* x, 93.
52. *Works* x, 118.
53. *Works* x, 93–9, ". . . conceive them free." For implicit parallel of two or more elements the quotient is 1.47; for all types of antithesis II, 2.13.
   Mrs. Thrale wrote of *Falkland's Islands*, " 'Tis Johnson . . . that interests us, and your style is invariably the same" (*Piozzi Letters* I, 318, quoted, *Life* III, 19, n.2).
54. *Ante* p. 26, n. 43.
55. *Works* II, 390–1.
56. *Works* II, 382, "His literature . . ."–388, ". . . reason wants not Horace

Yet it cannot be said that his genius is ever unprovided of matter, or that his fancy languishes in penury of ideas. His works abound with knowledge, and sparkle with illustrations. There is scarcely any science or faculty that does not supply him with occasional images and lucky similitudes; every page discovers a mind very widely acquainted both with art and nature, and in full possession of great stores of intellectual wealth. Of him that knows much, it is natural to suppose that he has read with diligence; yet I rather believe that the knowledge of Dryden was gleaned from accidental intelligence and various conversation, by a quick apprehension, a judicious selection, and a happy memory, a keen appetite of knowledge, and a powerful digestion; by vigilance that permitted nothing to pass without notice, and a habit of reflection that suffered nothing useful to be lost. A mind like Dryden's, always curious, always active, to which every understanding was proud to be associated, and of which every one solicited the regard, by an ambitious display of himself, had a more pleasant, perhaps a nearer way to knowledge than by the silent progress of solitary reading. I do not suppose that he despised books, or intentionally neglected them; but that he was carried out, by the impetuosity of his genius, to more vivid and speedy instructors; and that his studies were rather desultory and fortuitous than constant and systematical.

In the comparison of passages made in this chapter I have been thinking more of parallelism and antithesis than of diction. I have not much to say about the progress of Johnson's diction, to what degree at different times it was abstract, general, non-sensory, or philosophic—and this for the reason discussed above,[57] that these qualities of diction, being dependent on context, are not measurable or countable in words as such. Professor Taylor has proved beyond doubt, I think, that the average number of syllables in Johnson's words is as great in the *Lives of the Poets* as in the *Ramblers.*[58] This, however, need not persuade us to any further conclusion. There are long words and long words. It is conceivable that Johnson's words should have continued of the same average length yet have become less philosophic. And this, I believe, is

to support it," a passage of 1,500 words. For implicit parallel of two or more elements the quotient is 1.67; for all types of antithesis II, 1.93.

57. *Ante* pp. 55, 61.

58. *Taylor* p. 29. I present an ellipsis of his table of average word length.

Rambler 1st 10	1.54	
Last 10	1.59	° Sections from the lives of Addison, Prior,
Idler 1st 15	1.51	Pope, Cowley, Milton, Waller, Butler, and
Last 16	1.53	Dryden.
Lives of the Poets °		
Narrative	1.53	
Exposition	1.59	°° Sections from the lives of Savage [1744],
Eminent Lives °°	1.53	Drake [1740], and Boerhaave [1739].

what did happen. Certainly, even when they continue philosophic, they are less often exaggerated or freakish.[59] Another matter on which I have little to say is the decrease in sentence length which took place between the *Rambler* and the *Lives of the Poets*. Professor Taylor has already treated the matter thoroughly. His painstaking statistics show that in the *Ramblers* Johnson averaged 43.1 words per sentence, in the *Idlers*, 33.4, in the *Lives*, 30.1.[60] Perhaps this was an improvement in Johnson's writing; perhaps he may be read the more easily for it. But it would be difficult to say how far this is independent of the changes in subject matter which we have discussed, and more difficult to say whether anything peculiarly Johnsonian evaporated with the length of the sentence.[61]

59. Boswell says, "So easy is his style in these Lives, that I do not recollect more than three uncommon or learned words; one, when giving an account of the approach of Waller's mortal disease, he says, 'he found his legs grow *tumid*' . . . . Another, when he mentions that Pope *emitted* proposals . . . and a third, when he calls Orrery and Dr. Delaney, writers both undoubtedly *veracious* . . . ." But Dr. Hill supplies eight more examples (*Life* IV, 39 and n.1).

60. *Taylor* p. 35, Table II. These figures are for "indicated" (punctuated) sentence length. In another table Professor Taylor shows that both "indicated" and "real" (structural) sentence length decrease (p. 41, Table V).

61. Professor Taylor says of Johnson's later style, "All the old devices remained, even more pronouncedly often . . . [Cf. *post* Appendix B] but the sentences became shorter, the movement tense and energetic" (*Taylor* p. 33). Something like this may perhaps be conceded. Shorter sentences would seem to make shorter intervals between primary emphases and less distinction among emphases. Professor Sherman says, "Herein we see the essential difference between the condensed book-style and the condensed oral. The one . . . gains speed by leaving meaning to be implied within the sentence, the other outside of it." And he believes that the terseness of short sentences varies "according to the leap or omission of thought between. It is the length of the leap rather than the shortness of the periods that makes an author seem laconic" (L. A. Sherman, *Analytics of Literature* [Boston, 1893], pp. 301–2, 303, n. 1). I should say that between the short sentences of Johnson's later style there is a very short average leap, that they differ from the members of his earlier long sentences chiefly in the omission of connectives and change of punctuation.

It is interesting, however, to note that of all other English prose masters, only Dryden seems to have diminished his sentence in like degree as he grew older (Edwin H. Lewis, *The History of the English Paragraph* [Chicago, 1894], pp. 106–7, n. 2).

CHAPTER VI

Johnson's Theory—I

WHAT a man says about style, his theory of it, expresses a formulated, or fully conscious, preference, while what he does about style may proceed from a preference unrecognized by himself. In this sense the evidence of his theoretical pronouncements is more explicit and clearer than that of his practice. On the other hand the formulated preference suffers the disadvantage of generalization—a thing which comes partly from other minds (with the words used) and is an invasion which may set up the notions and lay out the lines which it is called in only to describe. It is not to be expected that any man should be able to define his own style adequately, even if we make the rash assumption that he is fully aware of it. We must add to this that Samuel Johnson is seldom formally addressed to the subject of his own style, that he lets fall cursory remarks, sometimes with his own style in mind, sometimes with that of others, sometimes with only a notion of style in general. The sort of evidence we are about to see is not so compelling as that already derived from Johnson's practice. It is not to be set on the same level and adduced against the practice.[1] At best it can be but corroboratory—or, where it is contradictory, be accepted as a contradiction, or perhaps as a puzzle. No one, for example, would care to argue on the basis of the following passage that Johnson disapproved of Latin and philosophic diction, yet here we see plainly that on one occasion at least he realized the futility of the philosophic tendency to invent a name for every concept. Boswell asks him for a synonym for "transpire."

'Why, Sir, (said he,) *get abroad*.' BOSWELL. 'That, Sir, is using two words.' JOHNSON. 'Sir, there is no end of this. You may as well insist to have a word for old age.' BOSWELL. 'Well, Sir, *Senectus*.' JOHNSON. 'Nay, Sir, to insist always that there should be one word to express a thing in English, because there is one in another language, is to change the language.'[2]

1. W. Vaughan Reynolds urges: "Johnson *opposed* Latin and Greek idioms" ("The Reception of Johnson's Prose Style," *Review of English Studies*, xi [1935], 150).

2. *Life* iii, 343–4.

In like manner it is easy to prove from a passage in the *Preface to the Dictionary* that he understood well enough that learning in other languages could produce corrupt English.

He that has long cultivated another language, will find its words and combinations crowd upon his memory; and haste and negligence, refinement and affectation, will obtrude borrowed terms and exotick expressions.[3]

In the face of passages like these, where Johnson seems to repudiate the preferences displayed in his own writing or to forget other critical statements made by himself, we must parallel Boswell's decision about his eating.

His practice, indeed, I must acknowledge, may be considered as casting the balance of his different opinions upon this subject; for I never knew any man who relished good eating more than he did.[4]

But there is a more deceptive class of statements, generalities and epithetical condemnations, where we can sometimes hardly

3. *Works* ix, 225–6. He could be severe on this fault when he detected it in another (*Works* x, 192, Review of *Memoirs of the Court of Augustus*). And from one whose own style is so definitely marked by a manner and so open to parody, some of his remarks in praise of an "equable" and "varied" style come curiously (*Lives* i, 418, *Dryden*, pars. 214–15; ii, 149–50, *Addison*, pars. 167–8; iii, 160, *Pope*, par. 172).

In the whole range of his criticism he says nothing at all in support of his favorite antithesis, but in two places, anticipating the criticism of Hazlitt, offers a keen analysis of its weakness (*Works* x, 286, *On the Bravery of the English Common Soldiers;* Walter Raleigh, *Johnson on Shakespeare* [London, 1929], p. 188, on Dryden's remarks about Mercutio).

The term "antithesis" as used by Johnson in *Lives* iii, 398–9, *Young*, par. 166, and in his criticism of a line in *Romeo and Juliet*, Walter Raleigh, *Johnson on Shakespeare*, p. 185, would seem to mean "paradox" or "oxymoron." Cf. *Works* vi, 438, *Rambler* No. 140.

In poetry at least Johnson objects to "inversions" (*Lives* i, 40, *Cowley*, par. 117; iii, 418, *Akenside*, par. 19; *Works* viii, 309, *Idler* No. 77, an example from Pope).

Twice, and only twice, so far as I have been able to find, Johnson admitted that he saw faults in his own style. When one of his *Ramblers* was read to him, he said: "too wordy" (*Life* iv, 5). And another time: "Sir, if Robertson's style be faulty, he owes it to me; that is, having too many words, and those too big ones" (*Life* iii, 173).

4. *Life* i, 468. I leave out of account the possibility that Johnson may at times simply not mean what he says. The evidence is plentiful that he often "talked for victory" (*Life* ii, 238; iii, 23, 80; iv, 111, 429; v, 352; *Misc.* i, 450, 452; *Works* i, 257; ix, 66), but it seems to me that he scarcely ever did so upon a literary topic, and on this point I find myself in agreement with another who surveyed the whole of Johnson's criticism, Joseph E. Brown (*The Critical Opinions of Samuel Johnson* [Princeton, 1926], p. xliv).

And I have found it impracticable to treat Johnson's theory chronologically. The evidence is often too scanty, and where there are contradictions, the later utterances do not contradict the earlier ones in any systematic way. Johnson's theory, like his style, seems to have undergone no great change from first to last. In this opinion I find myself again supported by Mr. Brown (*op. cit.*, pp. xlii–xliv).

prove what Johnson means, or where if we can, the meaning is what a reader of today might not at first be likely to conceive.[5] There is notably his *Idler* No. 36, on "The terrifick diction," where he speaks of "the ponderous dictator of sentences" and "the stately son of demonstration, who proves with mathematical formality what no man has yet pretended to doubt," and where he finds especially distasteful "a mode of style . . . by which the most evident truths are so obscured, that they can no longer be perceived."

This style may be called the *terrifick,* for its chief intention is to terrify and amaze; it may be termed the *repulsive,* for its natural effect is to drive away the reader; or it may be distinguished, in plain *English,* by the denomination of the *bugbear style,* for it has more terror than danger, and will appear less formidable as it is more nearly approached.[6]

I mean not to suggest that Johnson's own style deserves the epithets which he here applies to other styles, but that these epithets do suggest some of the criticisms of Johnson's style which we have quoted in earlier chapters. "Ponderous dictator of sentences," "stately son of demonstration," the *"terrifick"* style, "the *bugbear style.*" These recall what we have heard from Archibald Campbell, Horace Walpole, Hazlitt, or Macaulay. Fortunately Johnson proceeds to give us an actual "illustrious example" of what he means. In the *"Letters concerning Mind,"* [7] he says, "the author begins by declaring, that *the sorts of things are things that now are, have been, and shall be, and the things that strictly ARE.*" It is the tone of metaphysical mystification which seems to him "terrific." He might have been surprised to learn that a later critic should find the term "terrific diction" perfectly suitable to describe so different a thing as the ranting and abusive literary criticism of Swinburne.[8] The fact is that we all deplore terrific diction; there is scarcely anything on which we are more nearly unanimous. But we find ourselves sadly at variance when we set about comparing the objects, the phrases and words, which we actually call terrific. Epithets of this sort and all the more emphatic ways of expressing displeasure may give us a very vivid sense of what a critic dislikes in a given

Some of the notions to be treated in the following pages are touched upon by Hans Meier, *Dr. Samuel Johnsons Stellung zu den literarischen Fragen seiner Zeit* (Zürich, 1916), pp. 45–55; there is somewhat less in Sigyn Christiani, *Samuel Johnson als Kritiker* (Leipzig, 1931), pp. 78–81.

5. Into this class or into the preceding may fall Johnson's censure of the *Essay on Man* for truisms, which Mr. Christie amusingly puts beside Taine's censure of Johnson for the same fault (*Christie* pp. 16–17).

6. *Works* VIII, 143–4.

7. By John Petvin, publ. 1750 (*Courtney* p. 81).

8. *Macmillan's Magazine,* LIV (1886), 363–5, "The Terrific Diction," unsigned

kind of writing if we know what kind is meant, but by themselves they are small clue to what kind is meant.[9]

"The language is laboured into harshness," says Johnson. "The mind of the writer seems to work with unnatural violence. 'Double, double, toil and trouble.' He has a kind of strutting dignity, and is tall by walking on tiptoe." As everybody will recall, he is talking about the odes of Gray.[10] He says of the *Memoirs of the Court of Augustus:* "Sometimes the reader is suddenly ravished with a sonorous sentence, of which when the noise is past the meaning does not long remain." [11] Of Shakespeare: "The equality of words to things is very often neglected, and trivial sentiments and vulgar ideas disappoint the attention, to which they are recommended by sonorous epithets and swelling figures." [12] And one of the faults of the tragedies of Johnson's own day is a "perpetual tumour of phrase." [13]

In all these cases we know what Johnson is talking about, the work to which he is attributing the fault of excess, and from this we can infer at least approximately what form of excess is meant. If we did not know the work, we should know only that he was speaking of some form of the general fault of excess. In the following passage Johnson is speaking simply of bad writings that come under the inspection of Criticism. His range is the whole field of writing.

Some secret inequality was found between the words and sentiments, or some dissimilitude of the ideas and the original objects . . . incongruities were linked together, or . . . some parts were of no use but to enlarge the appearance of the whole, without contributing to its beauty, solidity, or usefulness.[14]

Who shall ever venture to illustrate this passage, to say what concrete shapes of bombast floated before the inner eye of Johnson as he generalized?

General expressions by Johnson and general conclusions based upon such expressions can afford us no satisfaction—even when

9. Johnson himself says of Dick Minim the critic: "He has several favourite epithets, of which he has never settled the meaning, but which are very commodiously applied to books which he has not read, or cannot understand. One is *manly*, another is *dry*, another *stiff*, and another *flimzy;* sometimes he discovers delicacy of style, and sometimes meets with *strange expressions*" (*Works* viii, 246–7, *Idler* No. 61).

10. *Lives* iii, 440, par. 48.

11. *Works* x, 192.

12. *Works* ix, 255, *Preface to Shakespeare.*

13. *Works* vi, 350, *Rambler* No. 125. Cf. *Life* iii, 37, on Thomson; iii, 256, on Potter's translation of Aeschylus.

14. *Works* v, 17, *Rambler* No. 3.

they do not seem at variance with his practice. To conclude, for example, that Johnson believed style should be "clear," "elegant," and suited to its theme [15] is not to give Johnson a theory of style that can be distinguished from any other person's theory. Everybody believes these things—in one sense or another—just as everybody despises terrific diction. More particularly, everybody in Johnson's day believed them. To find statements we need go no farther than the best known rhetorics of the day, Kames's or Campbell's or Blair's or the routine performance of Ward.[16] Just as in our study of Johnson's writing we were concerned to describe those characteristics of his style which distinguish it from other styles, so in this study we are most concerned to point out whatever explicit acknowledgments Johnson made of the characteristic preferences exhibited in his own writings.

ii

Either Johnson was not specifically aware of the characters of his style which we have called parallelism,[17] antithesis, and inversion, or he thought it not worth while to discuss them. On the whole matter of the structure of sentences and paragraphs, the arrangement of ideas, Johnson makes but few statements which seem helpful to us.[18] He has much to say, however, on the purpose of creative writing, the nature of general truth and its elaboration in writing, the relation of things and words, and the corollary question of diction.

Johnson's belief that art achieved grandeur through generality, that the streaks of the tulip were not to be numbered, is well enough

15. These three points and another, that style should be native, make Johnson's theory of style as seen by W. Vaughan Reynolds, "Johnson's Opinions of Prose Style," *Review of English Studies*, IX (1933), 436–43.

16. Henry Home, Lord Kames, *Elements of Criticism* (New York, 1823), II, 19, 21 (first published, 1762); George Campbell, *Philosophy of Rhetoric* (London, 1801), II, 1–5 (first published, 1776); Hugh Blair, *Lectures on Rhetoric and Belles Lettres* (Dublin, 1783), I, 219, 221–2; II, 26–7; John Ward, *System of Oratory* (London, 1759), I, 307–8, 319–20; II, 126.

17. "It is inelegant to vary the construction of Members of the same Period," said James Buchanan in his *Regular English Syntax*, 1767 (1780 ed., pp. xi–xii, quoted by Sterling A. Leonard, *The Doctrine of Correctness in English Usage 1700–1800* [Madison, 1929], p. 81).

18. But see *Rambler* No. 158, *Works* VII, 109 for evidence of Johnson's concern for coherence and transition. In a letter to Mrs. Thrale (*Letters* II, 138, No. 657) he chuckles over his own "graceful negligence of transition," the associative, accidental kind, and constructs a deliberate illustration by passing from Shakespeare and Nature to Mrs. Montagu. And cf. *ante* p. 90, n. 3.

On the topic of "cadence" Johnson made a few statements which I have thought important enough to discuss in Appendix D, *post* pp. 155–7.

known but may admit some illustration here. The tulip passage, in Imlac's account of the poet, is as follows:

The business of a poet . . . is to examine, not the individual, but the species; to remark general properties and large appearances; he does not number the streaks of the tulip, or describe the different shades in the verdure of the forest. He is to exhibit in his portraits of nature such prominent and striking features, as recall the original to every mind; and must neglect the minuter discriminations, which one may have remarked, and another have neglected, for those characteristics which are alike obvious to vigilance and carelessness.

And Imlac makes the same application to men and manners— human nature.

He must divest himself of the prejudices of his age or country; he must consider right and wrong in their abstracted and invariable state; he must disregard present laws and opinions, and rise to general and transcendental truths, which will always be the same.[19]

Johnson says something of this sort again and again. The metaphysicals fell short of the sublime because "great thoughts are always general, and consist in positions not limited by exceptions, and in descriptions not descending to minuteness."[20] Shakespeare is great because "nothing can please many, and please long, but just representations of general nature."[21]

19. *Works* xi, 31–2, *Rasselas*, chap. x. Cf. Arthur O. Lovejoy, *The Great Chain of Being* (Cambridge, Mass., 1936), esp. pp. 290–1.
20. *Lives* i, 21, *Cowley*, par. 58. Cf. i, 45, *Cowley*, par. 133.
21. *Works* ix, 242, *Preface to Shakespeare*. Cf. p. 243. For further statements see *Rambler* No. 36 (*Works* v, 235) and *Adventurer* No. 92 (*Works* ix, 74), on pastoral poetry; *Rambler* No. 143 (*Works* vii, 15) and *Adventurer* No. 95 (*Works* ix, 77), in which Johnson argues from the limitation of fit subjects (all these being generalities) to the likelihood of unconscious plagiarism; Preface to Payne's *New Tables of Interest* and Dedication to Mrs. Lennox's *Shakespear Illustrated* (Allen T. Hazen, *Samuel Johnson's Prefaces & Dedications* [New Haven, 1937], pp. 110, 143–4); *Rambler* No. 23 (*Works* v, 154). In *BP* xi, 137, "He thought that a man who had never traded himself might write well upon trade." He is said to have offered to write a *Dictionary of Trade and Commerce*, though admitting that he did not know "much . . . in the practical line" (*Misc.* ii, 162). Cf. *ante* p. 55.
Sir Joshua Reynolds spoke of "the invariable general form which nature most frequently produces, and always seems to intend in her productions" (*Idler* No. 82, Johnson's *Works* viii, 330). This was the beautiful, the subject of art. Cf. his discussion of verisimilitude in the painting of a violin (*Idler* No. 79, *Works* viii, 320); and his annotations to William Mason's verse translation of Du Fresnoy's *Art of Painting* (*Works of William Mason* [London, 1811], iii, 80–1); and Elbert N. S. Thompson, "The *Discourses* of Sir Joshua Reynolds," *PMLA*, xxxii (1917), 351–4. Cf. Dryden in his "Parallel of Poetry and Painting" prefixed to his 1695 version of Du Fresnoy (*Essays of John Dryden*, ed. W. P. Ker, [Oxford, 1926], ii, 118).
For the opposite view, the romantic recommendation of particularity, see Joseph Warton, *Essay on Pope* [London, 1806], i, 47. Cf. Aisso Bosker, *Literary Criticism in the Age of Johnson* (Groningen, 1930), pp. 255–6.

Johnson has insisted on an important truth, that a writing should tell something more than the circumstantial or accidental, that it should not be simply representational (if it could be). To our minds it must seem that he has missed another truth, which taken with the first makes the difficulty and debate over literary art. This is that a writing must be itself, original and ungeneralized. What makes both these truths possible is that the subject in art is not things (tulips or human nature) but concepts, visions of things, in the artist's head. The question of detail in the light of this doctrine is not one of "minuter discriminations, which one may have remarked, and another have neglected," but of discrimination between detail which is relevant and that which is irrelevant to the central concept. Johnson himself once connects the notion of relevance with that of generality.

> Instead of dilating his thoughts into generalities, and expressing incidents with poetical latitude, he [Shakespeare] often combines *circumstances unnecessary to his main design,* only because he happened to find them together.[22]

By his theory of generality Johnson could hardly account for his own experience as an artist or for the effect produced upon him by other literary art. It is not surprising to find him in occasional contradictions. In the "Essay on Epitaphs":

> There are no rules to be observed which do not equally relate to other compositions. The praise ought not to be general, because the mind is lost in the extent of any indefinite idea, and cannot be affected with what it cannot comprehend. When we hear only of a good or great man, we know not in what class to place him, nor have any notion of his character, distinct from that of a thousand others.[23]

And he complains that he cannot find in Rowe's plays "any deep search into nature, any accurate discriminations of kindred qualities, or nice display of passion in its progress; all is general and undefined."[24] In *Adventurer* No. 95 he is aware of the conflicting

22. *Works* IX, 234, *Proposals for Printing Shakespeare.* The italics are mine.
23. *Works* IX, 443.
24. *Lives* II, 76, par. 32. In the Review of Warton's *Essay on Pope* (*Literary Magazine,* 1756) he cannot regret that "Pope laid aside his design of writing American pastorals; for, as he must have painted scenes, which he never saw, and manners, which he never knew, his performance, though it might have been a pleasing amusement of fancy, would have exhibited no representation of nature or of life" (*Works* [Oxford, 1825], VI, 39–40; cf. VI, 42). Cf. *Rambler* No. 60, *Works* V, 384; *Life of Roscommon, Works* XIV, 417, n. †. In the *Life of Addison* (*Lives* II, 87, par. 23) he says of Addison's *Travels,* "of many parts it is not a very severe [i.e., excessive] censure to say that they might have been written at home." Cf. *Life* V, 285, praise of Burnet's *History; BP* VII, 70–1, advice to Boswell about Corsica; *Courtney* p. 99, advice to Baretti.

demands of generality and particularity and gropes toward a reconciliation. Though the passions are few, "the alterations which time is always making in the modes of life" are a source of variety. "Thus love is uniform, but courtship is perpetually varying." [25]

Thus Johnson wavered in favor of his varying immediate perceptions, but his allegiance to the rule was none the less real. The rule itself was a concrete and genuine part of his perception and of his performance. What he said about the dignity of generality has its most obvious reflection in the fact that his own writing may, as we have said, be characterized as exceptionally general and abstract. Johnson, the last great neoclassicist, the reactionary, was the one who most seriously attempted to put into artistic practice the neoclassic uniformitarian ideal. Pope might speak of following nature, of "what oft was thought," by nature he might mean only what was universal and comprehensible to reason, unmodified by accident of time or place, but Pope wrote about "flounce" and "furbelow," "Spadillio" and "captive trumps," about Atticus and Sporus and the Dunces. Johnson stuck to his principles; with relentless logic he not only theorized but practised the generality. In his elaborate system of parallelism and antithesis, in the "philosophic" pomp of his diction, he devised a way of lending to the abstract an emphasis, a particularity and thickness. He made a kind of poetry of abstraction; out of emptiness he conjured weight, out of the collapsible he made structures. By limiting himself faithfully to the abstract, he achieved more with it than did any other neoclassicist.

iii

One function of Johnson's theory—though not directly a stylistic one—appears in his estimate of certain types of literature. History he disdained.

As ethics or figures, or metaphysical reasoning, was the sort of talk he most delighted in, so no kind of conversation pleased him less I think, than when the subject was historical fact or general polity . . . . 'He never (as he expressed it) desired to hear of the *Punic war* while he lived: such conversation was lost time (he said), and carried one away from common life, leaving no ideas behind which could serve *living wight* as warning or direction.' [26]

25. *Works* IX, 81.
26. *Misc.* I, 201–2, Piozzi *Anecdotes;* cf. I, 202–3, where Fox talks of Catiline's conspiracy. When Johnson says (*Life* v, 39), "I love anecdotes," it would appear from what follows that he means by "anecdotes" something like short, pointed stories—stories told "aphoristically." Cf. *Life* II, 11.

And consistently, he "did not . . . much delight in that kind of conversation which consists in telling stories." [27] History, or story, tells what happened—in some particular time at some particular place. The event is told merely as itself, for itself. History gives an idea of this event, this thing, but no generally applicable idea; it carries one away from "common life." Johnson's dislike of history is directly antithetic to his great affection for biography. Arthur Murphy mentions the two together: "General history had little of his regard. Biography was his delight." [28] And we have the clear and authoritative record of Boswell:

MONBODDO. 'The history of manners is the most valuable. I never set a high value on any other history.' JOHNSON. 'Nor I; and therefore I esteem biography, as giving us what comes near to ourselves, what we can turn to use.' [29]

The events of biography are no less particular than those of history but are more generally applicable to the personal human problem, and hence may readily be thought of as more universally significant —especially if the thinker is, like Johnson, not interested in economics or government, but in private morals. Biography is what happened to a person, like oneself.

For narrative to be justified at all it must have some value as generality; it must be a "specimen of life and manners." [30] This condition is best fulfilled in biography—in other narrative hardly at all.[31] Events are facts, and hence narrative is an enumeration of

27. *Misc.* i, 265, Piozzi *Anecdotes.*
28. *Misc.* i, 451.
29. *Life* v, 79. Cf. *Life* i, 425. See Bergen Evans, "Dr. Johnson's Theory of Biography," *Review of English Studies*, x (1934), 301–10, esp. 301–2, 309–10, for a discussion somewhat similar to the present.
30. *Misc.* i, 348, Piozzi *Anecdotes.* The passage, if it is wholly reliable, shows Johnson dealing with the problem of truth in art and reaching a conclusion consistent with his concept of nature as the subject of art. Not only truth of probability, but truth of fact is what he demands. It is easy to see that if such truth is observed to the letter, the value of the story as generality, its significance, suffers sadly. This is another expression of the conflict between the general and particular, the reconciliation of which Johnson could not accomplish. Mrs. Piozzi's words are: "He scorned to embellish a story with fictitious circumstances, which (he used to say) took off from its real value. 'A story (says Johnson) should be a 'specimen of life and manners; but if the surrounding circumstances are false, as it is no more a representation of reality, it is no longer worthy our attention.'" It is not clear how this principle would apply to *Rasselas* or to a play by Shakespeare. Cf. *Life* ii, 433.
Dr. Johnson "never tires of telling us that poetry should aim not at the particular but at the general. He does not as a rule, however, associate his general truth with a right use of fiction, or, if one prefers, with a certain quality of imagination" (Irving Babbitt, *On Being Creative* [Boston, 1932], p. 84, "The Problem of the Imagination: Dr. Johnson").
31. "Those parallel circumstances and kindred images, to which we readily conform our minds, are, above all other writings, to be found in narratives of the lives

facts, differing from other enumerations, inventories and the like, chiefly in the observance of chronological order. When we arrive at this point, at the notion of fact, of statement of fact, of a series of statements of fact, we are at the heart of what Johnson disliked in writing and by antithesis have a good indication of what he did like.

Johnson's dislike of mere fact would perhaps not have been so clearly recorded for us were it not for his extreme dislike of the prose of another writer whose style was the antipodes of his own. Perhaps some personal rancor at times stimulated Johnson to the criticism of Swift,[32] but the criticism is too clear and too often reiterated to leave a doubt either that Swift's style was really offensive to Johnson or that there was an esthetic reason. At best Swift's style is for Johnson but an adequate vehicle for an inferior burden. In the *Life of Swift:*

This easy and safe conveyance of meaning it was Swift's desire to attain, and for having attained he deserves praise, though perhaps not the highest praise. For purposes merely didactick, when something is to be told that was not known before, it is the best mode, but against that inattention by which known truths are suffered to lie neglected it makes no provision; it instructs, but does not persuade.[33]

In Boswell's *Life* Johnson says of those who like and those who dislike Swift's style: "Both agree that Swift has a good neat style; but one loves a neat style, another loves a style of more splendour." [34] There are yet other passages where Johnson is less kind —where he explains in an unreserved, unmistakable, concrete manner, what he dislikes in Swift's writing. In the *Life of Swift* he says of *The Conduct of the Allies:*

Surely, whoever surveys this wonder-working pamphlet with cool perusal will confess that its efficacy was supplied by the passions of its readers; that it operates by the mere weight of facts, with very little assistance from the hand that produced them.[35]

Of the same pamphlet he had earlier said:

of particular persons; and therefore no species of writing seems more worthy of cultivation than biography . . . . The general and rapid narratives of history, which involve a thousand fortunes in the business of a day, and complicate innumerable incidents in one great transaction, afford few lessons applicable to private life" (*Works* v, 383, *Rambler* No. 60). Cf. *Idler* No. 84, *Works* viii, 339.

32. See *Misc.* i, 373, Murphy's *Essay;* and *BP* x, 195; and to the contrary *Life* v, 44. For a discussion of Johnson's whole attitude toward *Swift*, see Walter B. C. Watkins, *Perilous Balance* (Princeton, 1939), esp. pp. 26–31.

33. *Lives* iii, 52, par. 114.

34. *Life* ii, 191–2. Cf. *BP* ix, 96–7.

35. *Lives* iii, 19, par. 48.

Swift has told what he had to tell distinctly enough, but that is all. He had to count ten, and he has counted it right.[36]

At Mrs. Thrale's once he argued with a gentleman on the same subject.

At length you *must* allow me, said the gentleman, that there are *strong facts* in the account of the Four last Years of Queen Anne: 'Yes surely Sir (replies Johnson), and so there are in the Ordinary of Newgate's account.' [37]

Plainness of fact, not as opposed to fiction, but as opposed to elaboration—this must be understood as the opposite of what Johnson admired in writing. Swift comes no nearer to merit by the inventions of *Gulliver's Travels*. "When once you have thought of big men and little men, it is very easy to do all the rest." [38] What *Gulliver's Travels* and the "Ordinary of Newgate's account" have in common is that they deal with things, a constant succession of different things, not different aspects of the same things. It is the difference between multiplication for range ("the prince and princess") and multiplication for emphasis ("the constituent and fundamental principle").[39] The "so many *things*, almost in an equal number of *words*" of Sprat had been no vain exhortation to Johnson's predecessors. It had become a real and conscious rule. Swift himself praised the style of the Brobdingnagians thus: "Their style is clear, masculine and smooth, but not florid; for they avoid nothing more than multiplying unnecessary words, or using various expressions." [40] And this was precisely the aim of Johnson, to multiply words, to use various expressions, to deal not in things but in thoughts about things.[41] In this he is nearer to the romantic essayists than to the neoclassic. His is the more meditative, more poetic

36. *Life* II, 65.
37. *Misc.* I, 188. He says almost the same thing in the conversation on *The Conduct of the Allies, Life* II, 65. For further comments on Swift's style see *Lives* III, 51, par. 111; *Life* I, 452; II, 318–19; v, 44. In *Rambler* No. 122 he writes: "Some have doubted whether an *Englishman* can stop at that mediocrity of style, or confine his mind to that even tenour of imagination which narrative requires" (*Works* VI, 330).
Addison, a writer plain and neat but much less so than Swift, receives Johnson's considered praise (*Lives* II, 149–50, *Addison*, pars. 167–8; *Life* I, 225; *Misc.* I, 233). But Mrs. Piozzi says: "It was notwithstanding observable enough (or I fancied so), that he never did like, though he always thought fit to praise it" (*Misc.* I, 283).
38. *Life* II, 319.
39. *Ante* pp. 20–2.
40. Swift's *Works*, ed. Scott (London, 1883), XI, 167, quoted in *Lives* III, 52, n. 3.
41. Boswell once reflected: "Johnson *could* not give real scenes of life so clean as Fielding; *his were* always *covered* with *a* bulk of sentiment like earth, not clean lines as in *The Covent Garden Journal*" (*BP* XIII, 214, Thursday, 1 April 1779. The italicized parts are editorial expansions).

style. It pauses and develops the aspects and relations of things, works them into a thought pattern, attracts into the pattern reflections of other things.

iv

THE need for elaboration was one of the consequences of the taste for generality. There were two kinds of subject matter: things, such as Swift dealt with, which had to be new things in order to claim attention; and general truths, which being general and true must be already known and which hence must be enforced or recommended. This enforcement or recommendation was the proper scope of literary art.

The task of an author is, either to teach what is not known, or to recommend known truths by his manner of adorning them; either to let new light in upon the mind, and open new scenes to the prospect, or to vary the dress and situation of common objects, so as to give them fresh grace and more powerful attractions, to spread such flowers over the regions through which the intellect has already made its progress, as may tempt it to return, and take a second view of things hastily passed over or negligently regarded.[42]

This occurs in *Rambler* No. 3, where Johnson is explaining the plan of his work—the second alternative, "to recommend known truths by his manner of adoring them." In *Adventurer* No. 115 we find this distinction between the modes of writing repeated. If an author "treats of science and demonstration," he must have a "style clear, pure, nervous, and expressive." But "if his topicks be probable and persuasory," he must "recommend them by the superaddition of elegance and imagery . . . display the colours of varied diction, and pour forth the musick of modulated periods."[43] In *Rambler* No. 152: "Among the criticks in history it is not contested whether truth ought to be preserved, but by what mode of diction it is best adorned."[44]

It will be noted that Johnson is an ornamentalist, at least in his terminology. But it is likely that no great writer, or even able hack

42. *Works* v, 14, *Rambler* No. 3.
43. *Works* ix, 121; cf. *Adventurer* No. 137, *Works* ix, 154. But he attributes the Methodist success in preaching "to their expressing themselves in a plain and familiar manner, which is the only way to do good to the common people" (*Life* i, 458–9). Doubtless he thinks of his essay audience as not so common as that of the Methodist preacher.
44. *Works* vii, 71. The same conception may be seen in Johnson's criticism of devotional poetry. "The paucity of its topicks enforces perpetual repetition, and the sanctity of the matter rejects the ornaments of figurative diction" (*Lives* iii, 310, *Watts*, par. 310).

writer, was ever an ornamentalist in more than terminology. As a feat of composition or as a concrete critical state of mind, ornamentalism is perhaps impossible. When Johnson speaks of things and their ornamentation,[45] we should have no difficulty in recognizing that he is talking about things and aspects of, or ideas about, things. This is all he can be talking about. Both the things and the ideas about them are included in what we call meaning. Since Johnson was not concerned with our particular problem, he was content to look on things, truths, or facts, as solid "meaning" (though he did not employ the term) and on notional modulations as "ornament." We need not then quarrel with his theory while describing it, but must recognize what it means in our own terms.

His most direct statement in defence of his system of elaboration refers to a passage of narration in the *Western Islands*. If *things must* be his reason for writing, his main theme, they can yet be adorned with clustered notions. Lord Monboddo wrote to Boswell that Johnson's language was too rich.

JOHNSON. 'Why, Sir, this criticism would be just, if in my style, superfluous words, or words too big for the thoughts, could be pointed out; but this I do not believe can be done. For instance; in the passage which Lord Monboddo admires, "We were now treading that illustrious region," the word *illustrious,* contributes nothing to the mere narration; for the fact might be told without it: but it is not, therefore, superfluous; for it wakes the mind to peculiar attention, where something of more than usual importance is to be presented. "Illustrious!"—for what? and then the sentence proceeds to expand the circumstances connected with Iona. . . .'[46]

Johnson is giving the reason that justifies all epithetical or non-restrictive modification. When we use any word to tell not what thing we mean but only under what aspect we mean it, we have taken the first step away from plain style. The second step is to multiply the aspects under which we refer to a single object. The third, and extreme Johnsonian, step is to multiply aspects (or words apparently expressing different aspects) so that within the range of relevance they overlap—which is "multiplication for emphasis."

The question whether his style was a way of saying the same thing over and over—that is, giving the same meaning over and over—seems to have occurred to Johnson but not to have worried him. Had he been forced to the wall, he would probably have ad-

45. For other examples, see *Rambler* No. 152, *Works* VII, 72; *Life* II, 439; III, 437; *Letters* I, 108, No. 160.
46. *Life* III, 173–4; cf. *BP* XIII, 40–1.

mitted, needlessly, that elaboration involved repetition. The un-
shakable sense which all writers must have that a multiplication
of notions about one thing is not a repetition of one meaning would
have compelled him to defend his practice, but his bias for talking
of nature and facts, and not of meaning, would have made him
plead guilty of repetition and defend it as ornament.[47] Or, he might
have resolved the conflict in another way, and indeed has left some
hints that he partly did so. "Words," he says in the *Preface to the
Dictionary*, "are seldom exactly synonymous; a new term was not
introduced, but because the former was thought inadequate:
names, therefore, have often many ideas, but few ideas have many
names." [48] If few ideas have many names, that is, if each idea has
but one name proper to it (though one name may by turns do
service for a number of ideas), then the dignity of the idea, that is,
the difference of one idea from another, is asserted, and the correct
basis established for a discussion of words and meaning. Thus:

translate history, in so far as it is not embellished with oratory, which is
poetical. Poetry, indeed, cannot be translated. . . .' [49]

JOHNSON. You may translate books of science exactly. You may also
(This is no other than the Crocean view.) If different words do
correspond to different ideas—different meanings—then follows
the impossibility of translating works which deal in ideas rather

47. Johnson's refusal to see difference of thought (meaning) in difference of
words or ornament is well illustrated in a dispute which he had over Pope's couplet:
      True wit is Nature to advantage dress'd,
      What oft was thought, but ne'er so well express'd.
"Sir, what Pope means, if he means what he says, is both false and foolish. In the
first place, 'what oft was thought,' is all the worse for being often thought, because
to be wit, it ought to be newly thought . . . . How can the expression make it
new? It may make it clear, or may make it elegant; but how new? You are con-
founding words with things" (C. B. Tinker, *Dr. Johnson & Fanny Burney* [New
York, 1911], pp. 151–2).
      It is clear that Johnson makes a demand of *wit* which he does not make of his
own moral writing—namely, that there be newness of thought. Cf. the statement in
Lives I, 19–20, *Cowley*, pars. 54–6: "Pope's account of wit is undoubtedly errone-
ous; he depressed it below its natural dignity and reduces it from strength of
thought to happiness of language." Cf. *Works* VII, 314, *Rambler* No. 194.
      48. *Works* IX, 36; cf. BP XI, 243. Johnson criticized Lord Hailes for modernizing
John Hales of Eton. "An authour's language, Sir, (said he,) is a characteristical
part of his composition, and is also characteristical of the age in which he writes.
Besides, Sir, when the language is changed we are not sure that the sense is the
same" (*Life* IV, 315). But in *Idler* No. 69, on the history of translations (*Works* VIII,
278), he says: "There is undoubtedly a mean to be observed. *Dryden* saw very
early that closeness best preserved an author's sense, and that freedom best exhibited his spirit; he therefore will deserve the highest praise . . . who can convey the same thoughts with the same graces, and who when he translates changes
nothing but the language."

than in facts. Poetry and poetic prose deal in ideas. There can be no doubt that Johnson considered his own prose as leaning toward the poetic. Another step he might have taken in his dignifying of the idea and through it the term, and this would have been the identifying of the idea with the thing and hence the multiplication of as many things as there are ideas and the belief in a different thing for each word. This sort of idealism of course he never yielded to explicitly, but he may have leaned toward it wistfully. In the *Preface to the Dictionary* he wrote:

I am not yet so lost in lexicography, as to forget that *words are the daughters of earth, and that things are the sons of heaven.* Language is only the instrument of science, and words are but the signs of ideas: I wish, however, that the instrument might be less apt to decay, and that signs might be permanent, like the things which they denote.[50]

And in a *Rambler:* "The pebble must be polished with care, which hopes to be valued as a diamond; and words ought surely to be laboured, when they are intended to stand for things." [51] In an *Idler:* "Words are but the images of things." [52] Certainly he did believe that words could have the weight of things, or more weight, and that it was such weight that the writer ought to wield. If "a new term was not introduced, but because the former was thought inadequate," then each different term must have a justification for its existence and for its appearance in a composition. If "constituent" and "fundamental" were created to correspond to different ideas and through these ideas to stand for things, then there was no fault in saying "the constituent and fundamental principle."

50. *Works* ix, 199.
51. *Works* vii, 74, *Rambler* No. 152. Perhaps he had some misgiving about words standing for things when he wrote to Miss Boothby: "It affords me a new conviction, that in these books there is little new, except new forms of expression; which may be sometimes taken, even by the writer, for new doctrines" (*Letters* i, 49, No. 79).
52. *Works* viii, 280, *Idler* No. 70. Cf. *Works* ix, 255, *Preface to Shakespeare,* quoted *ante* p. 92.

CHAPTER VII

Johnson's Theory—II

IN an earlier chapter we have referred to and disqualified as a question of style Johnson's severe canon of correctness in vocabulary. From the *Plan of a Dictionary* and the *Preface* one has no trouble whatever in showing that Johnson said he detested the adulteration of English with foreign words and uses, particularly with French, which seemed to him the most insidious threat of his own day. He would not be reduced to "babble a dialect of France." [1] Perhaps only a wavering distinction may be drawn between Johnson's objection to certain classes of words as incorrect, not English, and his objection to others as unfit for elegant composition, inexpressive of what he thought most worth expressing. And certainly correctness was for him one of the conditions of expressiveness. But an opinion about correctness is an opinion about the limitation of a language, about what liberties may be taken with a conventional medium of expression. This is to be distinguished from an opinion about how language may be most effectively used as an expressive medium, which is an opinion about style.

First we may notice what kind of word was stylistically objectionable to Johnson. "Low" is perhaps his most generic term of censure. He makes his use of the term very clear.

We are all offended by low terms, but are not disgusted alike by the same compositions, because we do not all agree to censure the same terms as low. No word is naturally or intrinsically meaner than another; our opinion therefore of words, as of other things arbitrarily and capriciously established, depends wholly upon accident and custom . . . . Words become low by the occasions to which they are applied, or the

1. For an array of evidence on this point, see W. Vaughan Reynolds, "Johnson's Opinions on Prose Style," *Review of English Studies*, IX (1933), 437–9; *Christie* pp. 24–7; Joseph E. Brown, *The Critical Opinions of Samuel Johnson* (Princeton, 1926), pp. 69–70. Or see esp. Johnson's *Works* IX, 214, 225, 226, *Preface to the Dictionary;* X, 190, Review of *Memoirs of the Court of Augustus; Lives* I, 190, *Milton,* par. 270; *Life* I, 221. It will be noticed (See esp. *Works* IX, 214) that besides words which were foreign and too new, Johnson discountenanced archaic words, those used only in the "time of rudeness antecedent to perfection." For a broader treatment of Johnson's views on lexicography and the fixation of language, see Hermann M. Flasdieck, *Der Gedanke einer Englischen Sprachakademie in Vergangenheit und Gegenwart* (Jena, 1928), pp. 108–20.

general character of them who use them; and the disgust which they produce, arises from the revival of those images with which they are commonly united.[2]

Or, as we might say today, low words are those which have low meanings. Since the meaning of words depends precisely upon "the occasions to which they are applied," we should have no difficulty in admitting that words applied to low occasions are to that degree low. Our essential quarrel with Johnson would be over what meanings should be called low, or whether any meaning is so low as to be irredeemable, whether, in fact, lowness or familiarity is not one of the elements that transform most readily into the poetic. When in the same *Rambler* Johnson goes on to pick out as low terms the "*dunnest* smoke of hell" and "*knife*" and "*peep through the blanket of the dark*,"[3] we know full well that our difference is not about diction but about the very center of meaning. What makes is possible for the question to seem one of diction is Johnson's habit, already noted, of speaking as if things were meaning, and diction (with its accompanying ideas) but the dress of meaning—or, more accurately, as if there were a part of thought that was central and determined, according to the things denoted by words, and this was meaning, while the connotation of the words, the ideas about things conveyed in the names given them, was not meaning. In this way it is quite possible to form a thorough-going theory of lowness in diction.

Language is the dress of thought; and as the noblest mien or most graceful action would be degraded and obscured by a garb appropriated to the gross employments of rusticks or mechanicks, so the most heroick sentiments will lose their efficacy, and the most splendid ideas drop their magnificence, if they are conveyed by words used commonly upon low and trivial occasions, debased by vulgar mouths, and contaminated by inelegant applications.[4]

And it follows that there is also a poetic diction, that is, a body of words never applied to low occasions and hence felt to be suited to the lofty occasions of poetry.

2. *Works* vii, 164–5, *Rambler* No. 168. "Low" was also for Johnson a term of lexicographic censure. Mr. Harold B. Allen's paper, "Terms of Linguistic Censure in Johnson's Dictionary," read at the Annual Meeting of the Modern Language Association of America, 28 Dec. 1938, contained some interesting statistics for Johnson's use of various terms of censure, such as "low," "improper," "corrupt," "barbarous," "unauthorized," "lacking etymology."

3. See also *Works* v, 241, *Rambler* No. 37, an example from the *Shepherd's Calendar;* x, 191, examples from the *Memoirs of the Court of Augustus;* Walter Raleigh, *Johnson on Shakespeare* (London, 1929), p. 111, an example from *Richard II.*

4. *Lives* i, 58, *Cowley,* par. 181; cf. *Works* vii, 164, *Rambler* No. 168.

There was . . . before the time of Dryden no poetical diction: no system of words at once refined from the grossness of domestick use and free from the harshness of terms appropriated to particular arts.[5]

The concept of low diction and lofty diction and of low thoughts (or matter) and lofty thoughts (or matter)—four separate things —leads to some interesting consequences. It has to be conceded, for example, that some "thoughts by their native excellence secure themselves from violation, being such as mean language cannot express." [6] Again, low diction is sometimes suitably employed when the matter is low. "Yet ne'er looks forward farther than his nose." Boswell "objected to the last phrase, as being low. JOHN-SON. 'Sir, it is intended to be low; it is satire. The expression is debased, to debase the character.' " [7] And lofty diction—this may be debased by application to low matter. "To degrade the sounding words and stately constructions of Milton, by an application to the lowest and most trivial things [as in the *Splendid Shilling*], gratifies the mind with a momentary triumph over that grandeur which hitherto held its captives in admiration." [8] On the other hand lofty diction may be successful in disguising low matter. "When the matter is low or scanty [as in Addison's *Battle of the Pigmies and Cranes, Barometer,* and *Bowling Green*] a dead language, in which nothing is mean because nothing is familiar, affords great conveniences; and by the sonorous magnificence of Roman syllables the writer conceals penury of thought and want of novelty, often from the reader, and often from himself." [9]

ii

IN the passage quoted above from the *Life of Dryden* "the grossness of domestick use" is coupled with "the harshness of terms appropriated to particular arts." Low terms and terms of art are condemned together. It is even possible that many words were to Johnson objectionable on both counts. The following passage which he quotes from Blackmore would seem to be full of examples.

I am not free of the Poets' Company, having never kissed . . . [their] governor's hands [. . .]: mine is therefore not so much as a permission-

5. *Lives* I, 420, *Dryden,* par. 220. See *ibid.,* n. 2 for Dryden's expression of the theory in the Dedication of his *Aeneis.*
6. *Lives* I, 217, *Butler,* par. 50. The subject of discussion is *Hudibras.*
7. *Life* v, 83. The line quoted is from the *Essay on Man,* IV, 224.
8. *Lives* I, 317, *J. Philips,* par. 10.
9. *Lives* II, 83, *Addison,* par. 11.

poem, but a downright interloper. Those gentlemen who [. . .] carry on their poetical trade in a joint stock would certainly do what they could to sink and ruin an unlicensed adventurer, notwithstanding I disturbed none of their factories nor imported any goods they had ever dealt in.

"Language such as Cheapside easily furnished," says Johnson in introducing this passage. And he follows it with the laconic comment, "He had lived in the city till he had learned its note." [10] These terms of commerce were objectionable to Johnson as such, and used in facetious analogy as they are, they seem to us, as well as to him, expressions of a cheap meaning.

It had been part of the diversitarianism of the Renaissance, just as it is part of romantic and modern local-color technique, to cultivate terms of art. Ronsard spoke out for them.[11] English Elizabethan plays are full of them. Dryden and Milton were still using them—though at moments with rather sour effect, and with misgivings on the part of Dryden.[12] Rymer implied such terms were "gross and trumpery." [13] Pope criticizes their use in Dryden.[14] Addison criticizes it in both Milton and Dryden.[15] From his "Dictionary of Rhyme" Edward Bysshe omits without argument "all uncommon Words, and that are of a generally unknown Signification; as the *Names* of Distempers that are unusual; most of the terms of Arts and Sciences." [16] Johnson's objection to terms of art is something of his age, though something in which he outdoes the age.

"Words too familiar or too remote," he continues in the passage from the *Life of Dryden*, "defeat the purpose of a poet." And of the second case he explains: "Words to which we are nearly strangers, whenever they occur, draw that attention on themselves which they should transmit to things." In another part of the *Life of Dryden* he says: "It is a general rule in poetry that all appropriated terms of art should be sunk in *general* expressions, because

10. *Lives* II, 238, *Blackmore*, par. 8.
11. *Œuvres Complètes*, ed. Gustave Cohen (Paris, 1938), II, 999–1000.
12. For the contradictory opinions of Dryden on technical terms in poetry, see *Essays of John Dryden*, ed. W. P. Ker (Oxford, 1926), I, 13, Preface to *Annus Mirabilis*, 1667; II, 236, Dedication of the *Aeneis*, 1697; cf. I, xxxiii; and J. E. Spingarn, *Critical Essays of the Seventeenth Century* (Oxford, 1908), I, xlv; II, 333.
13. J. E. Spingarn, *op. cit.*, II, 170, Preface to *Rapin*, 1674; cf. II, 222, *Short View of Tragedy*, 1693.
14. *Works of Alexander Pope*, VI (ed. Whitwell Elwin, London, 1871), 107, Letter 23.
15. *Morley* p. 428, *Spectator* No. 297.
16. Edward Bysshe, *Art of English Poetry*, 7th ed. (London, 1725), Vol. II, A *Dictionary of Rhymes* (1724), p. iii.

poetry is to speak an universal language." [17] The italics are mine. Here we find the notion of generality invested with another value for Johnson—that of comprehensibility. Swift's particularities about the reign of Queen Anne were poor writing because as particularities they lacked the significance or importance of general truth. Push particularity further—to the degree of technicality— and to insignificance is added incomprehensibility. Or, since technicality is but an extreme of particularity, incomprehensibility is an extreme of insignificance. Johnson's objection to technical terms in poetic use is clearly expressed again and again in the *Lives*, and exemplified. From Dryden's *Annus Mirabilis* he quotes three stanzas, underlining the nautical terms. It will suffice to quote but two lines here:

> Some the *gall'd* ropes with dawby *marling* bind,
> Or sear-cloth masts with strong *tarpawling* coats.

"I suppose," says Johnson, "here is not one term which every reader does not wish away." [18]

What Johnson disliked in poetry there is every reason to believe he disliked also in the creative prose of the general and moral essay. Even in essays of technical literary criticism he strove to deny himself the use of critical terms. In the first of the *Ramblers* on Milton's versification he realizes the difficulty of the feat but resolves upon it.

I am desirous to be generally understood, and shall therefore studiously decline the dialect of grammarians; though, indeed, it is always difficult, and sometimes scarcely possible, to deliver the precepts of an art, without the terms by which the peculiar ideas of that art are expressed, and which had not been invented but because the language already in use was insufficient. If therefore I shall sometimes seem obscure, may be imputed to this voluntary interdiction, and to a desire of avoiding that offence which is always given by unusual words.[19]

In the last *Rambler* he ranked "criticism . . . among the subordinate and instrumental arts." [20] He said elsewhere: "An art cannot

17. *Lives* I, 433, par. 255.
18. *Lives* I, 434, par. 256. For other expressions by Johnson of the same censure, see *Lives* I, 440, 462, *Dryden*, pars. 279, 336; I, 188, *Milton*, par. 263; *Works* x, 191, Review of *Memoirs of the Court of Augustus; Misc.* II, 441, letter to Rev. Edward Lye.
Johnson had also a lexicographical difficulty over technical terms. Like foreign words and archaic words, some technical words were not to be admitted as parts of the English language. Frequently, in fact, technical words were foreign words. See esp. *Works* IX, 168–9, *Plan of an English Dictionary;* IX, 204, 213, 220, *Preface to the Dictionary.*
19. *Works* VI, 92, *Rambler* No. 86.
20. *Works* VII, 396, *Rambler* No. 208.

be taught but by its proper terms, but it is not always necessary to teach the art." [21]

iii

Iт is a truth verging on paradox that Johnson's favorite words, the "philosophic" or scientific words which we discussed in an earlier chapter, should be special and technical just as much as the hated words of art. Both terms of art and philosophic terms have a tone of recondite currency; they suggest the accuracy of a special familiarity or erudition. This much "marling" and "tarpawling" have in common with "adscititious" and "equiponderant." Johnson himself is aware of the affinity in the following important passage from the *Idler* in defence of "hard words."

The state of every . . . art is the same; as it is cursorily surveyed or accurately examined, different forms of expression become proper. In morality it is one thing to discuss the niceties of the casuist, and another to direct the practice of common life. In agriculture, he that instructs the farmer to plough and sow, may convey his notions without the words which he would find necessary in explaining to philosophers the process of vegetation.[22]

Here "morality" as well as "agriculture" is considered as an art, and the experts in agriculture are "philosophers."

The same passage is further important as it suggests the question how Johnson himself thought he was using words in his essays. Was he discussing the "niceties of the casuist" in philosophic terms, or was he directing the "practice of common life" in common terms? The answer must be that he conceived himself as doing neither simply, but as combining the means of the former with the purpose of the latter: that is, he was turning philosophic diction to the purpose of moral instruction or discussion of general truths. We have his own word for it, unmistakably, in the last *Rambler*.

When common words were less pleasing to the ear, or less distinct in their signification, I have familiarized the terms of philosophy, by applying them to popular ideas.[23]

21. *Works* viii, 281, *Idler* No. 70, "Hard words defended," where Johnson also states very plainly the case for technical words in their place. "Every hour produces instances of the necessity of terms of art . . . . They that content themselves with general ideas may rest in general terms; but those whose studies or employments force them upon closer inspection, must have names for particular parts, and words by which they may express various modes of combination, such as none but themselves have occasion to consider."

22. *Works* viii, 282, *Idler* No. 70.

23. *Works* vii, 395, *Rambler* No. 208. That Johnson is using the term "philosophic" in the sense of scientific there can be no doubt. It is his common use. For example, in the *Journey to the Western Islands* he says: "The cuddy is a fish of which I

Johnson, therefore, approved philosophic terms in elegant prose, though terms of art he did not. The antithesis lies in the various degrees of generality and hence comprehensibility, significance and dignity, which the various arts, sciences, or philosophies, possess. If we construct a scale of four examples, sailing, agriculture, chemistry, morals, it is impossible to say that the terms of any upper group of these sciences would have been for Johnson "philosophic" and those of the lower, "terms of art." But it may be said that he would have tended to use the terms of the upper end of the scale, accepting the whole vocabulary of morals, picking and rejecting in chemistry and agriculture, and shunning nautical terms, as he wished that Dryden and Milton had done. The point is that the less a set of principles and facts and their terms were the business of practical and active men and the more they were the object only of study and the creation of learning, the more generally comprehensible and applicable were the terms—and of course the more worthy of the attention of learned or intelligent men outside the particular science. Further, and not so obviously, the comprehensibility of such scientific terms had a kind of inevitability and sanction—whereas the words growing from the rub of active life, the need to refer to this or that thing or part of a special business, were adventitious and bastard; they came from without the authority and tradition.[24] "These accidental and colloquial senses are the disgrace of language, and the plague of commentators," Johnson once wrote.[25] And while he was not referring here to terms of art,

know not the philosophical name" (*Works* x, 406). In a letter to Dr. Brocklesby he gives the name of "philosophers" to people interested in balloons (*Life* IV, 356). Presumably he means the same when he says of Browne: "He must . . . . be confessed to have augmented our philosophical diction" (*Works* IV, 612, *Life of Browne*). Cf. *New English Dictionary*, "Philosopher," 1; "Philosophic," 1.b; "Philosophical," 1.b.

From some examples given in the *Preface to the Dictionary*, it is plain that "hard words" include philosophic. "Sometimes easier words are changed into harder, as *burial* into *sepulture* or *interment*, *drier* into *desiccative*, *dryness* into *siccity* or *aridity*, *fit* into *paroxysm*" (*Works* IX, 212).

24. For this reason the special talk of drawing rooms was no more elegant than that of sailors. It was equally accidental and unauthorized. "Those who aspire to gentle elegance, collect female phrases and fashionable barbarisms, and imagine that style to be easy which custom has made familiar. Such was the idea of the poet [Pope, "On the Countess of Burlington . . ."] who wrote the following verses to a *countess cutting paper*:

> *Pallas* grew *vap'rish once and odd*,
>   She would not *do the least right thing*
> Either for Goddess or for God,
>   Nor work, nor play, nor paint, nor sing.
>   (*Works* VIII, 308, *Idler* No. 77)

25. Note to *The Merry Wives of Windsor*, IV, iii, 12–13, Walter Raleigh, *Johnson on Shakespeare* (London, 1929), p. 95.

the association of "accidental" and "colloquial" is telling. He made this even clearer in the *Preface to the Dictionary*.

Of the laborious and mercantile part of the people, the diction is in a great measure casual and mutable; many of their terms are formed for some temporary or local convenience, and though current at certain times and places, are in others utterly unknown. This fugitive cant, which is always in a state of increase or decay, cannot be regarded as any part of the durable materials of a language, and therefore must be suffered to perish with other things unworthy of preservation.[26]

If meanings which arose colloquially, from the actual use of men, were "accidental," what kind of meanings were not accidental? What kind existed by prescription or inherently? One must presume that Johnson had in mind meanings fixed or derivable from the etymology of words—that is, meanings determined by *ancient* rather than by *recent* colloquial use.[27] These were meanings so long established that they were capable of modulation, combination and extension into new meanings that demanded recognition, were not accidental, but inherent in the word roots."It is my serious opinion," Johnson once said, "that our living languages must be formed quite slavishly on the model of the classics, if our writings are to endure."[28] This attitude of Johnson's is part of an attitude general among eighteenth-century grammarians, that language is a logical institution, pristinely perfect but debased through usage and needing to be restored and preserved by reason. Johnson is here closely akin to Horne Tooke, who would by etymology reduce all parts of speech to nouns and verbs;[29] to George Campbell, who attempts (despite his disavowal of the principle)

26. *Works* IX, 221.
27. "*Tiff*," says Johnson in the *Dictionary*, "a low word, I suppose without etymology." *Chouse* is "perhaps a fortuitous and cant word, without etymology." Cf. *Courtney* pp. 51–3. "Dr Johnson," wrote George Campbell, ". . . hath declared the name *punch*, which signifies a certain mixt liquor very well known, a cant word, because, being to appearance without etymology, it hath probably arisen from some silly conceit among the people. The name *sherbet*, which signifies another known mixture, he allows to be good, because it is Arabic; though, for aught we know, its origin among the Arabs, hath been equally ignoble or uncertain" (*Philosophy of Rhetoric*, 2d ed. [London, 1801], p. 342, n.*).
28. In the *Monthly Magazine*, IX (1800), 149–51, appeared "A German Traveller's Account of His Interview with Dr. Johnson; and some Remarks of his Writings." Mr. H. L. Levy has recently offered a new translation of this account and has pointed out the author as the diplomatist H. P. Sturz, who visited Johnson 18 Aug. 1768 at Mr. Thrale's (*Times Literary Supplement*, XXXIX [1940], pp. 80, 339).
29. *Diversions of Purley*, ed. Richard Taylor (London, 1829), I, 46, 103 ff.; II, 18 ff. Cf. Otto Funke, *Englische Sprachphilosophie im Späteren 18. Jahrhundert* (Bern, 1934), pp. 109, 135–7.

to determine by etymology the "proper signification" of words.[30] The meaning of a word like "marling" depended on the usage of sailors, and hence was accidental, limited, insignificant, undignified, and incapable of modulation and extension. The meaning of a word like "adscititious" depended on a form of the Latin verb *adsciscere,* which in turn was an inceptive form of the verb *scire,* whose meaning was one of the most basic and simple of our ideas. Such a word as "adscititious" may itself not have been current in any science, but it might have been or ought to have been; it was formed on the pattern of scientific words; it was a term of the most universal science, that of generality, *Allerlei-Wissenschaft;* it was of the native vocabulary of philosophers. "Marling" was a word which many might understand but which few needed or ought to understand. "Adscititious" was a word which few might understand, but which all should understand—all who knew the roots of the language and could put two and two together. For the same reason the learned man might invent his "three or four" [31] words, provided they were of the philosophic language, not inventions at all, but extensions.

> Et nova fictaque nuper habebunt verba fidem si
> Graeco fonte cadant, parce detorta.[32]

And it followed that philosophic words, being of inherent literal validity, should have a strong claim to metaphorical use, and hence that their currency in the language should increase. "As by the cultivation of various sciences, a language is amplified, it will be more furnished with words deflected from their original sense; the geometrician will talk of a courtier's zenith, or the eccentrick virtue of a wild hero, and the physician of sanguine expectations and phlegmatick delays." [33] Johnson himself, as we have seen in our analysis of his writing, relied continually on both the literal and

30. *Philosophy of Rhetoric,* 2d ed. (London, 1801), I, 334–5; cf. Sterling A. Leonard, *The Doctrine of Correctness in English Usage 1700–1800* (Madison, 1929), pp. 132–6.
31. " 'These people, Sir, that Gerrard talks of, may have somewhat of a *peregrinity* in their dialect, which relation has augmented to a different language.' I asked him if *peregrinity* was an English word: he laughed, and said, 'No.' I told him this was the second time that I had heard him coin a word. When Foote broke his leg, I observed that it would make him fitter for taking off George Faulkner . . . . Dr. Johnson at that time said, 'George will rejoice at the *depeditation* of Foote;' and when I challenged that word, laughed, and owned he had made it, and added that he had not made above three or four in his *Dictionary"* (*Life* v, 130).
32. Horace, *Ars Poetica,* 11. 52–3, quoted by Boswell, *Life* I, 221.
33. *Works* IX, 224, *Preface to the Dictionary.*

figurative [34] use of philosophical diction, on "inundations" and "momentaneous excursions," on "catharticks of vice, or lenitives of passion." As Boswell puts it, "He delighted to express familiar thoughts in philosophical language." [35]

More simply Johnson accounted for his usage with the formula: big words for big meaning. "He that thinks with more extent than another will want words of larger meaning." [36] Thus he expresses it in the *Idler* in defence of "hard words." And Mrs. Piozzi writes: "Though he was accused of using big words as they are called, it was only when little ones would not express his meaning as clearly, or when perhaps the elevation of the thought would have been disgraced by a dress less superb." [37] Johnson's notion is echoed at length by Boswell in conversation with a young Scotch friend.

He mentioned the Ridicule . . . called *Lexiphanes*, written by one Campbell. "Sir," said I, "nothing can be more unfair. Mr. Johnson's language is suitable to his sentiment. He gives large words because he has large ideas. If Campbell clothes little paultry ideas with these big words, to be sure the effect must be ridiculous. The late King of Prussia's tall Regiment looked very stately with their large grenadier caps. If Campbell had taken these caps and clapped them on the heads of a parcel of blackguard children in the street, it would be highly ridiculous; but does that prove anything against the caps when properly applied? No, Sir, Mr. Johnson has gigantick thoughts, and therefore he must be allowed gigantick words." This was quite in Mr. Johnson's own stile.[38]

And "We may," says Boswell also, "with the utmost propriety, apply to his learned style that passage of Horace, a part of which he has taken as the motto to his Dictionary." [39] A smaller part of the same passage had been taken already by Johnson as the motto of *Rambler* No. 88, on Milton's versification. And part of this we may quote:

34. Cf. Johnson's reduction of words to their original or etymological meanings and his statement about this in the *Preface to the Dictionary* (*ante* p. 66).

35. *Life* I, 217. And Boswell quotes the passage from *Rambler* No. 208. Murphy too echoes *Rambler* No. 208. Johnson "pours along, familiarizing the terms of philosophy" (*Misc.* I, 470). Cf. *Life* III, 284, n. 4; *BP* XIII, 40; *Letters* I, 384, n. 4; Nathan Drake, *Essays . . . Illustrative of the Rambler, Adventurer, and Idler* (London, 1809), I, 256–7.

36. *Works* VIII, 280, *Idler* No. 70. Boswell quotes this in *Life* I, 218. Here may be mentioned Johnson's warnings against big words for little matters (*Life* I, 471; III, 303; v, 141; *Works* x, 192).

37. *Misc.* I, 344.

38. *BP* VII, 174, Oxford, 27 March 1768. Murphy says: "The thought seems to expand with the sound of the words" (*Misc.* I, 467).

39. *Life* I, 220.

Audebit quaecunque minus splendoris habebunt,
Aut sine pondere erunt, et honore indigna ferentur,
Verba movere loco.

and with it the translation by Creech, which Johnson adds:

what words appear
Too light and trivial, or too weak to bear
The weighty sense, nor worth the reader's care,
Shake off.[40]

For the big thoughts and the big words the proper organ was the
big voice, a part of Johnson's technique well recognized by his
contemporaries. "His *bow-wow way*," Lord Pembroke called it.[41]
Boswell described it more respectfully. "He had a loud voice, and a
slow deliberate utterance, which no doubt gave some additional
weight to the sterling metal of his conversation." [42] And in a note
he offers another figure:

The *Messiah*, played upon the *Canterbury organ*, is more sublime than
when played upon an inferior instrument . . . . *While therefore Dr.
Johnson's sayings are read, let his manner be taken along with them.*

On the island of Skye, Ulinish heard Johnson talk of tanning and
milk and making whey and said: "He is a great orator, Sir; it is
musick to hear this man speak." [43]

40. *Works* VI, 103; cf. *Life* I, 220.
41. *Life* II, 326, n. 5; and V, 18, n. 1.
42. *Life* V, 18; cf. IV, 428–9. For other statements, see *Letters* I, 295, n. 2; *Life* II,
326–7; *Misc.* I, 451, Murphy's *Essay.*
Boswell says Johnson's recitation of a passage from *Macbeth* was "grand and
affecting" (*Life* V, 115); cf. *Life* II, 212; *Misc.* I, 347. Miss Reynolds found his
manner "injudicious" in reading "familiar subjects, narrations, essays, letters, &c."
(*Misc.* II, 266–7, *Recollections*). For Johnson's theory of styles in reading, see
the *Preface to the Preceptor* (*Works* IX, 408).
43. *Life* V, 246.
A few words on imagery might be expected in this chapter. But just as Johnson's imagery has, beyond a certain etymological quality, little to make it peculiarly his own, so it seems to me that his utterances on imagery have no very
specific relation to his practice. See esp. *Life* III, 174, 403; IV, 166, 247 and n. 4;
V, 228, 291; *Letters* I, 337, No. 409; *Lives* II, 228, *Congreve*, par. 33; III, 229, *Pope*,
par. 329; *Works* XI, 30, *Rasselas*, chap. X; *Dictionary*, "Imagery."
Johnson frequently uses the term "imagination" in the pejorative sense of "idle
reverie" or "daydream," as in the title of Chapter XLIII of *Rasselas*, "The Dangerous
Prevalence of Imagination" (*Works* XI, 121). Cf. *Rambler* No. 89, *Works* VI, 110;
Life IV, 208; *Misc.* I, 25, *Prayers and Meditations;* Irving Babbitt, *On Being Crea-
tive* (Boston, 1932), pp. 80–2, 87; Stuart G. Brown, "Dr. Johnson, Poetry, and
Imagination," *Neophilologus*, XXIII (1938), 203–7.

CHAPTER VIII

Antecedents of Johnson's Style

W E have detached Johnson from the rest of English letters, so far as such a thing is possible, and have discussed
his style and his theory of style as it were *in vacuo*. When
we compared him to Addison and Hazlitt, we refrained from
chronological implications. To complete a study of Johnson's style,
it is just these implications which would have to be explored; but
to do so would be to undertake not so much the completion of the
present study as a sequel to it. Such a work would have to make
more general, more exclusive statements, be based on a far wider
canvass of negative evidence. In the fullest sense it is a task probably not worth doing—for example, if it includes finding out how
many newspaper writers of the latter half of the eighteenth century assumed Johnsonian manners. In this chapter and the next I
pretend to say only some things relevant to the history of the Johnsonian style.

The question how Johnson's style was formed has not of course
had to wait until now for answers. Johnson himself made some
suggestions, perhaps jocular, perhaps but careless. His biographers
made more. Sir John Hawkins was the least restrained; in scatter-
shot statements he named the "old English writers" More, Ascham,
Hooker, Spenser, Sandys, Jewel, Chillingworth, Hales of Eton; [1]
"the divines and others of the last century," Sanderson, Taylor,
Sir Thomas Browne, Cowley.[2] Boswell too delivered a broadside
opinion.

The style of Johnson was, undoubtedly, much formed upon that of the
great writers in the last century, Hooker, Bacon, Sanderson, Hakewell,
and others.[3]

Altogether fourteen writers, and "others" not named. But how far
Johnson "owed his excellence," as Hawkins phrases it, to these

1. *Works* I, 96–7. Johnson censured Lord Hailes for modernizing the language
of Hales of Eton (*ante* p. 102, n. 49).

2. *Works* I, 271. The passage goes on to record Johnson's disapproval of the
"tinsel of Sprat," the "smooth verbosity of Tillotson," the "involved" style of Ham-
mond and Barrow and the latter's prolixity. Cf. *Works* I, 463, 542.

3. *Life* I, 219. One may add that Mary Lepell, Lady Hervey, wrote that the
Ramblers reminded her of William Melmoth's *Letters . . . by . . . Sir Thomas
Fitzosborne, Bart.* (*Letters* [London, 1821], pp. 61–2. Cf. *Courtney* p. 26). Cf. *post*
p. 129.

divines and others of the last century and others of the century before that, how far he formed on their style a "new one" or was inspired by them to "original phrases and new combinations of integral parts of sentences," might admit a wide solution. He himself told Boswell "that Bacon was a favourite authour with him; but he had never read his works till he was compiling the English Dictionary, in which" Boswell "might see Bacon very often quoted."[4] In the *Preface to the Dictionary* he thought that the "terms of natural knowledge" might be "extracted" from Bacon alone.[5] He did quote Bacon often in the *Dictionary* and quoted him or referred to him on numerous other occasions.[6] Perhaps the cut or sectional structure of Bacon's *Essays*, their curt Senecan style, had something to do with the *Ramblers*. It is to be remarked that when read in the folio edition, with separated paragraphs and capitalized initial words of paragraphs, the *Ramblers* assume clearly a character somewhat disguised by more continuous printing. They seem then to read, each one not so much a single essay as a collection of paragraphic essays, sometimes parallel, sometimes antithetic. Perhaps also Johnson recruited some of his vocabulary from Bacon's "terms of natural knowledge."[7] And so for Hooker, from whose work and the Bible Johnson thought the "language of theology" might be "extracted."[8]

Hawkins was right in stressing Johnson's interest in the "divines . . . of the last century," "the great English church-men." Johnson wrote:

Our own language has, from the reformation to the present time, been chiefly dignified and adorned by the works of our divines, who, considered as commentators, controvertists, or preachers, have undoubtedly left all other nations far behind them . . . . Of morality little is necessary to be said because it is comprehended in practical divinity, and is perhaps better taught in *English* sermons than in any other books ancient or modern.[9]

Sir Edmund Gosse thinks that we ought to regard Johnson in the *Rambler* as "taking up the task of a lay-preacher, and as deliberately

4. *Life* iii, 194.
5. *Works* x, 215.
6. See, for example, *Life* iii, 194, n. 1, 510, App. F; v, 89, 220, 232; *Works* vi, 226, 420, 436 (*Rambler*, Nos. 106, 137, 140); ix, 61 (*Adventurer* No. 85); Letters i, 252, n. 2; *Lives* iii, Index; and Joseph E. Brown, *Critical Opinions of Samuel Johnson* (Princeton, 1926), pp. 282–3.
7. Johnson's heavily marked volume of Bacon's English writings, from the 1740 edition of the works, is in the Yale Library, and Johnson's method with it has been described by Gordon S. Haight, "Johnson's Copy of Bacon's Works," *Yale University Library Gazette*, vi (1932), 67–73.
8. *Works* ix, 215, *Preface to the Dictionary*.
9. *Works* viii, 367, *Idler* No. 91.

competing with the popular theologians of his youth," in whose hands the sermon at "the beginning of the century had been as popular as the novel is to-day."[10] Johnson's own sermons, laden with the peculiarities of his style, were apparently preachable enough in his own day.[11] It is strange that Hawkins, with his attention upon the divines, failed to mention certain sermon-writers more nearly contemporary with Johnson. South, for example, a copy of whose sermons was given away by Johnson in his last illness and upon whom Johnson seems a number of times to draw.[12] Or Clarke, whose sermons Johnson "valued above all other" and in his last illness recommended to the Deist Dr. Brocklesby.[13] Sermons, by various divines, and other religious writings seem to have claimed a good deal of Johnson's attention,[14] though many of these, such as Law's *Serious Call*,[15] must have had little if any effect on his notions of literary excellence. In the Hebrides Johnson read aloud and praised Ogden's sixth sermon on prayer, from which Boswell quotes a "specimen of Ogden's manner," a specimen which does not, one must concede, promise a rich yield of Johnsonian antecedents.[16]

ii

AMONG the writers of the seventeenth century, however, there was one other whom Boswell reserved for separate mention.

Sir Thomas Brown, whose life Johnson wrote, was remarkably fond of Anglo-Latian diction; and to his example we are to ascribe Johnson's sometimes indulging himself in this kind of phraseology.[17]

10. *Leaves and Fruit* (New York, 1927), p. 362, "The Prose of Dr. Johnson."

11. *Courtney* p. 170; *Life* III, 181, 506–7, App. F; IV, 381, n. 1 (on p. 383). Cf. W. Fraser Mitchell, *English Pulpit Oratory from Andrewes to Tillotson* (London, 1932), esp. p. 125.

12. *Life* IV, 505, 530, App. J; *Misc.* I, 185, n. 3, Piozzi *Anecdotes*; *Letters* II, 183, n. 2, 439, App. C. Cf. W. Fraser Mitchell, *op. cit.*, pp. 313–20; Norman Mattis, "Robert South," *Quarterly Journal of Speech*, XV (1929), esp. pp. 552–5. I mean not to suggest that the relatively plain style of South was an important model for Johnson; but Hawkins might have mentioned South as plausibly as he did some others. In *Life* III, 247–8 Johnson praises the sermon style of Atterbury, South, Seed, Jortin, Sherlock, and Smalridge, but takes exception to that of Tillotson.

13. *Life* IV, 416 and n. 2; *Misc.* II, 387, Windham's *Diary*; 156, Hoole's *Narrative*; *Works* I, 365, 577.

14. *Life* I, 38–9; II, 505, App. B; IV, 311–12, 484, App. J; *Letters* I, 357, n. 4; *Works* I, 163, 317, 542; XI, 206, 207, 211. *Courtney* p. 45 lists some religious writers quoted in the *Dictionary*.

15. William Law's *Serious Call to a Devout and Holy Life* appeared in 1728. For Johnson's acquaintance with it see *Life* I, 68; II, 122; III, 445, App. A; IV, 311; *Letters* I, 31, 52; *Works* I, 563–4; *BP* XVIII, 234.

16. *Life* V, 351.

17. *Life* I, 221–2. "The observation . . . ," he adds in a footnote, "has been made by many people." Cf. *Life* I, 308.

The same theory was advanced by Murphy.

How he differed so widely from such elegant models [Cowley, Dryden, Tillotson, Temple, Addison, Swift, Pope] is a problem not to be solved, unless it be true that he took an early tincture from the writers of the last century, particularly Sir Thomas Browne. Hence the peculiarities of his style, new combinations, sentences of an unusual structure, and words derived from the learned languages.[18]

And earlier than this Vicesimus Knox, as Boswell points out in his footnote, had selected from the *Pseudodoxia Epidemica* some examples of learned diction such as he thought must have been Johnson's model in the *Rambler*.

Intellectual acquisition is but reminiscential evocation.

We hope it will not be unconsidered that we find no constant manuduction in this labyrinth.

a faraginious concurrence of all conditions

Being divided from truth themselves, they are yet further removed by advenient deception.[19]

That there is some resemblance between the diction of Johnson and that of Browne's scientific writing, especially the *Pseudodoxia*, cannot be denied. Johnson himself confessed that Browne had "augmented our philosophical diction." [20] But the resemblance may perhaps be qualified in one important way, a way suggested by such words in Knox's examples as "manuduction" and "faraginious" and clearly illustrated when Johnson himself censures Browne's diction.

[He] poured in a multitude of exotick words; many, indeed, useful and significant, which, if rejected, must be supplied by circumlocution, such as *commensality* for the state of many living at the same table, but many superfluous, as a *paralogical* for an unreasonable doubt; and some so obscure, that they conceal his meaning rather than explain it, as *arthritical analogies* for parts that serve some animals in place of joints.[21]

18. *Misc.* I, 467.
19. *Winter Evenings* (London, 1790), I, 192, "On Dr. Johnson's Prayers, with a Remark on his Style." The first edition appeared in 1788. Knox quotes three other examples: "For not attaining the deuteroscopy, they are fain to omit the superconsequences, coherences, figures, or tripologies, and are not some time persuaded by fire beyond their literalities." "Their individual imperfections being great, they are moreover enlarged by their aggregation." "Deluding their apprehension with ariolation."
He says it has "always appeared" to him that Johnson imitated Browne, and he believes it "is now generally thought." Cf. *Life* I, 308.
20. *Works* IV, 612, *Life of Browne*.
21. *Ibid.*, p. 612.

"Arthritical analogies" is such a philosophical term as we shall not find in Johnson, partly because, as he says, it is so unusual as to conceal meaning, but further because it has a quality of meaning quite different from that of Johnson's usual philosophic term. "Arthritical analogies" is a philosophic term which refers not to anything abstract or very general, but to so particular and concretely tangible a class of objects as "parts that serve some animals in place of joints." This is not Johnson's way. "Wit," it will be recalled, he changed to "vitality," and he once changed "drunken" to "vinous," [22] but, speaking of a bulldog's shape, he changed "tenuity" to "thin part." [23] He selects his philosophic terms from the range of the more abstract sciences, or if he takes from the others, it is for a metaphorical use. His terms are those of that broad science of which we spoke, the philosophy of things in general, by which he achieves the "grandeur of generality." Browne too uses terms within this range, as some of the examples adduced by Knox illustrate. But his tendency is constantly the other way, toward the particular, the recondite, the freakish, the unheard-of. He deals in the bric-a-brac of philosophic terminology. And even his terms of general philosophy are so mixed with Pharaoh and mummy or the powder of the golden calf, or spotted with scorpion and salamander, that the whole texture of the writing suggests strange places and bizarre experiences. He deserves the name "exotick" which Johnson applies to him, a name which would sit most curiously on Johnson himself. Where Browne uses remote terms to make us think of remote things, Johnson "familiarizes." One of the strongest impressions we receive on reading Johnson's work is that we know where we are. No matter how philosophic his words become, we know all along that he is talking about quite common things. Such is the friendly office of generality.

While it is plain that the chief resemblance between Browne and Johnson seen by Boswell, Murphy, and Knox was in vocabulary, yet Murphy speaks of "new combinations, sentences of an unusual structure." One might be most tempted to compare Johnson's inverted substantive clauses with those of Browne. The chief difference between them seems to be in the direction of emphasis. Browne's are falling or fading inversions. They express hesitation or doubt or mere perfunctory affirmation. When the substance of the clause has been presented, it is left suspended, as if only hypothesized, or with perhaps a whisper of a statement following.

22. *Life* III, 41.
23. *Life* III, 190.

But whether the virtuous heathen, who lived better than he spake, or erring in the principles of himself, yet lived above Philosophers of more specious Maximes, lye so deep as he is placed; at least so low as not to rise against Christians, who beleeving or knowing that truth, have lastingly denied it in their practise and conversation, were a quaery too sad to insist on.[24]

Here is a termination subdued out of all positiveness, buried beneath the mournful weight of the sentence's whole problem, expressive of reluctance, of reverence, of a bowed head before a profound and somber mystery. For contrast we may take the opening sentence of our *Rambler* No. 2.

That the mind of man is never satisfied with the objects immediately before it, but is always breaking away from the present moment, and losing itself in schemes of future felicity; and that we forget the proper use of the time now in our power, to provide for the enjoyment of that which, perhaps, may never be granted us, has been frequently remarked; and as this practice is a commodious subject of raillery to the gay, and of declamation to the serious, it has been ridiculed, with all the pleasantry of wit, and exaggerated with all the amplifications of rhetorick.[25]

"Has been frequently remarked"—but Johnson will not leave his inverted clauses here; they were not introduced for this purpose. With "this practice," referring immediately to "frequently remarked," he catches up the syntactic end before it is well dropped, and marches forward to the peak of his sentence, holding his emphasis to the last thumping "amplifications of rhetorick."

iii

To say that Johnson went back to Sir Thomas Browne for philosophic diction may be to seek too remote and too literary a source. It may be rather that Johnson and Browne derived their diction from the same kind of source—the physician and scientific speculator, from his proper scientific reading,[26] and the moralist, philosopher and chemical dabbler, from departments of his own reading. This would best account for the result—the similarity and the difference between the dictions of the two so different doctors.

24. *Religio Medici and Other Writings,* "Everyman's Library," p. 130, *Hydriotaphia.*
25. *Works* v, 7–8.
26. Cf. Geoffrey Keynes, *Bibliography of Sir Thomas Browne* (Cambridge, England, 1924), pp. 182–4, sale catalogue of Browne's library; Robert R. Cawley, "Sir Thomas Browne and His Reading," *PMLA*, xlviii (1933), esp. 437, 442; Malcolm Letts, "Sir Thomas Browne and his Books," *Notes and Queries,* 11th series, x (1914), 322–3, 343.

Johnson's interest in physical science, his experiments, his laboratories, are so well known that we need no more than mention them.[27] The general interest of cultivated people during that time in physical sciences and the effects of this interest on writing can hardly be described in brief. Smollett says of the reign of George II: "Natural philosophy became a general study; and the new doctrine of electricity grew into fashion . . . . the art of chemistry was perfectly understood and assiduously applied to the purposes of sophistication." [28] At the time when Johnson frequented the Ivy Lane Club, says Hawkins, "Dyer was going through a course of chemistry under Dr. Pemberton, of Gresham College, and would sometimes give us such descriptions of processes as were very entertaining, particularly to Johnson, who would listen to them attentively." [29] Bishop Watson's chemical lectures at Cambridge from 1766 to 1769 had crowded audiences "of persons of all ages and degrees, in the University." [30] In the carriage on the way to Southill in 1781 Johnson divided his attention between his own *Prince of Abyssinia* and the Bishop's *Chemical Essays.*[31]

"The anatomist and chemist," confesses Gibbon, "may sometimes track me in their snow." [32] Johnson never made a similar confession. But he says of his collecting authorities for the *Dictionary:* "I . . . extracted from philosophers principles of science; from historians remarkable facts; from chymists complete processes; from divines striking exhortations . . . ." [33] And Murphy believed that Johnson's "pomp of diction . . . was first assumed in the *Rambler"* because in compiling the *Dictionary* at the same time "he grew familiar with technical and scholastic words." [34] Johnson

27. *Misc.* I, 307, Piozzi *Anecdotes; Letters* I, 179, n. 2, 189; II, 165, n. 2; *Life* I, 140, 436; II, 55; III, 398; IV, 237, 293; *BP* XI, 181–2.

28. *History of England from the Revolution to the Death of George II* (Edinburgh, 1805), Vol. V, p. 321, Bk. III, chap. xiv, sec. xxiv. Cf. Marjorie Nicolson, *The Microscope and English Imagination,* "Smith College Studies in Modern Languages," Vol. XVI, No. 4 (Northampton, 1935), esp. pp. 2–3, 34–49.

29. *Works* I, 414.

30. Richard Watson, *Anecdotes* (London, 1817), pp. 29, 33.

31. *Life* IV, 118.

32. *Miscellaneous Works* (London, 1814), I, 229. After the publication of the first volume of his *History* Gibbon had attended a course of anatomy and some lessons in chemistry.

33. *Works* IX, 212–13, *Preface to the Dictionary. Courtney* pp. 44–5 lists some scientific treatises and technical dictionaries used by Johnson for the *Dictionary.* According to *Courtney* p. 59, the Reverend H. J. Todd's edition of the *Dictionary,* 1818, contains at the end of the fourth volume a list of most of the works from which Johnson quotes. Johnson's library contained a number of scientific treatises (*Catalogue of the Valuable Library of Books of the Late Learned Samuel Johnson* [London, 1785], esp. pp. 14, 15, 27. Cf. S. C. Roberts, "Johnson's Books," *London Mercury,* XVI [1927], esp. 616–17).

34. *Misc.* I, 466.

was familiar with such writers as "the learned, philosophical and pious Dr. Cheyne," whose *Essay of Health and Long Life* appeared in 1724 and *English Malady,* in 1733. Johnson recommended both of these books to Boswell and was fond of referring to the second.[35] On page after page of either book he could have read passages like the following:

A certain Degree of Heat, in the same *Fomentation,* will *dissolve* and *dissipate* a Tumor, and a higher Degree of it will harden and make it *schirrous;* and thus, Mercury, in moderate Doses, will break, *dissolve,* and *attenuate* the Blood and Juices, whose *Viscidity* and consequent *Compression* on the Nerves, *interrupt* their *Vibrations* and Action, and so produce a Palsy which a gentle *Salivation* will remedy and *antidote.*[36]

Johnson knew a score or so of other books on medicine, electricity, pharmacy and the like. The references to them may be found sprinkled through his writing and conversation.[37] And many of them he might have read as a very young man. Professor Cooper has quoted from Arbuthnot's *Essay Concerning the Nature of Aliments* a passage which he says Johnson copied piecemeal as illustration for the *Dictionary.*

Barley is *emollient,* moistning and expectorating. Oats have some of the same qualities. Barley was chosen by Hippocrates as proper food in *inflammatory distempers.* Rice is the food of, perhaps, two thirds of mankind; it is most kindly and *benign* to human *constitutions,* proper for the *consumptive,* and such as are subject to *haemorrhages.* Next to rice is wheat, the bran of which is highly *acescent* and stimulating; therefore the bread that is not too much *purged* from it is more wholesome for some *constitutions.* Rye is more acid, *laxative,* and less nourishing than wheat. Millet is *diarrhoetick,* cleansing, and useful in diseases of the kidneys. Panick *affords* a soft *demulcent nourishment,* both for *granivorous* birds and mankind. Mays *affords* a very strong *nourishment,* but more *viscous* than wheat. Pease being *deprived* of any *aromatick* parts, are mild, and *demulcent* in the highest degree; but being full of *aerial particles,* are *flatulent* when *dissolved* by *digestion.* Beans

35. *Life* I, 65; III, 26–7, 87, 473, App. F; V, 154, 210; *BP* X, 216; XII, 106; *Letters* I, 358–9; II, 198, n. 3; *Works* X, 227.

36. *The English Malady* (London, 1733), p. 241, chap. xii, sec. ii, "Of the Nature and Cause of Palsies." I have altered some of the author's italics in order to distinguish my own. Cf. *An Essay of Health and Long Life,* 6th ed. (London, 1725), p. 177, chap. vii, sec. 2, "Why most Persons are seized with chronical Diseases about the Meridian of Life; and why some sooner." At times the learned author betrays a consciousness of his own diction. "The Reason why the *Scurvy* is so °*endemick* a Distemper . . . is, that it is produced by *Causes* mostly special and particular to this Island." In a footnote he explains "*endemick*": "Peculiar to this Country" (p. 178).

37. *Life* III, 34, 476, App. F; V, 247; *Misc.* II, 431; *Letters* II, 321; *Works* IX, 82, 272, 416; X, 258; XI, 212.

resemble them in most of their qualities. All the forementioned plants are highly *acescent,* except pease and beans.[38]

The italics are mine. A harvest of philosophic words. "Such books as these," says Professor Cooper, "would dispose the mind of Johnson to be what we call 'scientific.' "[39]

Johnson's own *Dictionary* was not the only one on which he worked. There was Dr. James's *Medicinal Dictionary,* published in 1743, to which Johnson seems to have contributed lives of physicians and part of an article on botany.[40] Under the title "Aer" in this *Dictionary* is inserted a large section of Boerhaave's lectures on *Air,* from his *Chemistry,* and the life of Boerhaave in the *Dictionary* is an expansion of the *Life* which Johnson contributed to the *Gentleman's Magazine* in 1739.[41] The great scientist Boerhaave, deeply religious and orthodox, antagonistic to the philosophies of Hobbes and Spinoza, may well have been something like a hero for the young Johnson, such an exponent of rhetoric as well as of physical and metaphysical sciences as Johnson set himself to become. "Nor was he unacquainted with the art of recommending truth by elegance," runs the *Life,* "and embellishing the philosopher with polite literature." [42] And Boerhaave's Latin account of his dropsy and shortness of breath, so like Johnson's own later memoranda, "deserves not only to be preserved as an historical relation of the disease which deprived us of so great a man, but as a proof of his piety and resignation to the divine will." [43]

Whether or not Johnson drew from Boerhaave's Latin or the English of Arbuthnot or Cheyne, it is apparent that some of his words are derived directly from scientific reading. At times he uses them raw, unassimilated, as they came from their original context, torn bleeding. Thus in a letter to Mrs. Thrale:

38. Lane Cooper, "Dr. Johnson on Oats and Other Grains," *PMLA,* lii (1937), 789. He quotes the second edition of Arbuthnot's book, 1732, which he thinks may be that used by Johnson.
He shows also Johnson's dependence on Philip Miller's *Gardener's Dictionary* (6th ed., 1752) and his use of Mortimer's *Whole Art of Husbandry* (2d ed., 1708) (*loc. cit.,* pp. 788–95).
39. In publishing *A System of Vegetables,* 1783, the Botanical Society at Lichfield paid grateful acknowledgment "to that great Master of the English tongue, Dr. Samuel Johnson, for his advice in the formation of the botanic language" (*Courtney* p. 156).
40. Allen T. Hazen, *Samuel Johnson's Prefaces & Dedications* (New Haven, 1937), p. 70 and n. 3.
41. He drew this *Life* from the *Oratio academica in memoriam Hermanni Boerhaavii* of Albert Schultens, published at Leyden in 1738 (*Courtney* p. 10).
42. *Works* iv, 354, *Life of Boerhaave.* Cf. *Works* ix, 64, *Adventurer* No. 85.
43. *Works* iv, 349–50. Perhaps another hero was Barretier. "Accumulating learning (and the example of Barretier, whose life he wrote) shewed him how to arrive at all science" (*Misc.* ii, 339, Tyers' *Sketch*).

The two vesicatories which I procured with so much trouble did not perform well, for, being applied to the lower part of the fauces, a part always in motion, their adhesion was continually broken.[44]

At times they are partly assimilated, by metaphorical use or shading with the context, as in *Rambler* No. 156:

Every government, say the politicians, is perpetually degenerating towards corruption, from which it must be rescued at certain periods by the resuscitation of its first principles, and the re-establishment of its original constitution. Every animal body, according to the methodick physicians, is, by the predominance of some exuberant quality, continually declining towards disease and death, which must be obviated by a seasonable reduction of the peccant humour to the just equipoise which health requires.[45]

It is such terminology which Johnson usually succeeds in depriving of its medical or laboratory flavor, denaturalizes, as it were, and employs in his writing to produce the general philosophic character, the tone of the man who knows whereof he speaks.

iv

PROBABLY it was sentence structure which Johnson had in mind when he once told Boswell that "he had formed his style upon that of Sir William Temple, and upon Chambers's Proposal for his Dictionary," [46] or more specifically, "upon about twenty lines" of Chambers' Proposal.[47] Tyers says that Johnson "set for his emulation," not Chambers' Proposal, but the Preface to Chambers' *Cyclopedia*,[48] and fixes the beginning of this emulation, on Johnson's authority, at the time of the *Plan of a Dictionary*. Boswell says of both Johnson's suggestions, "He certainly was mistaken," and adds: "Or if he imagined at first that he was imitating Temple, he was very unsuccessful; for nothing can be more unlike than the simplicity of Temple, and the richness of Johnson." [49]

Dr. Hill could find no copy of Chambers' Proposal, and the "most Johnsonian" passage he could find in the Preface [50] inclines one to

44. *Letters* II, 304, No. 851. Cf. *Letters* II, 235, 348; *Life* IV, 354–5; *Works* X, 266.
45. *Works* VII, 95. Cf. *Works* VIII, 10, *Idler* No. 3. In *Works* VIII, 27, *Idler* No. 7, occurs an interesting example of analogy drawn from science but not involving scientific terms. "It is discovered by *Reaumur*, that spiders might make silk, if they could be persuaded to live in peace together. The writers of news, if they could be confederated, might give more pleasure to the publick."
46. *Life* I, 218–19.
47. *Boswell's Note Book*, ed. R. W. Chapman (London, 1925), p. 19.
48. *Misc.* II, 347–8.
49. Cf. *BP* XVII, 66, London, 6 Feb. 1788.
50. *Life* I, 219, n. 1.

agree with Boswell that Johnson was mistaken, or to decide that he had his tongue in his cheek. For Temple a better case may be made. A number of times Johnson shows himself to be specifically familiar with Temple's works.[51] In a passage from the *Life* which I have quoted in Appendix D,[52] where Johnson says it was Temple who gave cadence to English prose, and where he implies that cadence means putting the emphasis at the end of the sentence, Johnson indicates in what respect he may have considered himself indebted to Temple. The passages from Temple selected by Dr. Hill [53] show at least that the indebtedness is possible. Temple, like Dryden, is careful of the ends of his sentences. Sometimes he uses the reënforcement of a doublet. He has, furthermore, a considerable antithetic tendency.

But again it seems to me unnecessary to find Johnson's antecedents in any single author. There is another possibility, so obvious a part of neoclassic literature as to be easily overlooked. "We may wonder," writes Sir Edmund Gosse, "that, while his early verse owes so much to the teaching of Pope, his early prose shows no tincture of Steele or Swift." [54] To which Johnson might have replied, as he did once to Boswell, "Sir, you *may* wonder." Swift's whole way of writing, we have seen, was repugnant to Johnson; Steele's perhaps but little less. The one who could teach him something was Pope—or rather it was the whole school of couplet writers.

For more than a century a special rhetoric had been evolving which the young Johnson was to find ready to his needs—a rhetoric from which the rhetoric of Johnson seems to proceed by a very short step, across the line from verse to prose. The rhetoric of the neoclassic couplet had been in its origins related to the curt form of Senecan prose, the style of writers like Bacon and Feltham. With the triumph of "plain" prose style in the second half of the seventeenth century, the more pointed rhetoric survived and was developed chiefly in the couplet; it became distinctly a verse style. A didactic and epigrammatic purpose first shaped the tendency toward closure in the couplet, toward emphatic completeness. As early as 1589 we find Puttenham describing the chief means of closure, three rhetorical figures, *antimetabole* or inversion,[55] *antith-*

---

51. *Life* II, 234, n. 4, 421; III, 330; IV, 379; *BP* xv, 197; *Letters* II, 128, No. 647.
52. *Post* p. 156, from *Life* III, 257.
53. *Life* I, 218, n. 3.
54. *Leaves and Fruit* (New York, 1927), p. 361, "The Prose of Dr. Johnson."
55. *Antimetabole* is simply a special kind of chiasmus—the inversion of identical terms. Cf. *New English Dictionary*, where definition and example from Puttenham are cited.

eton or antithesis, and *parison*. "Parison involves the notion of balance as well as parallelism, for it means similarity of *form* between the equal rhythmic members of *isocolon*." [56] "Punish my fault, or pitie mine estate," writes Drayton in "Rosamond to Henry." Fairfax, translating Tasso into English *ottava rima*, constantly falls into "lines and pairs of lines built on co-ordinated parallelism." "A common extension is the balanced antithesis with reversed order." "High were his thoughts, his heart was bold in flight." [57] Such is the rhetoric of which Waller and Denham became the first thoroughgoing exponents, and which reached its perfection in Pope—the rhetoric of parallel, of antithesis, of chiasmus.

In his earliest efforts Johnson shows his interest in these characters of the couplet. When he is perhaps nineteen years old, "Thy form more lovely, more adorn'd thy mind," he writes "To a Young Lady on her Birth-Day." [58] "Bless with a smile, or with a frown destroy," he writes for some other young ladies; "Each youth admires, though each admirer dies"; "Vex ev'ry eye, and every bosom tear"; "No maid to flatter, and no paint to hide." [59] The whole piece has a *Rape-of-the-Lock* tone. A few years later the "Verses to a Lady, on receiving from her a sprig of Myrtle" contain a further assortment. "Now grants, and now rejects a lover's prayer." "The myrtle crowns the happy lovers' heads, The unhappy lovers' grave the myrtle spreads." "Soon must this bough, as you shall fix his doom, Adorn Philander's head, or grace his tomb." [60] And so through Johnson's two great neoclassic satires one may pick out specimens.

LONDON

1. I praise the hermit, but regret the friend.
2. Let such raise palaces, and manors buy,
   Collect a tax, or farm a lottery.
3. Others with softer smiles, and subtler art,
   Can sap the principles, or taint the heart;

56. George Williamson, "The Rhetorical Pattern of Neo-Classical Wit," *Modern Philology*, xxxiii (1935–36), 61–4. See the whole article (pp. 55–81) for a treatment of the theoretical development of couplet rhetoric and the relation of this rhetoric to Senecan prose. One of the characteristics of the curt form of Senecan prose was asymmetry (absence of parallel). Cf. George Williamson, "Senecan Style in the Seventeenth Century," *Philological Quarterly*, xv (1936), esp. pp. 338–40, 346–7; Morris W. Croll, "Attic Prose," *Studies in Philology*, xviii (1921), pp. 79–128.

57. Ruth C. Wallerstein, "The Development of the Rhetoric and Metre of the Heroic Couplet, Especially in 1625–1645," *PMLA*, L (1935), 172–81. Cf. Geoffrey Tillotson, *The Poetry of Pope* (Oxford, 1938), pp. 124–30.

58. *Life* i, 54.

59. *Life* i, 55–6.

60. *Life* i, 92 and n. 2.

With more address a lover's note convey,
Or bribe a virgin's innocence away.
4. Spurn'd as a beggar, dreaded as a spy,
   Live unregarded, unlamented die.
5. Behold the warrior dwindled to a beau.

THE VANITY OF HUMAN WISHES

6. Increase his riches and his peace destroy.
7. Dart the quick taunt, and edge the piercing gibe.
8. Hate dogs their flight, and insult mocks their end.
9. The golden canopy, the glitt'ring plate,
   The regal palace, the luxurious board,
   The liv'ried army, and the menial lord.
10. The festal blazes, the triumphal show,
    The ravish'd standard, and the captive foe,
    The senate's thanks, the gazette's pompous tale.
11. His fall was destin'd to a barren strand,
    A petty fortress, and a dubious hand.
12. The fruit autumnal, and the vernal flow'r.[61]

To copy every specimen, even every more regular one, would be to copy a greater part of the poems. Here are antithesis,[62] chiasmus, and several degrees of parallel making the very texture of the composition. The parallels in the later poem become more frequent and more complicated. Examples 7 and 8 above are doublets of three elements of implicit parallel. In 9 there are six members of two elements, a degree of parallel very rare, perhaps not found in his prose. In 10 he reaches four members, then changes the syntax of the elements. In 11 he offers a pretty example of the triplet of two parallel elements so common in his prose, but rather disguised here by the trenchancy of the nonphilosophic diction and the effect of the rhyme falling at the end of the first and third members and setting up another parallel pattern (the couplet). The last two members of the triplet are put against the first member and the sentence stem from which the triplet branches. It is this possibility of various counter patterns which makes the rhetoric of parallel and antithesis susceptible of more subtlety in the couplet than in

61. *Works* xi, 319 (1), 321 (2), 322 (3, 4), 323 (5), 332 (6), 333 (7, 8), 334–5 (9), 337 (10), 338 (11), 339 (12).
62. As an example of "antithesis" for the *Dictionary* Johnson chooses not a prose passage but a part of the famous lines from *Cooper's Hill:*
            Though gentle, yet not dull;
      Strong without rage; without o'erflowing, full.
And there is a passage in Johnson's *Life of Pope*—"He first endeavours to wound, and is then afraid to own that he meant a blow" (*Works* iv, 57)—which reminds one curiously of something Pope had said about Atticus.

prose and which tends to make it seem a different thing in the couplet. Perhaps Johnson never stated the identity to himself. But in his couplet satires he was employing a rhetoric which needed only to be taken out of verse and inflated to solemnity by philosophical diction to become the rhetoric of his *Ramblers.*[63]

v

IF the antecedents of Johnson's prose style lie chiefly in books of natural philosophy and in the neoclassic couplet, that is, in writings outside the course of English literary prose, one may consider how far other writers of English literary prose, before Johnson, contemporary with and after him, were affected by the same antecedents, whether Johnson was alone in borrowing a strange idiom for prose or but went to a conspicuous extreme where others ventured moderately; and so, whether some writers who followed him chronologically were really his imitators.

In Johnson's time, thinks Leslie Stephen, Addison is "still a kind of sacred model," but "the best prose writers are beginning to aim at a more complex structure of sentence, fitted for the expression of a wider range of thought and emotion." [64] Johnson's own friends Hawkins and Murphy were aware of this difference but spoke of the new writing only as Johnson's.[65] A writer in the *Monthly Review* for December 1793 gives us a fortunate glimpse at an opinion of more scope.

63. A form of composition which may also have had something to do with Johnson's structural rhetoric is the short prayer, especially the collect. I have placed a brief discussion of this point in Appendix E, *post* pp. 157–8.

Under the head of structural antecedents would come the question whether Johnson's unidiomatic inversions were made acceptable to his mind by his immersion in Latin. Of this I think there can be no doubt. We know first that Johnson did possess much Latin. (See Percy H. Houston, *Doctor Johnson* [Cambridge, 1923], pp. 12–17.) Hawkins says he spoke it with "great fluency and elegance" (*Works* XI, 199). The young Boswell conjectured that he "was so much accustomed to the Roman language as almost to think in it" (*BP* I, 70, 21 Sept. 1762). Secondly, there is hardly need of example to show that Latin takes advantage of its explicit morphology to bring any part of syntax into prominence at the start of a sentence. "Rem publicam, Quirites," begins an oration which every schoolboy used to know, and only after six more objects, some adverbial and participial phrases, comes the verb "videtis," the last word of the sentence (Cicero, *Third Oration Against Catiline*).

64. *Samuel Johnson* (New York, n.d.), p. 171.

65. *Works* I, 269–70; *Misc.* I, 467–70. Cf. *Life* I, 224 and n. 1. Macaulay speaks of "the question of precedence between Addison and Johnson, a question which, seventy years ago, was much disputed" (*Miscellaneous Writings and Speeches* [London, 1871], p. 381, the *Encyclopedia Britannica* article of 1856; this passage is omitted from the article in the eleventh edition of the *Encyclopedia,* quoted elsewhere in the present work).

During our course of critical labours, which have now continued through nearly half a century, we have had occasion to remark a gradual change in the public taste with respect to style. At the time when our work commenced, Addison and Swift were esteemed our best models in prose writing; perspicuity, ease, and harmony, were the chief points at which our most classical writers aimed; and, provided these excellencies were attained, unnecessary diffuseness, feebleness, and even colloquial inelegance, were scarcely perceived to be faults. After this time, a stricter attention to precision and elegance of expression prevailed, through a set of writers among whom Mr. Melmoth makes a principal figure; till, by degrees, a fastidiousness of taste has been introduced, which shrinks from familiar and idiomatic phraseology, and which can only be gratified by a closely-condensed and highly-ornamented diction, as remote as possible from the ease of colloquial discourse. Our great masters in this style are the late Dr. Johnson and Mr. Gibbon.[66]

It will be noted that the writer considers the new style to have been originated not by Johnson but by an earlier "set of writers," among whom the principal figure was Mr. Melmoth, and that the mastery of the style is shared by Johnson with Gibbon. It was Melmoth, as we have already noted, whose *Letters . . . by . . . Sir Thomas Fitzosborne* were likened by Lady Hervey to the *Rambler*.[67] But as a model for Johnson's style Melmoth's would be scarcely more satisfactory than that of Chambers. The following passage shows more resemblance than most.

To say truth, my friend, the longer I lived in the high scenes of action, the more I was convinced that nature had not formed me for bearing a part in them: and though I was once so unexperienced in the ways of the world as to believe I had talents, as I was sure I had inclination, to serve my country, yet every day's conversation contributed to wean me by degrees from that flattering delusion.[68]

66. *Monthly Review*, 2d Series, XII (1793), 361, a review of *The Reveries of Solitude* (London, 1793), attributed by the reviewer to Shenstone's friend the Reverend Mr. [Richard] Graves. Professor B. C. Nangle tells me that the editorial copy of the *Monthly* in the Bodleian Library indicates that the reviewer was William Enfield.

William Rider in his *Historical and Critical Account of the Lives and Writings of the Living Authors of Great Britain* (1762) is apparently referring to the same difference in styles when he writes that Goldsmith has "happily found out the secret to unite Elevation with Ease, a Perfection in Language, which few Writers of our Nation have attained to, as most of those who aim at Sublimity swell their Expressions with Fustian and Bombast, whilst those who affect Ease, degenerate into Familiarity and Flatness" (p. 14).

67. *Ante* p. 115, n. 3.

68. *Letters on Several Subjects by the Late Sir Thomas Fitzosborne, Bart.* (London, 1748), p. 91, Letter XX, to Clytander, "Reasons for the author's retirement." These *Letters* first appeared in 1742. Perhaps the moral topics and the classical

Where we need not expect to find models for Johnson's style, we may, however, find at work the same expressive tendencies as had full scope in his style. Melmoth, even Chambers, may to some extent illustrate this. Where the illustration is to begin and end is indeed dubious. The whole range of writers from the age of Anne to the late Johnsonian era is open to suspicion. What, for example, of Pope himself? If the writing of couplets could affect Johnson's prose, might it not affect Pope's? It would seem that it did, not so much in parallel multiplications, but markedly in antitheses. In his letter to Mr. Bridges, for example, he writes:

It is more advantageous to a scribbler to be improved in his judgment than to be soothed in his vanity.

as much celebrated for their knowledge of the original, as . . . decryed for the badness of their translations

Men . . . never approve any other's sense, but as it squares with their own.[69]

In the second year of Johnson's *Rambler* we find the obscure scribbler Robert Shiels writing a description of Edinburgh:

They may be said to be hospitable, but not complaisant, to strangers. Insincerity and cruelty have no existence among them; but if they ought not to be hated they can never be much loved, for they are incapable of insinuation, and their ignorance of the world makes them unfit for entertaining sensible strangers. They are public-spirited, but torn to pieces by factions. A gloominess in religion renders one part of them very barbarous, and an enthusiasm in politics so transports the genteeler part, that they sacrifice to party almost every consideration of tenderness.[70]

names of the correspondents made Lady Hervey compare them with the *Rambler*.
     Letter XVI contains a praise of Temple and Addison for "a graceful *manner*" in writing (pp. 77–8); Letter XXIV concerns "oratorical numbers" or "numerous composition" (esp. p. 113).
     Johnson wrote to Mrs. Thrale, 1 May 1780: "From the authour of 'Fitzosborne's Letters' I cannot think myself in much danger. I met him only once about thirty years ago, and in some small dispute reduced him to whistle; having not seen him since, that is the last impression" (*Life* III, 423–4).
     69. *Lives* III, 253–4, *Pope*, par. 383.
     70. From the *Life of Samuel Boyse* in *The Lives of the Poets of Great Britain and Ireland to the Time of Dean Swift, by Mr. Cibber* (1753), quoted by Walter Raleigh, *Six Essays on Johnson* (Oxford, 1910), pp. 121–2. For Shiels's authorship, see p. 120, n. 1, and cf. *Life* III, 29–30 and n. 1.
     The *Life of Richard Savage, Esq.* in this collection is admittedly compiled from Johnson's *Life* (*Courtney* p. 17).

"Consciously or unconsciously," says Sir Walter Raleigh, this author "had formed his literary style wholly on the Johnsonian model." Lord Chesterfield, writing in the *World* one year later on Johnson's *Dictionary*, had not formed his style on the Johnsonian model, but he furnishes this example.

I presume that obedience can never be expected when there is neither terror to enforce, nor interest to invite it.[71]

Just as readily as Johnsonian constructions, Johnsonian philosophic diction might be accumulated to surfeit from the first half of the century. Foote is said to have come before Dr. Gower of Worcester College bringing a large dictionary in which to find the meaning of the Doctor's words.[72] As early as 1714, in *Spectator* No. 617, occurs a criticism of the humor which consists in "the affectation of strained and pompous expressions, fetched from the learned languages." The example which is given is certainly not Johnsonian, but it contains phrases like this: "If any one at the Board could have so far articulated, as to have demanded intelligibly a Reinforcement of Liquor, the whole Assembly had been by this time extended under the Table." [73] Or there is the more amusing because more serious use of big words in Blackmore's *Lay Monastery*. These essays record the conversations of a group of retired and pensive gentlemen, of whom the intellectual leader is, oddly enough, a Mr. Johnson. (See the *Life of Blackmore* for our Johnson's comment on this fictitious prototype.) [74] In No. 31 Mr. Johnson and the writer are taking a walk and see a rainbow. "This prospect" gives the writer "occasion to mention Sir I. Newton's Principles."

You see . . . in this instance, that the beams of the sun being intercepted, modified, and refracted by the black surface of the cloud, can no longer keep their complication entire; but the coalition is dissolved, and the parts are actually disunited. Here we plainly discern the threads

71. *The World*, No. 100, 28 Nov. 1754, *British Essayists*, ed. Alexander Chalmers (London, 1817), xxvii, 258. In Chesterfield's *Miscellaneous Works*, 1, 229, are included two speeches written by Johnson (*Life* i, 505, App. A).

Mr. Louis L. Martz in his Yale doctoral dissertation *Tobias Smollett's Association with Travel-Books* (1939) devotes a chapter (Part I, chap. vii, pp. 149–78) to showing that Smollett in revising the language of various travel books and histories for his *Compendium of Voyages* (1756) persistently created parallel structures and adopted diction such as we should call "philosophic."

72. John Forster, *Historical and Biographical Essays* (London, 1858), ii, 307. Cf. William King, *Anecdotes of his Own Times* (Boston, 1819), p. 132.

73. *Morley* p. 864.

74. *Lives* ii, 244, *Blackmore*, par. 26.

of this shining aggregate unravelled, and displayed in their native colours.[75]

This is philosophic diction in the raw.

75. *Lay Monastery* No. 31, 25 Jan. 1713, in *The Gleaner*, ed. Nathan Drake (London, 1811), I, 30.

John Constable, *Reflections Upon Accuracy of Style* (London, 1731), blames writers of his day for emulating seventeenth-century writers like Owen Feltham in the use of strange words, "newly coin'd or forg'd" (pp. 84–7).

CHAPTER IX

Effects of Johnson's Style

WHATEVER the number of writers who were trifling with philosophic diction or parallel or antithesis, one fact remains indisputable, that Johnson's style, from the time it had its first full opportunity in the *Rambler,* was recognized by his contemporaries as something extraordinary, a prodigy or monstrosity, a huge phenomenon—of grandeur or at least of pomposity, "A large party," says Macaulay, "pronounced the style perfect, so absolutely perfect that in some essays it would be impossible for the writer himself to alter a single word for the better. Another party, not less numerous, vehemently accused him of having corrupted the purity of the English tongue." [1]

Those who found fault with the style were partly those whom we have had occasion to quote in earlier chapters, partly others more vituperative, but less enlightening, a variety of professional critics, parodists, and satirists. There was the irresponsible William Kenrick in 1766, with his *Defence of Mr. Kenrick's Review of Dr. Johnson's Shakespeare;* there was the clumsy Archibald Campbell in 1767, with his *Lexiphanes.* J. Thomson Callender in 1782 selected for publication *The Deformities of Dr. Johnson.* A more distinguished enemy was Horace Walpole, who for a period of nine years, in his letters from 1773 to 1782, noticed Johnson's style with a scorn which he gathered into a "General Criticism of Dr. Johnson's Writings" for his collected works in 1798. [2] Vicesimus

1. *Encyclopedia Britannica,* 11th ed. (Cambridge, England, 1911), xv, 466–7. For a general statement about the reception of Johnson's writings in America see Daniel Robert Lang, *Dr. Samuel Johnson in America, A Study of His Reputation: 1750–1812 (Abstract of a Thesis,* University of Illinois, 1939) (Urbana, 1939), esp. pp. 16–17.
2. In listing the above critics I have drawn from W. Vaughan Reynolds' instructive article "The Reception of Johnson's Prose Style," *Review of English Studies,* xi (1935), 146–52. Reynolds quotes also Charles Churchill's *Ghost,* 1762, Archdeacon Francis Blackburne's *Remarks on Johnson's Life of Milton,* 1780, and George Colman's *Prose on Several Occasions,* 1787. Cf. *Courtney* pp. 27–9, 104–5; *Life* iv, 314, n. 3, 499–500, App. J; Charles Russell, "Dr. Johnson and Walpole," *Fortnightly Review,* New Series, cxiv (1923), 658–66; *The Works of Horatio Walpole, Earl of Orford* (London, 1798), iv, 361–2; *Horace Walpole's Correspondence with Rev. William Cole,* ed. W. S. Lewis and A. Dayle Wallace (New Haven, 1937), i, 310.

Knox, a writer on the whole well disposed toward Johnson, in his *Essays Moral and Literary* had to confess that he found Johnson guilty of "an affected appearance of pomposity" and "perpetual triplets." [3] The Reverend Robert Burrowes, for whose criticism we have shared Boswell's respect, was perhaps the only one who censured with sobriety and precision. During Johnson's life and for a while after it, the casual objections to his style are too numerous to be accounted for. [4]

Those who wrote in praise of Johnson's style were chiefly such as we have quoted in earlier chapters, his friends and biographers, the members of his literary set and of adjacent sets—Boswell, Hawkins, Mrs. Piozzi, Towers, Murphy, and others. [5] The casual praises of Johnson's style are, like the censures, far too numerous to be accounted for. [6] We may quote Shenstone, who in 1760 writes: "I have lately been reading one or two volumes of the Rambler; who, excepting against some few hardnesses in his manner, and the want of more examples to enliven, is one of the most nervous, most perspicuous, most concise, most harmonious prose writers I know. A learned diction improves by time." [7] A reviewer of the *Lives* in the *Gentleman's Magazine* for May 1781 knew not "which most to admire, the sense or diction, the elegance or penetration." [8] Finally, as there were the *Deformities*, so there were the *Beauties of John-*

3. *Essays Moral and Literary*, 5th ed. (London, 1784), i, 136, No. 28, "On the Periodical Essayists."
Robert Potter, with his *Inquiry into . . . Dr. Johnson's Lives of the Poets*, 1783, and *Art of Criticism . . . in Dr. Johnson's Lives*, 1789, is an important critic of Johnson who neglects any extended discussion of the style but is at least not a great admirer of it (Herbert G. Wright, "Robert Potter as a Critic of Dr. Johnson," *Review of English Studies*, xii [1936], 305–21).
4. See, for example: William Cowper, *Letters* (London, 1820), p. 21, 18 Oct. 1765; Mary Wortley Montagu, *Letters and Works*, ed. Lord Wharncliffe (London, 1837), iii, 92, 23 June 1754; *Series of Letters between Mrs. Elizabeth Carter and Miss Catherine Talbot*, ed. Montagu Pennington (London, 1809), i, 349, 28 May 1750; 357, 20 Oct. 1750; *Correspondence of Thomas Gray*, ed. Paget Toynbee and Leonard Whibley (Oxford, 1935), iii, 1290, App. Z, *Reminiscences* of Norton Nicholls; *Life* i, 208, n. 2; iv, 433, App. A; *Misc.* i, 270 and n. 5; *BP* i, 70.
5. W. Vaughan Reynolds, "The Reception of Johnson's Prose Style," *Review of English Studies*, xi (1935), 155–6, quotes the opinion of each of the above except Boswell. For Boswell see esp. *Life* i, 214–25; *BP* x, 123–4.
6. See, for example: *Life* i, 169, 209–10; ii, 201; v, 48, 407–8; *Courtney* pp. 15, 26, 38; *Misc.* i, 397–8, Murphy's *Essay*; *BP* xiii, 299–300; xviii, 233–4; Thomas Twining, *Recreations and Studies of a Country Clergyman of the Eighteenth Century* (London, 1882), p. 112.
7. *Life* ii, 452–3. The letter was to the Reverend Richard Graves, the author considered in the passage quoted from the *Monthly Review ante* p. 129.
8. *Gentleman's Magazine*, li (1781), 224. I have made no extended search through the various periodical reviews of Johnson's works. Those in the *Monthly Review* have been collected by John K. Spittal, *Contemporary Criticisms of Dr. Samuel Johnson* (London, 1923). Cf. *Courtney* pp. 147–8.

son, which appeared in 1781 and 1782 in two parts, the first of which was reprinted twice before the end of 1782.[9]

ii

As the sincerest form of flattery is imitation, we might expect to find among Johnson's closest friends and warmest admirers those who imitated his style most closely. Hawkesworth comes immediately to mind—Hawkesworth, who like Johnson had his amateur interest in science,[10] who denied that he was an imitator of Johnson,[11] but was thought to be so by Johnson himself [12] and was praised for the happiness of his imitations by Boswell.[13] Miss Talbot was deceived into writing of the *Adventurer:* "I discern Mr. Johnson through all the papers that are not marked A, as evidently as if I saw him through the keyhole with the pen in his hand." [14] Perhaps as early as 1744 Hawkesworth had in taking over the *Debates in Parliament* in the *Gentleman's Magazine* begun to model his style upon Johnson's.[15] By the time he came to edit the *Adventurer* he was able, where there was occasion to generalize, as at the beginning or end of an essay, or in introducing or taking leave of the series, to produce some paragraphs of Johnsonian writing. The following from the last *Adventurer* is a fair example.

As I was upon these principles to write for the young and the gay; for those who are entering the path of life, I knew that it would be necessary to amuse the imagination while I was approaching the heart; and that I could not hope to fix the attention, but by engaging the passions. I have, therefore, sometimes led them into the regions of fancy, and sometimes held up before them the mirror of life; I have concatenated events, rather than deduced consequences by logical reasoning; and

9. *Life* iv, 500, App. J; Allen T. Hazen, "The Beauties of Johnson," *Modern Philology*, xxxv (1938), 289–95. Cf. *Life* i, 214, n. 1; *Misc.* ii, 351, n. 1; *Courtney* p. 35.

10. *Works* i, 252; cf. *ibid.*, p. 292.

11. *Life* i, 252–3.

12. *Life* ii, 216; cf. *Life* i, 190, n. 3; *Letters* ii, 8, No. 514; *Lives* iii, 1, Swift, par. 1.

13. *Life* i, 252. William Rider, in his *Historical and Critical Account of the Lives and Writings of the Living Authors of Great-Britain* (London, 1762) wrote of the *Adventurer:* "The Author has so carefully copied the Stile of Mr. *Johnson*, that the Imitation cannot but be obvious to every body" (p. 14).

14. *Series of Letters between Mrs. Elizabeth Carter and Miss Catherine Talbot*, ed. Montagu Pennington (London, 1809), ii, 109. She made an opposite mistake about the *Ramblers:* "Mr. Johnson would, I fear, be mortified to hear that people know a paper of his own by the sure mark of somewhat a little excessive, a little exaggerated in the expression" (i, 357).

15. *Life* i, 511–12, App. A; Alexander Chalmers, *British Essayists* (London, 1817), xxiii, v, x.

have exhibited scenes of prosperity and distress, as more forcibly persuasive than the rhetoric of declamation.[16]

Beyond this there is little that can be called imitation by the men of Johnson's circle. Johnson was surprised that Croft wrote the *Life of Young* so well.[17] A few crabbed sentences are Johnsonian.[18] "All the nodosities of the oak without its strength," said Burke.[19] Sir Joshua Reynolds was notably "of Johnson's school." [20] Of a passage in the *Discourses* Johnson once observed, "I think I might as well have said this myself." [21] But Reynolds' style on the whole could scarcely be taken for Johnson's.[22] One might expect that Boswell, whose mind was so "strongly impregnated with the Johnsonian aether," would have cultivated Johnson's style more than he appears to have done. He thought that some of his own sentences in the *Hypochondriack* were as good as some in the *Rambler*.[23] But the fact is that Boswell's style in the *Hypochondriack* is hardly for a sentence Johnsonian.[24] More suggestive of Johnson are occasional pieces of philosophic diction in the *Life*. Johnson's spirit is "grievously clogged by its material tegument." In a china factory at Derby "a boy turned round a wheel to give the mass rotundity." In the Hebrides Johnson's stick was of great use for their "wild peregrination." [25]

16. *British Essayists* (London, 1817), xxv, 305, *Adventurer* No. 140.

Cf. Hazlitt, *Howe* vi, 104, *Lectures on the English Comic Writers*, v, "On the Periodical Essayists."

For Johnson in the *Adventurer*, see L. F. Powell, "Johnson's Part in *The Adventurer*," *Review of English Studies*, iii (1927), 420–9.

Alexander Chalmers points out that Joseph Warton too when writing for the *Adventurer* betrays the fact that "he kept company with Dr. Johnson." "The beginning of No. 139," he thinks, "if found detached, might have been attributed to Dr. Johnson" (*British Essayists* [London, 1817], xxiii, xxxii).

17. *Life* iv, 482, App. J.

18. *Lives* iii, 370, par. 40; 373, par. 52; 374, pars. 55, 59; 379, par. 80; 381, par. 96.

19. *Life* iii, 59.

20. *Life* iii, 261, n. 1; iii, 369 and n. 3; *Misc.* ii, 230; Charles R. Leslie and Tom Taylor, *Life and Times of Sir Joshua Reynolds* (London, 1865), ii, 461.

21. *Life* iv, 320.

22. Cf. *Misc.* ii, 231, n. 1. Of course the imitations which Reynolds wrote show that he knew Johnson's conversational style very well (*Misc.* ii, 233–48). For the extent to which Johnson helped Reynolds with his earlier *Discourses* and for that to which Malone helped with the later, see *Life* iii, 529–30, App. F; Frederick W. Hilles, *The Literary Career of Sir Joshua Reynolds* (Cambridge, England, 1936), pp. 134–43, 190. Cf. Elbert N. S. Thompson, "The Discourses of Sir Joshua Reynolds," *PMLA*, xxxii (1917), esp. 341.

23. *BP* xii, 172, 22 Oct. 1778.

24. Miss Bailey believes that the phrasing is often "strongly suggestive" of the *Rambler* (*The Hypochondriack*, ed. Margery Bailey [Stanford University, 1928], i, 34; cf. i, 67).

25. *Life* ii, 289; iii, 163; v, 318. It is possible that these are examples of conscious parody.

Johnson's three female collaborators in the *Rambler,* Miss Talbot, Miss Mulso, and the learned Mrs. Carter, hardly attempted his style.[26] Yet there were other ladies who did. The one who had been closest to Johnson, Mrs. Piozzi, wrote for the most part a chit-chat style, or could write, as in the Preface to her *Anecdotes,* a sort of Euphuism, what Walpole called "high-varnished." [27] But in the midst of chitchat she succumbed often to the temptation to be dignified.

If, however, I ventured to blame their ingratitude, and condemn their conduct, he would instantly set about softening the one and justifying the other.

His talk therefore had commonly the complexion of arrogance, his silence of superciliousness.[28]

And poor old Johnson's "auricular organs . . . never could perform their functions." [29] The Swan of Lichfield, Anna Seward, did not tune her voice for Johnson's sake,[30] but she praised him for his

In his *Poetical Review of the Literary and Moral Character of Dr. Johnson,* John Courtenay put among the prose writers of Johnson's "brilliant school" Reynolds, Dr. Burney, Malone, Steevens, Hawkesworth, and Boswell. He named Goldsmith and [Sir William] Jones as poets of the school (*Life* i, 62, n. 3, 222–3).

Professor C. B. Tinker quotes some passages from Goldsmith's *Life of Nash* and *Life of Voltaire* which suggest that Goldsmith at times had the desire, though not quite Johnson's "ability to sum up a whole department of things in one telling sentence" (*Dr. Johnson & Fanny Burney* [New York, 1911], p. xxxiv). Cf. *Life* ii, 209, 216.

Arthur Murphy was a friend of Johnson's who seems to have been little if at all affected by Johnson's style. In his *Gray's Inn Journal,* which followed (29 Sept. 1753 to 21 Sept. 1754) close on the *Rambler,* he is more like the *Tatler* and *Spectator.* In one number (No. xxxiii, folio ed., pp. 197–8) he perhaps ridicules the *Rambler.* And even when in No. 38 he makes the mistake of retranslating a French translation of *Rambler* No. 190 (*Misc.* i, 306), the narrative character of this *Rambler* and the freedom of the French translation (*Journal Étranger,* April 1754, pp. 97–111) prevent Murphy's English from showing many Johnsonian traits. Cf. Curtis B. Bradford, "Arthur Murphy's Meeting with Johnson," *Philological Quarterly,* xviii (1939), 318–20; *Samuel Johnson's 'Rambler'* (Yale doctoral dissertation, 1937), pp. 175–9.

26. Miss Talbot and Miss Mulso, the one with an allegorical letter in the character of Sunday and the other with four "billets" in different town characters, had little opportunity for Johnsonism. See *Courtney* p. 25; D. Nichol Smith, "The Contributors to *The Rambler* and *The Idler,*" *Bodleian Quarterly Record,* vii (1935), 508–9. Miss Mulso was the author also of Nos. 77, 78, 79 of the *Adventurer,* the story of Fidelia, where again she could hardly be Johnsonian (Alexander Chalmers, *British Essayists* [London, 1817], xxiii, xxxiii). Mrs. Carter, speaking seriously in the figure of Religion, could be somewhat Johnsonian for a sentence or two (*Works* v, 286–7, *Rambler* No. 44); she also contributed *Rambler* No. 100 (*Courtney* p. 25). She is noticed in *Christie* p. 34, n. 6.

27. *Misc.* i, 143–5.

28. *Misc.* i, 292, 347; cf. i, 269.

29. *Misc.* i, 152; cf. *Misc.* i, 282, a passage which includes the word "alembicated."

30. Margaret Ashmun, *The Singing Swan* (New Haven, 1931), pp. 201–3.

"strength and glow of . . . fancy," [31] and in the prose of her letters there are frequent workings of a kind of Johnsonian masculinity. The short biography of her by Mr. Hesketh Pearson needs no other source of humor than its plentiful studding of her philosophic phrases. "Domiciliary dilapidation," "umbrageous eminences," "nineteen oceanic immersions." Or one may be reminded of something better in Johnson by "the native gaiety of my spirit eternally eclipsed." [32] And all the world knows that by far the most deplorable effect of Johnson's style was upon that young member of the Streatham set, Fanny Burney. The change from the maiden graces of *Evelina* to the mature pretensions of *Cecilia, Camilla, The Wanderer,* and the *Memoirs of Dr. Burney* has become through Macaulay a notorious event in the history of the English language.[33]

It is a curious evidence both of the susceptibility of the human mind and of the hypnotic power of Johnson's patterns of emphasis that among his imitators may be listed not only his friends but his critics and among the latter the most severe. The Reverend Robert Burrowes, as Boswell remarks, was not only an acute critic of Johnson's style but an imitator of it.[34] We may illustrate Boswell's statement with a quotation from Burrowes' "Essay." Who will not be reminded of the *Preface to the Dictionary?*

The distinctions of words esteemed synonimous, might from his writings be accurately collected. For thoughts the most definite, he has language

Cf. P. Laithwaite, "Anna Seward and Dr. Johnson," *Times Literary Supplement,* XXXI (1932), 12.

31. *Life* I, 40, n. 3.

32. *The Swan of Lichfield* (London, 1936), pp. 21, 23, 32, 33. She could sustain briefly the Johnsonian construction, as in a letter to Boswell praising his *Tour to the Hebrides* and in a much later one to Scott (*Letters of Anna Seward* [Edinburgh, 1811], I, 130; VI, 13–14). For an indication that she revised her letters on leaving them for publication, see James L. Clifford, "Further Letters of the Johnson Circle," *Bulletin of the John Rylands Library,* XX (1936), 283, n. 1.

33. Otto Jespersen, *Growth and Structure of the English Language* (New York, 1923), pp. 148–9. See *Life* IV, 389; *Select Essays of Macaulay,* ed. Samuel Thurber (Boston, 1892), pp. 173, 176, 177.

But Professor C. B. Tinker believes that Johnson's influence upon Fanny Burney has been overestimated. He quotes some passages from *Evelina* which suggest that her tendency to formality was original. And Miss Burney herself recorded that "Mrs. Montagu had pronounced the dedication [of *Evelina*] to be so well written that she could not but suppose it must be the doctor's" (*Dr. Johnson & Fanny Burney* [New York, 1911], pp. xx, 98).

Even poor Miss Reynolds, struggling with sentences in her *Recollections of Dr. Johnson,* could be Johnsonian for one word. "Very rarely . . . was he intentionally asperous" (*Misc.* II, 280).

34. *Life* IV, 386. Boswell quotes an example from Burrowes' Preface to the volume of *Transactions of the Royal Irish Academy* in which the "Essay" on Johnson's style appeared.

the most precise; and though his meaning may sometimes be obscure, it can never be misunderstood.[35]

As late as 1802 William Mudford in his *Critical Enquiry into the Moral Writings of Dr. Samuel Johnson* compared Addison and Johnson in an antithetic passage which strongly recalls Johnson's comparison of Dryden and Pope. "Johnson possessed powers unattainable by Addison; and Addison moved in a circle where Johnson could not approach. Addison is gay and lively; Johnson grave and sententious," and so forth.[36] Hazlitt himself, most vigorous of all critics of Johnson's style, in the very stride of his criticism, falls into the Johnsonian manner.

He dares not trust himself with the immediate impressions of things, for fear of compromising his dignity; or follow them into their consequences, for fear of committing his prejudices. His timidity is the result, not of ignorance, but of morbid apprehension.[37]

And the Earl of Orford, in his ultimate "General Criticism of Dr. Johnson's Writings"—had he for a moment fallen under the spell?

He destroys more enemies with the weight of his shield than with the point of his spear. . . . He excites no passions but indignation: his writings send the reader away more satiated than pleased.[38]

The logic of Johnson's style, exactly what is attacked, its settled pattern and answering of part to part, exercises a mastery and strong sway. The critic of less ponderous mind in attempting to describe the great motion, to keep time with the majestic rolling, is caught up and carried with it. He begins to rebuke Johnson in his own language. He finds himself enlisted in a mode of thinking and compelled into a method of rhetoric. Without seeing the heresy he has embraced a new ritual. He does not censure by analysis, but defines by parody. He derives his momentum from the force which he is attempting to resist, and contributes as much to sustain the school of Johnsonian style as the most earnest admirer, the most energetic defender, or the most obsequious imitator.

35. *Burrowes* p. 40; cf. pp. 27, 28, 42, 44.
The anonymous author of *Taxation, Tyranny, Addressed to Samuel Johnson, L.L.D.* (London, 1775) at the start of his political assault pays tribute to Johnson's style and in the act approaches it (pp. 1–2).
36. Quoted by W. Vaughan Reynolds, "The Reception of Johnson's Prose Style," *Review of English Studies*, xi (1935), 156–7. Cf. *Courtney* pp. 28–9. For Johnson's comparison of Dryden and Pope see *Works* iv, 107–10. Cf. Murphy's comparison of Johnson and Addison (*Misc.* i, 467–70).
37. *Howe* vi, 102, *Lectures on the English Comic Writers* (1819), Lecture v, "On the Periodical Essayists."
38. *Works of Horatio Walpole, Earl of Orford* (London, 1798), iv, 362.

iii

WHEN we pass from the circle of those who in some way immediately attach themselves to the name of Johnson, either his personal friends or enemies, or the critics of his writing, we pass into the wide field of English prose history. Here the influence of Johnson is diffused and mingled with similar forces or shaded by the various motives that were working toward romantic prose. Here, as much as in the period before Johnson, must be considered the direct effect of popular "philosophic" reading and the general prose absorption of the neoclassic couplet rhetoric. Johnson's share in the style of a given writer is very difficult to estimate. Nathan Drake named Robertson, Blair, Gibbon, Burke, Leland, Madame D'Arblay, Ferguson, Knox, Stuart, Parr, Gillies, Nares, Mackenzie, Chalmers, Roscoe, and Anderson "as having, in a greater or less degree, founded their style on that of the author of the Rambler." [39] Boswell quotes from Robertson's *History of America*, Gibbon's *Decline and Fall*, Nares's *Elements of Orthoepy*, Mackenzie's *Mirror* and Knox's *Essays* passages which suggest in varying degrees either that Johnson's writing was the model, or that the forces which had affected him were widely prevalent. [40] Robertson confessed that he had read Johnson's *Dictionary* twice over. [41] Johnson spoke once of "the verbiage of Robertson" and another time said, "Sir, if Robertson's style be faulty, he owes it to me; that is, having too many words, and those too big ones." [42] Of all the Johnsonian school Gibbon and Burke were the most elastic and sinewy. "Many experiments," Gibbon tells us, "were made before I could hit the middle tone between a dull chronicle and a rhetorical declamation." [43] Like Johnson he is not content with the chronicle, the list of facts. But he is more cautious than Johnson of the epithetical elaboration of facts, the multiplication of notions. To Burke it seemed that Robertson composed "in a dead language" which he understood but could not speak. [44] Burke was the inspiration of the youthful Hazlitt and model of his style. He had, says Hazlitt, "noth-

39. *Essays, Biographical, Critical, and Historical, Illustrative of the Rambler, Adventurer, & Idler* (London, 1809), i, 282–3.

40. *Life* iv, 388–90.

41. *Works* i, 345.

42. *Life* ii, 236; iii, 173. Boswell reports that Blair in his oral lectures had criticized Johnson's style and imitated it, changing a passage from *Spectator* No. 411, "Their very first step out of business is into vice or folly," into, "Their very first step out of the regions of business is into the perturbation of vice, or the vacuity of folly" (*Life* iii, 172).

43. *Memoirs*, ed. George B. Hill (London, 1900), pp. 189–90.

44. Margaret Forbes, *Beattie and his Friends* (Westminster, 1904), p. 81.

ing of the *set* or formal style, the measured cadence, and stately phraseology of Johnson, and most of our modern writers." [45]

From the first time I ever cast my eyes on any thing of Burke's (which was an extract from his letter to a Noble Lord . . . in 1796), I said to myself, "This is true eloquence: this is a man pouring out his mind on paper." All other style seemed to me pedantic and impertinent. Dr. Johnson's was walking on stilts; and even Junius's (who was at that time a favourite with me) with all his terseness, shrunk up into little antithetic points and well-trimmed sentences. But Burke's style was forked and playful as the lightning, crested like the serpent. He delivered plain things on a plain ground; but when he rose, there was no end of his flights and circumgyrations.[46]

One might suppose that in the field of the periodical essay the *Rambler* would cast a long shadow, but it seems doubtful that it did. Boswell was able to find in *Mirror* No. 16 a passage which has something of Johnson's regular structure (though certainly little of his diction),[47] but Mackenzie and the friends who projected the *Mirror* and the *Lounger* were men of sentiment and sensibility, who aimed on the whole at an Addisonian suavity and lightness. Mackenzie's style, says his biographer, "has the polish of Addison with the tenderness of Steele." [48] And after all he is called not the Johnson but the Addison of the North. What Mackenzie and the other periodical writers of that time seem to owe to Johnson is an occasional parallel or pointed antithesis and much more occasionally a philosophic word—and of so much they were probably conscious. The *Country Spectator* of 1793 is perhaps one of the clearest examples. In his farewell paper, after a strongly Johnsonian complaint that the papers have been "written during short intervals stolen from continued interruption, when the spirits were exhausted with fatigue or the mind sickened with disgust," the Spectator confesses:

45. *Howe* vii, 310, *Eloquence of the British Senate* (1807), "Character of Mr. Burke."

46. *Howe* xii, 228, *The Plain Speaker* (1826), Essay xx, "On Reading Old Books."

47. *Life* iv, 390. For a better example, see *Mirror* (London, 1809), i, 84, No. 14, on the thoroughly Johnsonian topic of "Indolence."

48. Harold W. Thompson, *A Scottish Man of Feeling* (London, 1931), p. 198. See the whole discussion of the *Mirror* and *Lounger* (pp. 186–213). Walter Graham, *English Literary Periodicals* (New York, 1930), p. 119, points out that the *Rambler* and later periodical essays were four- or six-page, single-column papers, whereas the periodicals of the *Tatler* and *Spectator* era consisted of a single leaf with two or three columns, but it seems to me too much to say that the *Mirror* was one of the "truest imitators of the *Rambler*," that it "followed the tone as well as the form of Johnson's work." Of *Periodical Essays,* 1780, he says the same. I have not seen this paper.

I have sometimes endeavoured to lead the Reader into abstract specu-
lation, and sometimes I have prattled about the nonsense of the day: in
some instances I have paid regard to the rotundity of periods and correctness of composition; in others I have attempted to be colloquial,
and have been negligent from design.[49]

But the chief series in the second half of the century, the *Mirror*
and *Lounger,* the *World,* the *Connoisseur,* the *Observer,* and most
of the minor ones, seem, with the exception of a paragraph here
and there (principally in papers on Johnson) to have avoided the
mighty effort of the *Rambler* and to have continued clear in the
prattling town-talk tradition of the *Spectator* and *Tatler.*[50]

To what extent Johnson deflected the course of common English
prose cannot easily be reckoned. Malone said that "Johnson had
made an aera in the english language. Every body wrote a higher
style now, even Christie in Advertisements." [51] Boswell said that
the imitation of Johnson had been so general that even the newspaper writers aspired to it, and the two examples which he offers [52]
are to the point. Hawkins said: "Some of the most popular orators
of this country now living, have not only proposed . . . [Johnson's
style] to themselves as a model for speaking, but for the purpose of
acquiring the cadence and flow of his periods, have actually gotten
whole essays from the Rambler by heart." [53] To me it seems that
among those most influenced by Johnson may have been the anti-

49. *Country Spectator* (Gainsborough, 1793), p. 264, No. xxxiii. The thirty-three
numbers ran weekly from Tuesday, 9 Oct. 1792 to Tuesday, 21 May 1793. Walter
Graham, *op. cit.,* p. 140, believes that No. xxvii, "*Wilson* and *Mary;* a tale," is "told
in the manner of Johnson." Perhaps this is so, but after all it is not in a tale that
one finds the most characteristic Johnsonian manner.

50. Mr. Curtis B. Bradford in his Yale doctoral dissertation *Samuel Johnson's
'Rambler'* (1937), pp. 217–26 reports of some twenty-eight periodical essays, including the above-mentioned, that the chief Johnsonian influence is in the occasional
discussion of similar topics.

51. *BP* xvi, 120, London, 15 Aug. 1785. At the auctioneer James Christie's
"Great Room in Pall Mall" Johnson's library had earlier in the year been sold
(*Catalogue of the Valuable Library of Books of the Late Learned Samuel Johnson*
[London, 1785], p. 1). It will be recalled that Johnson thought that in his own
day nobody wrote as poorly as Martin had in his account of the Hebrides, but
there is no indication that Johnson attributed this improvement to his own example
(*Life* iii, 243).

52. From the *Diary* of 9 Nov. 1790 and from the *Dublin Evening Post* of 16 Aug.
1791 (*Life* iv, 381, n. on p. 384).

53. *Works* i, 291. *Taylor* p. 56 quotes a passage heavy with parallel and antithesis
from Bishop Lowth's *Letter to the Right Reverend Author of the Divine Legation
of Moses,* 1765. Johnson's own sermons, "about forty . . . given or sold . . . to
different persons, who were to preach them as their own" (*Life* iv, 381, n. 1,
on p. 383), are good evidence of the favor which his style found with the clergy.
Cf. *Life* iii, 181, 506–7, App. F; *Courtney* p. 170.

It is possible that Johnson exercised some influence upon parliamentary style.
But Saintsbury is misleading when he suggests that Sydney Smith's peroration of a

quarian and philological writers. Tyrwhitt, for example, would say
of conjectural criticism: "When it assumes an air of gravity and
importance, a decisive and dictatorial tone; the acute Conjecturer
becomes an object of pity, the stupid one of contempt." [54] Or
Thomas Warton would wind up his *Enquiry into . . . Thomas
Rowley* with the strong assertion that "external arguments have
seldom served to any other purpose, than to embarrass our reasoning, to mislead the inquisitive, and to amuse the ignorant." [55]

About the turn of the century there were still some who thought
Johnson had changed English prose style. Anderson, Chalmers,
and Drake write to this effect. "The attempt to imitate him . . .
has elevated the style of every species of literary composition . . . .
He not only began a revolution in our language, but lived till it was
almost completed." [56] And in 1835 Carlyle could speak of "the
whole structure of our Johnsonian English breaking up from the
foundations." [57]

Perhaps Johnson's sway over certain classes of minor writers,
philological clergymen, for example, or juridical lecturers, continued far into the nineteenth century. Certainly the sturdy weed
of philosophic diction still flowered.[58] Among major writers, one
may mention Scott [59] in an occasional moment of grandiloquence,

speech for Mackintosh is a caricature of Johnson's style (George Saintsbury, *History
of English Prose Rhythm* [London, 1912], p. 271 and n. 1). Smith has only Mackintosh in mind, though it must be admitted the parody might be of Johnson (*Memoir
of the Reverend Sydney Smith by his Daughter Lady Holland*, ed. Mrs. Austin
[New York, 1856], i, 340–2).

54. *Observations and Conjectures Upon Some Passages of Shakespeare* (Oxford,
1766), p. 20.

55. *Enquiry into the Authenticity of the Poems Attributed to Thomas Rowley*
(London, 1782), p. 125.

56. Alexander Chalmers, *British Essayists* (London, 1817), xix, xli–xlii. Cf.
Robert Anderson, *Life of Samuel Johnson* (London, 1795), pp. 231–2; Nathan
Drake, *Essays . . . Illustrative of the Rambler, Adventurer, & Idler* (London,
1809), i, 283.

57. *Letters of Thomas Carlyle to John Stuart Mill, John Sterling and Robert
Browning*, ed. Alexander Carlyle (London, 1923), p. 192. Carlyle is talking about
vocabulary—"whole ragged battalions of Scott's-Novel Scotch . . . Irish, German,
French, and even Newspaper Cockney . . . storming in on us." Perhaps he is
thinking more of the *Dictionary* than of the *Ramblers*.

58. For a survey of philosophic diction in the nineteenth century, see Otto Jespersen, *Growth and Structure of the English Language* (New York, 1923), pp.
149–52.

59. There are some examples in the *Life of Dryden*. "His mind was amply stored
with acquired knowledge, much of it perhaps the fruits of early reading and application. But, while engaged in the hurry of composition, or overcome by the lassi-
tude of continued literary labour, he seems frequently to have trusted to the
tenacity of his memory, and so drawn upon this fund with injudicious liberality,
without being sufficiently anxious as to accuracy of quotation, or even of assertion"
(Walter Scott, *Life of John Dryden* [London, 1808], p. 532). Cf. Scott's memoir of
Johnson, *Lives of the Novelists* (Paris, 1825), ii, 79–90.

or Ruskin,[60] as disciples of Johnson.

But even by the turn of the century the vanguard writers were occupied with far different ideals. Contemporary with Chalmers' and Drake's preservative efforts comes the first of Hazlitt's indignant condemnations. And "I rather believe," ventures old Richard Cumberland, "the style of . . . [the *Ramblers*] is not now considered as a good model." [61]

iv

WE may conclude our discussion on an affirmative note by adverting to the numerous intentional imitators or parodists of Johnson. It seems safe to say that no other English writer (with the possible exception of Burton) has sustained so large a school.[62] The earliest of these, though one of the least effective, was Bonnell Thornton, of whose *Rambler* No. 99999 in the third issue of the *Drury Lane Journal* the best part is the title.[63] Others achieved at least a hilarious lavishment of philosophic diction, as in the anonymous newspaper ode to Mrs. Thrale, "Cervisial coctor's viduate dame." [64] There were genteel efforts, like the elder George Colman's "Letter from Lexiphanes; containing Proposals for a *Glossary* or *Vocabulary* of the *Vulgar Tongue*." [65] There were attempts like the *Lexiphanes* of Campbell, not only crude but im-

60. When Ruskin's father took the *Rambler* and *Idler* on foreign journeys, their "turns and returns" fastened themselves in the youth's "ears and mind." "Nor was it," he says, "possible for me, till long afterwards, to quit myself of Johnsonian symmetry and balance in sentences intended, either with swordsman's or paviour's blow, to cleave an enemy's crest, or drive down the oaken pile of a principle" (*Praeterita* [London, 1900], I, 415–16). For some examples, see *Selections from the Works of John Ruskin*, ed. C. B. Tinker (Boston, 1908), pp. 106, 142, 157. Our inquiry into the architectural merits of St. Mark's, says Ruskin, need not "be disturbed by the anxieties of antiquarianism, or arrested by the obscurities of chronology."

61. *Memoirs of Richard Cumberland, Written by Himself* (London, 1807), I, 362 (first published in 1806).

62. It may be mentioned in passing that there flourished a school of imitators and mimics of his speech—Boswell, Garrick, Henderson the actor, Davies and Allen the booksellers, Goldsmith and others (*Life* I, 391, 412 and n. 1; II, 249, 326 and n. 2 and n. 5; III, 269–70; IV, 92, 490, App. J; *Misc.* II, 195 and n. 7, 399; *Works* I, 416; *BP* III, 14; VI, 50–1; VII, 75; IX, 264; X, 157; XI, 275; C. B. Tinker, *Dr. Johnson & Fanny Burney* [New York, 1911], pp. 203, 207, 221–2, 245. Even Mrs. Thrale "had his tones, which sat very ill on her little French person" (*Memoirs of Miss Hawkins*, I, 79, quoted in *Misc.* I, 347, n. 1).

63. *Have At You All or the Drury-Lane Journal* (London, 1752), pp. 67–71, No. 3, 30 Jan. 1752.

64. *Life* IV, 387. Such must have been the magazine verses on the *Dictionary* from which Boswell quotes, "Little of Anthropopathy has he" (*Life* V, 273).

65. *Life* IV, 387, where Boswell quotes a sample. Cf. *ante* p. 133, n. 2. Boswell thought the "most perfect imitation" of Johnson was John Young's *Criticism on the Elegy Written in a Country Churchyard*, but Johnson would not even cut the leaves (*Life* IV, 392 and n. 1).

polite.[66] "I could caricature my own style much better myself," said Johnson of one which he distinguished as best among a "rude mass" of criticisms of the *Western Islands*.[67] "Bombast in them is the sublime in thee," wrote Johnson's admirer the Reverend Percival Stockdale.[68]

Another time Johnson said, "No, Sir; the imitators of my style have not hit it," but he added, "Miss Aikin has done it the best; for she has imitated the sentiment as well as the diction." [69] Miss Anna Laetitia Aikin, later Mrs. Barbauld, in her essay "On Romances, An Imitation" had indeed "imitated the sentiment" in the sense that she had set out quite seriously to develop a suitable theme, the appeal of romances, and to do so in the Johnsonian manner. The essay is an altogether humorless, flat-footed procession of Johnsonian doublets, triplets, and antitheses in an array of Johnsonian diction that includes the word "adscititious" and the phrase "frigid indifference." [70] Johnson might admit, if he liked, that she had imitated his sentiment, but certainly it was without any of his conviction.

There was another lady who undertook to imitate Johnson not in an essay but through the course of a whole book, a continuation of *Rasselas*. Miss Ellis Cornelia Knight's *Dinarbas* appeared in 1790 and enjoyed a number of editions, being printed with *Rasselas* as late as 1846.[71] "The inundation having subsided, the prince and princess, with their companions, left Cairo, and proceeded on the way to Abissinia." On the "long and tedious" journey—and through the whole tedious book—they entertained such "reflections" as that "activity is natural to man; and he who has once tasted the joys of liberty and action will . . . [not] be contented with perpetual rest and seclusion." [72] It is to be suspected that the Johnsonian school of lady imitators was more enduring than the history of published parodies can ever show. Let us deviate from this history long enough to recall one of the last of the Johnsonian ladies, who

66. For a quotation see *Life* II, 44, n. 5. Cf. Robert C. Whitford, "A Little Lyttelton," *Philological Quarterly*, III (1924), 302–8.

67. *Life* II, 363. Cf. Walter Graham, *English Literary Periodicals* (New York, 1930), pp. 141–2; *Misc.* II, 421 and n. 1 and n. 2; and the address of "Johnsonoddle" in Henry Man's *Cloacina; a Comi-Tragedy*, anon. (London, 1775), pp. iv, 12.

68. *The Remonstrance*, anon. (London, 1770), p. 17. Cf. *Life* II, 112–13.

69. *Life* III, 172 and n. 3. Cf. *BP* XIII, 40–1.

70. *Miscellaneous Pieces in Prose, By J. and A. L. Aikin* (London, 1773), pp. 40, 45. See "frigid indifference" in Johnson's *Works* X, 339, *Journey to the Western Islands*. Cf. "cold indifference," *Works* XI, 28, *Rasselas*, chap. ix; and XI, 114, *Rasselas*, chap. xxxviii; "frigid tranquillity," *Works* IX, 229, *Preface to the Dictionary*.

71. *Courtney* p. 94. Cf. *Misc.* II, 171, n. 1.

72. *Rasselas; a Tale, by Dr. Johnson. Dinarbas; a Tale: being a Continuation of Rasselas* (London, 1817), pp. 133–4, *Dinarbas*, chap. i.

lived at Cranford, but was doubtless typical of a spirit that in 1853 was lingering in many places throughout England. Miss Deborah Jenkyns was the daughter of a deceased rector of the town. "On the strength of a number of manuscript sermons, and a pretty good library of divinity, [she] considered herself literary." She despised Mr. Boz, and when *The Pickwick Papers* were read aloud at her party, she said: "Fetch me 'Rasselas,' my dear, out of the book-room." And after she had read out a counterblast, "Dr. Johnson's style," she said, "is a model for young beginners. My father recommended it to me when I began to write letters—I have formed my own style upon it." [73]

In so far as that which is parodied must be familiar, we have good evidence that for nearly thirty years after his death Johnson's style was a vivid part of the literary consciousness of educated people. In 1812 Horace and James Smith selected the "Ghost of Dr. Johnson" to deliver one of their *Rejected Addresses* for the reopening of Drury Lane Theater.[74] The next year appeared Eaton Stannard Barrett's *Heroine,* in which the burlesque of Gothic novels is diversified by the Memoirs of the poet James Higginson, one of the cleverest and most telling of all Johnsonian parodies. The circumstances of Johnson's own early life are hinted in a narrative that shows all the Johnsonian traits but particularly the short statement and inversion of oblique cases which are most noticeable in the *Lives.*

Of genius, the first spark which I elicited, was my reading a ballad in the shop, while the woman who had sold it to me was stealing a canister of snuff. This specimen of mental abstraction shewed that I would never make a good tradesman; but it also evinced, that I would make an excellent scholar. A tutor was accordingly appointed for me; and during a triennial course of study, I had passed from the insipidity of the incipient *hic, haec, hoc,* to the music of a Virgil, and to the thunder of a Demosthenes.

My first series of teeth I cut at the customary time, and the second succeeded them with sufficient punctuality. This fact I had from my mamma.[75]

The exploit remained feasible throughout the nineteenth century [76] and even in the twentieth has had revivals. Herbert Vivian

---

73. Elizabeth C. Gaskell, *Cranford,* "Everyman's Library," pp. 12–13. See one of Miss Jenkyns' letters on pp. 20–1.

74. *Rejected Addresses* (Boston, 1860), pp. 106–13.

75. *The Heroine,* ed. Michael Sadleir (London, 1927), pp. 78–81, Letter IX. Cf. *Courtney* p. 139.

76. Cf. *Courtney* pp. 93, 106; George Saintsbury, *History of English Prose Rhythm* (London, 1912), p. 271 and n. 2, a misleading statement about Susan Ferrier; cf. her *Inheritance* (Edinburgh, 1824), I, 62.

thought British politics of the years 1901 and 1902 needed the voice of "Toryism" in *Ramblers* No. 209 to 260. True, there was, particularly in the later numbers, not much Johnsonism besides a few big words and the original folio format and eighteenth-century type. But in No. 209 a letter from Johnson among the shades was a more sustained effort at Johnsonian construction and diction and included the word "adscititious." "The true Function of a Government," warns Johnson, "is to govern, not to proceed from Error to Error by persistent Subjection to the Demands of popular Vacillation." [77]

There can be little doubt that even in the present day the number of Johnsonian parodies is such that "a deeper search, or wider survey" might collect a considerable chrestomathy. Hugh Kingsmill, for example, contributes to the *English Review* for November 1931 some "Remarks by Dr. Johnson on Certain Writers of the Present Age, Collected by J-m-s B-sw-ll Esquire." "Shaw's frenzy is of the mind alone. His notions are vehement, his feelings are cool. To the characters in his plays he cannot impart what he lacks himself: they have nothing of passion, and little of life." [78] Kingsmill's parody has the excellence of being a genuine expression. He says of Shaw, Wells, Chesterton, Belloc, and Inge something appropriate and something like what Johnson would have said.

The most recent parody of Johnson to come to my notice is in the *Oxford Magazine* for 9 June 1938. The Reverend Canon Adam Fox has been elected to the Professorship of Poetry. Apropos of the event appears a considerable extract "From Johnson's *Life of Fox*." I suppose that almost every sentence of this parody has a prototype somewhere in the works of Johnson. By the election of Fox "no rival was mortified and no faction embittered."

Since the modes of error are agitated by continual change while truth remains always the same, his poetry now shines with undiminished lustre when the false wit of the *Fantasticks* is neglected by the polite,

The Reverend H. F. Cary's "Continuation of Johnson's Lives" in the *London Magazine*, 1821–24 (collected edition, *Lives of English Poets* [London, 1846]) is not very Johnsonian in style.

77. *The Restored Rambler*, I (1901), 1248. This *Rambler* ran from Saturday, 29 June 1901 to Thursday, 26 June 1902. It was in effect a small magazine, with red, and later blue, paper cover, miscellaneous contents contributed by various authors, verses, cartoons, photographs, book advertisements, quotations of press comment.

78. *English Review*, LIII (1931), 737. There is some restrained parody of Johnson's speech in G. K. Chesterton's three-act play *The Judgment of Dr. Johnson* (London, 1927). A. Edward Newton's *Doctor Johnson, a Play* (Boston, 1923) is a composite of parody and genuine Johnsonian utterance from Boswell's *Life* and Johnson's works, the genuine being in preponderance (p. xi).

condemned by the judicious, and read by the learned with frigid indifference.[79]

"Frigid indifference"! From Miss Aikin to the *Oxford Magazine,* the use of such a doleful term or of a hard word like "adscititious" is a chief reliance of the Johnsonian parodist. The last two examples from which we have quoted are certainly of a more refined sort than the parody which flourished in Johnson's own day. Yet if Johnsonian parody is capable of advancement, it is restricted too by the fact that it must conform to its model. That which is read with admiration in the pages of Johnson, may be discovered with amusement in the imitations of his immediate successors, but the further the imitation is protracted by posterity, the greater must be the danger that the effort will excite but a murmur of polite disgust or a smile of frigid indifference.

79. *Oxford Magazine,* LVI (1938), 737–8. And see the *New Statesman and Nation,* New Series, XIV (1937), 698–9, "Result of Competition No. 396," a Johnsonian conversation on intervention in Spain, by A. K. Milne; and XV (1938), 62, "Result of Competition No. 405," Johnson on Boswell's character, by Richard Pennington.

APPENDICES

Appendix A

Cf. *ante* p. 63.

A TOPIC which the reader may have expected to find discussed in Chapter IV is punctuation. It is true that punctuation is related to meaning. It may be of great importance in forestalling misinterpretation, especially if a composition, such as a play of Shakespeare, is to be read aloud or recited—"trippingly on the tongue." [1] But even in such a case punctuation is rather a help to recording than a part of meaning. Punctuation bears somewhat the same relation to meaning as does the art of printing. It cannot be said that a text of Cicero in a school edition, punctuated according to modern English convention, has acquired more meaning than a manuscript where the words run together. Nor would there seem to be in the difference between eighteenth-century and twentieth-century punctuation a difference in meaning. Punctuation is a typographical convention adopted by degrees to serve notice of the presence of syntactic forms of meaning. A difference between punctuation marks may be as much a mere typographical difference as that between a Gothic and a Roman letter. It is true that a comma and a semicolon within one convention, say that of the twentieth century, correspond to differences in meaning (though they do not consistently); yet a comma of the twentieth century may at times find its complete equivalent in a semicolon of the eighteenth century. Since the eighteenth century a shift in punctuation has taken place which has been a shift not in a whole way of thinking, but simply in the values assigned to a set of ink marks. The proof of this is that to try to assign a twentieth-century value to eighteenth-century punctuation is often to make nonsense of the writing. [2]

Professor Taylor has summarized the peculiarities of Johnson's punctuation in a passage [3] which seems to me to answer itself—that is, to pose punctuation as a problem of meaning and then implicitly to dismiss the problem.

1. Cf. J. Dover Wilson, *The Manuscript of Shakespeare's Hamlet* (Cambridge, England, 1934), II, 195–200.

2. In averaging words per sentence in Chaucer, Fabyan, Ascham, Spenser, Lyly, and Joseph Hall, Professor L. A. Sherman was forced to a like conclusion ("On Certain Facts and Principles in the Development of Form in Literature," *The University Studies of the University of Nebraska*, I [1892], 337–8).

3. *Taylor* pp. 37–8.

[Johnson] over-punctuates. The flow of his prose is arrested beyond the reckoning of man by commas, semicolons, and colons, separating into segments the smallest elements, islanding words and phrases, bringing the sweeping current of the thought headlong against unexpected formal pause-marks.

This sounds like a serious enough complaint. But Professor Taylor continues, "One learns very quickly to pay little attention to interfering semicolons . . . . Johnson is relatively consistent in his excess."

Another difficulty:

Besides over-punctuating within a sentence of normal length, he is given to the creation, markedly in his pre-Dictionary period but always to a degree, of long stringy sentences that a well-taught twelve-year-old would divide several times.

In a sentence which Professor Taylor offers as an example there are "eight main clauses which would be expressed more nearly to the heart's desire of the present age . . . in three separate sentences." Again serious, but again, fortunately, "It is perfectly clear as it stands, and is doubtless satisfactory enough to the average mortal."

In other words: Johnson's punctuation is so different from our own that if we were forced to assign to all his punctuation marks their present value, we should unhinge his writing. But the sense of the words themselves comes to our aid and shows us after a little what values to assign to the punctuation.[4]

Appendix B

Cf. *ante* pp. 18–19, 24–32.

STATISTICIANS of Johnson's style have reached somewhat different conclusions by the process of using the same words, "triplet" or "doublet," but under the protection of these counting quite different things, or

---

4. A study of the punctuation of Johnson's texts is further disqualified as a study of style by the fact that the punctuation may often represent not Johnson's but the printer's choice. In his Cornell doctoral dissertation *Johnson's Lives of the Poets* (1938) George L. Lam reports of the 1779–81 and 1783 editions of the *Lives:* "The variants in punctuation are numerous. *1783* frequently omits commas, changes commas into semicolons or semicolons into colons" (p. 176). And this cannot be taken with certainty as Johnson's own revision. A collation with the ms. of the *Life of Rowe* in the R. B. Adam Library shows that "in the use of semicolons Johnson is much more sparing than either *1779–81* or *1783*. Subordinate clauses are invariably marked off by commas instead of semicolons" (pp. 204–5). Cf. Ronald B. McKerrow, *An Introduction to Bibliography* (Oxford, 1927), p. 250; and review, *Philological Quarterly,* VII (1928), 157.

For the question of punctuation it is particularly unfortunate that Professor Taylor fails to indicate on what text of Johnson's works he has based his study.

counting in quite different places. Professor Reynolds would seem, from the examples he offers, to include in his definition of the triplet all triple multiplications except perhaps those of single words. But in sampling the *Lives* (*Savage, Milton, Pope, Dryden*) he chooses the "first thirty" paragraphs of each. Since these paragraphs are chiefly narrative, one need not wonder that he finds in all only eight triplets. From other samples of Johnson's prose his figures for triplets are nearer what one might predict: *Preface to Lobo*, 4; *Plan of a Dictionary*, 8; *Rambler* No. 5, 2; *Rambler* No. 70, 7; *Rambler* No. 141, 1; *Rambler* No. 173, 3; *Rambler* No. 208, 3; *Idler* No. 65, 3.[5]

Mr. O. F. Christie says: "Of 'triplets' I have counted in *The Rambler* 27 instances, in *The Adventurer* 2, and in *The Idler* 4."[6] In only five *Ramblers* I myself have counted 25 triplets, so that in the 203 *Ramblers* by Johnson I should expect to find about 1,015 triplets. But Mr. Christie's definition of a triplet is narrower. "The simplest 'triplets,'" he says, "consist of three sets of double nouns." This rules out all triplets of single words and all triple multiplications without implicit parallel and perhaps also all those of two elements of implicit parallel consisting of nouns with adjectives, or verbs with adverbs, or verbs with nouns. This seems quite arbitrary, in the sense that it is decided without any reference to the nature of triplets as parallels.

Professor Taylor's definitions also are somewhat different from mine; he measures elements of parallel not in words but in sets of "minor word-groups or phrases." It is plain from his examples that he includes antitheses of type I, and that he counts as parallel what I have called identical elements. He differentiates between perfect and imperfect examples, the latter having "one homologous element missing" or being "slightly ineffective rhythmically." The following example is classified as a doublet of four elements, and I presume the intended division is as I have marked it:

engaged / without design / in numberless / competitions
and mortified / without provocation / with numberless / afflictions.

In my own classification this would be a doublet of three elements, the analogous but different words only being considered parallel: i. e., "engaged," "design," "competitions": "mortified," "provocation," "afflictions." Professor Taylor's statistics are not altogether univocal with mine but may be found to suggest the same conclusions. In the first ten *Ramblers*, for example, he finds 88 doublets of two elements of implicit parallel; in the last ten, 90; in the first fifteen *Idlers*, 85; in the last sixteen, 95. In the *Lives of the Poets* he distinguishes between narrative and exposition and finds in 16,593 words of exposition 118 such doublets, but in nearly the same number of words of narrative, only 50,[7] thus offering

5. W. Vaughan Reynolds, "A Note on Johnson's Use of the Triplet," *Notes and Queries*, CLXV (1933), 23–4.
6. *Christie* p. 31.
7. *Taylor* pp. 44–7, Table VII.

support for my contention that the large tracts of narrative in the *Lives* are in great measure responsible for their average lightness.

Appendix C

Cf. *ante* p. 83, n. 42.

THE extensive revisions of the *Rambler* first studied by Alexander Chalmers in 1802 [8] go back to the fourth edition, of 1756, and the second edition, of 1752. And Mr. Curtis Bradford has shown that Johnson not only pruned excess adverbs, straightened out awkward constructions and altered his diction, but eliminated words and phrases which formed integral parts of just such constructions as we have considered peculiarly Johnsonian, doublets and triplets of various degrees of implicit parallel. He reduced triplets to doublets and doublets to single words and phrases.[9] It is possible, further, to compare these revisions with those which Johnson made for two later works. He revised *Rasselas* in 1759 for a second edition which appeared but a few months after the first. He revised the *Lives of the Poets* for the edition of 1783. A glance at Mr. Chapman's textual notes to *Rasselas* will show the revisions to be minute beside those of the *Rambler*.[10] The revisions of the *Lives*, while somewhat heavier than those of *Rasselas*, again fail by far to match those of the *Rambler*.[11] These comparisons tempt the inference that Johnson found a heavy revision of the *Rambler* necessary because it was a work of his middle period and full of his excesses, but could allow his later works, in a more restrained style, to stand more nearly as he wrote them.

And this seems sound in so far as it means that in the *Rambler* Johnson made more mistakes than he did later when by long practice he had become more assured. But it can hardly mean that the revision of the *Rambler* represents any change in Johnson's theory or practice of style. The edition of 1787, on which this study is based, follows the revised fourth edition of 1756.[12] As a test, I have collated the 1787 and 1751 folio texts of three *Ramblers*, Nos. 2, 129, and 180. I chose No. 180 because according to Mr. Bradford it "is among those *Ramblers* most thoroughly

8. *British Essayists* (London, 1817), XIX, xxvii–xxxix.

9. Curtis B. Bradford, "Johnson's Revision of *The Rambler*," *Review of English Studies*, XV (1939), 302–4, 307, n. 1, 308–9.

10. *Rasselas*, ed. R. W. Chapman (Oxford, 1927). The editions had been collated before by Professor O. F. Emerson, *Anglia*, XXII (1899), 499–509. Cf. D. Nichol Smith, "Johnson's Revisions of his Publications," in *Johnson & Boswell Revised*, by D. Nichol Smith *et al.* (Oxford, 1928), esp. p. 13.

11. George L. Lam, *Johnson's Lives of the Poets* (Cornell doctoral dissertation, 1938), pp. 75 ff. See especially p. 109, where it appears that Johnson's revisions did not affect at all the passage from the *Life of Pope* used in our analysis.

12. I have collated *Rambler* No. 77 in the 1787 edition with a critical text based on the fourth edition, in Appendix II of Curtis B. Bradford's Yale doctoral dissertation *Samuel Johnson's 'Rambler'* (1937).

revised." [13] Here, it is true, if the revisions were reversed, the effect upon a tabulation of Johnsonian elements in the 1787 edition would be quite noticeable. We should have to add one doublet of three elements of implicit parallel, two of one element, and five without implicit parallel; two triplets of two elements, and one without implicit parallel; and one antithesis of type II. Yet even in this *Rambler* we should have to subtract one doublet of two elements of implicit parallel.[14] Nos. 129 and 2, both of which I have used in my analysis of Johnson's style, are on moral subjects, the type which according to Mr. Bradford is the most heavily revised. In these the effect upon our tabulation would be far less. To the more heavily revised, No. 129, we should have to add two doublets of two elements of implicit parallel, four of one element, and three without implicit parallel. To No. 2 we should have to add only one doublet without implicit parallel.

A certain further light is thrown on the matter by Mr. Bradford's study of changes in diction. Supposing that Johnson's style had improved, one might have expected some decrease in the number of "hard" or "philosophic" words. Mr. Bradford reports, "I have collected 40 good examples of changes from hard words to simpler, and 50 of changes from simple to hard." [15] And this haphazardness of substitution is attested by the examples Mr. Bradford adduces.

An entry in Strahan's ledger shows that Johnson made the latest of these revisions before September of 1754, not two years and a half later than the last number of the *Rambler* on 14 March 1752.[16] They are the revisions not of a man whose taste and style have improved with the years but of one who has been away from his composition long enough to recognize its defects. Though numerous, the revisions are miscellaneous. Johnson corrected faults which originally he would not have made had he not been too close to his composition or too much hurried.[17] That there are not an equal number of corrections in later works means that the older Johnson was able to do more satisfactory work at first draft.

Together with revision we may briefly mention a kindred process,

13. Curtis B. Bradford, *op. cit.*, p. 20, n. 1. Alexander Chalmers prints the original text of this *Rambler* and indicates by italics the parts later revised (*British Essayists* [London, 1817], xix, xxxii–xxxviii).

14. The count is actually a more complicated matter of addition and subtraction. For example, Johnson destroys four doublets of one element of implicit parallel but creates two others, the effect in our reversal of revisions being two plus. The destruction of one form frequently creates another. "He glutted them with delicacies, he cheared them with wine, he softened them with caresses, and by degrees" in the 1751 edition, but in the 1787 (*Works* vii, 231) he merely "glutted them with delicacies, and softened them with caresses." Also Johnson creates some altogether new elements. "Moral truth" in the 1751 edition is "moral and religious truth" in the 1787 (*Works* vii, 236).

15. *Loc. cit.*, p. 312, n. 1.

16. Curtis B. Bradford, *loc. cit.*, p. 304.

17. We have good evidence that not only the *Ramblers* but the *Debates in Parliament,* the *Idlers, Rasselas,* and the *Lives* were written in haste (*Life* i, 71, n. 3, 331, 341; iv, 409; *Misc.* i, 96, *Prayers and Meditations*).

recasting. Johnson's "Life of Roscommon" which appeared in the *Gentleman's Magazine* of 1748 [18] was the matrix of the later composition included in the *Lives of the Poets*. The life of 1748 had long notes which were incorporated in the text of the later. Professor Taylor counts nineteen sentences retained from the twenty-nine of the life of 1748 and compares them with the fifty-nine additional sentences, finding a decrease in indicated and actual sentence length and in predication, and an increase in the percentage of simple sentences and in the proportion of critical expository sentences to narrative.[19] It is the last, a difference in subject matter, which accounts for a slight increase in the number of Johnsonian constructions.

The first twelve paragraphs of the later life are chiefly narrative, consisting of text and notes (many of these quotations) from the earlier, with some unimportant rearrangement. Next are inserted four paragraphs in discussion of linguistic academies, and as the subject is more general, Johnson becomes more peculiarly himself.

> In this country an academy could be expected to do but little. If an academician's place were profitable, it would be given by interest; if attendance were gratuitous, it would be rarely paid, and no man would endure the least disgust. Unanimity is impossible, and debate would separate the assembly.[20]

Then come four paragraphs of narrative taken from the earlier life, but with two changes to Johnsonism. Where Roscommon, delayed by gout, had before been merely "impatient," he becomes now "impatient either of hinderance or of pain." And where before his "distemper" was "driven up" into his bowels, now his "disease" is "repelled" into his bowels.[21] The next six paragraphs, a poetical character, partly specific, are taken without change from the early version. Then come eleven new paragraphs, all specific criticism—concerning a story borrowed from Boileau for the *Essay on Translated Verse*, concerning the "interposition of a long paragraph of blank verse," and so forth. Only in a final paragraph does Johnson once more wax general and Johnsonian.

> Of Roscommon's works, the judgement of the publick seems to be right. He is elegant, but not great; he never labours after exquisite beauties, and he seldom falls into gross faults. His versification is smooth, but rarely vigorous, and his rhymes are remarkably exact. He improved taste, if he did not enlarge knowledge, and may be numbered among the benefactors of English literature.[22]

18. *Gentleman's Magazine*, xvii (1748), 214–17.
19. *Taylor* p. 48, Table viii.
20. *Works* ii, 209.
21. *Works* ii, 210; *Gentleman's Magazine*, xvii (1748), 216.
22. *Works* ii, 215.

Appendix D

Cf. *ante* p. 93, n. 18.

JOHNSON several times uses the term "cadence" in a way that is quite indeterminate. In the oft-quoted passage of the last *Rambler* he says: "Something, perhaps, I have added to the elegance of its construction, and something to the harmony of its cadence." [23] More often he uses the term in talking of verse. "The resemblance of poetick numbers, to the subject which they mention or describe, may be considered as general or particular; as consisting in the flow and structure of a whole passage taken together, or as comprised in the sound of some emphatical and descriptive words, or in the cadence and harmony of single verses." [24] Here certainly "cadence" means nothing more determinate than it does in his *Dictionary:* "Cadence. . . . The flow of verses, or periods." [25] Another term which Johnson uses in the same way and which perhaps has the same kind of meaning is "modulation." "Then begin the arts of rhetorick and poetry, the regulation of figures, the selection of words, the modulation of periods." [26] "The next requisite is . . . if his topics be probable and persuasory, that he be able to . . . pour forth the musick of modulated periods." [27] "Modulation," says the *Dictionary:* "1. The act of forming any thing to certain proportion. . . . 2. Sound modulated; harmony; melody."

Fortunately, on one occasion when Johnson used the term "cadence" he gave a specific clue to what he meant. "In my opinion," said James (*Hermes*) Harris, "the chief excellence of our language is numerous prose." Harris doubtless intended the word "numerous" to refer to some quality of words as "music," as merely sound.[28] But Johnson made plain by his answer that the word "cadence" when applied to prose style

23. *Works* VII, 395, *Rambler* No. 208.

24. *Works* VI, 143, *Rambler* No. 94; cf. VI, 145. Cf. *Works* VI, 137, *Rambler* No. 92. In the *Life of Waller* (*Lives* I, 292, par. 140) he writes: "Repentance, trembling in the presence of the judge, is not at leisure for cadences and epithets."

25. Apparently Boswell means something else when he writes (*Life* I, 386), "It was too late in life for a Caledonian to acquire the genuine English cadence." Cf. *New English Dictionary,* "Cadence," 1, 1, 2.b, 2.c.

26. *Works* VIII, 253, *Idler* No. 63.

27. *Works* IX, 121, *Adventurer* No. 115. R. S. Crane (*Philological Quarterly*, XIII [1934], 122) suggests that a commentary on this passage might bring "into relief the importance which Johnson attached to 'harmony of cadence,' 'the musick of modulated periods.'"

28. See the *New English Dictionary,* "Numerous," 5, where the meaning given is "measured, rhythmic, harmonious, musical." This use of the term by Harris is quoted and just before it: "Men grew excessively fond of the numerous Stile, and readily sacrificed the Strength and Energy of their Discourse to the Harmony and Cadence of their Language," from John Mason's *Essay on the Power and Harmony of Prosaic Numbers* (1749), p. 4. See this essay for a detailed grammar of "numerous" prose.

meant practically and concretely for him a certain management of sense through sound. He said: "Sir William Temple was the first writer who gave cadence to English prose. Before his time they were careless of arrangement, and did not mind whether a sentence ended with an important word or an insignificant word, or with what part of speech it was concluded." [29] In short, cadence means putting emphasis at the end. On the expectation that the end of a period will say something important—because unless something important is to be said, there is no reason why the period should be continued beyond the preceding important thing—the mind (through the ear) is satisfied to find at the end of a period a word emphatic (or important) in sense and supported by an emphasis or weight of sound. This is a rule of emphasis which Johnson himself hardly ever disregards.[30]

Johnson's concrete interpretation of the word "cadence" when applied to verse as well as to prose is perhaps illustrated in a certain repeated criticism of rhymes. Of Cowley he says: "His rhymes are very often made by pronouns or particles, or the like unimportant words, which disappoint the ear and destroy the energy of the line." [31] He says something like this of Denham, Waller, and Pope.[32] One of his examples from Denham is:

> if it might have stood
> By any power, by this right hand it shou'd.

And of the Earl of Carlisle's tragedy *The Father's Revenge* he wrote: "A rigid examiner of the diction might . . . wish . . . some lines more rigorously terminated." [33]

The principle with which Johnson is concerned is clearly enunciated by a contemporary rhetorician. In his *Lectures on Rhetoric and Belles Lettres* Hugh Blair writes:

> The same holds in melody, that I observed to take place with respect to significancy; that a falling off at the end, always hurts greatly. For this reason, particles, pronouns, and little words, are as ungracious to the ear, at the conclusion, as I formerly shewed they were inconsistent with strength of expression. It is more than probable, that the sense and the sound have here a mutual influence on each other. That which hurts the ear, seems to mar the strength of the meaning; and that which really degrades the sense, in consequence of this primary effect, appears also to have a bad sound.

29. *Life* III, 257. As a matter of fact Dryden had done this before Temple and had been studious of it. In his revision of the *Essay of Dramatic Poesy* he frequently put before its object at the beginning of a clause a preposition which had been at the end. In the *Defence of the Epilogue* he noted his former fault (*Essays of John Dryden*, ed. W. P. Ker [Oxford, 1900], I, xxvii, 168). See Pope on the same subject, Joseph Spence, *Anecdotes*, ed. Samuel W. Singer (London, 1820), p. 213.
30. Cf. *ante* p. 32, n. 70; p. 37.
31. *Lives* I, 60, par. 187.
32. *Lives* I, 82, par. 40; I, 294, par. 146; III, 258, pars. 398–9.
33. *Life* IV, 247.

How disagreeable is the following sentence of an Author, speaking of the Trinity: "It is a mystery which we firmly believe the truth of, and humbly adore the depth of." And how easily could it have been mended by this transposition: "It is a mystery, the truth of which we firmly believe, and the depth of which we humbly adore." [34]

One notes that Blair is attempting to treat "melody" as separate from "significancy"—despite the plain lesson of his example and his own suspicion that "it is more than probable, that the sense and the sound have here a mutual influence on each other."

Appendix E

Cf. *ante* p. 128, n. 63.

THAT Johnson was so familiar with the *Book of Common Prayer* as to have it almost a daily part of his mind is hardly to be questioned. "When he was a child in petticoats," his mother set him a collect to commit to memory, and he had it by the time she had gone upstairs.[35] Hawkins tells us that he began translating collects into Latin in his early years and continued through life,[36] and to corroborate this testimony we have among Johnson's *Poemata* four such verse translations.[37] As an example let us see the first as Johnson knew it in the *Book of Common Prayer*.

O GOD, Whose nature and property is ever to have mercy and to forgive, receive our humble petitions; and though we be tied and bound with the chain of our sins, yet let the pitifulness of Thy great mercy loose us, for the honour of JESUS CHRIST, our Mediator and Advocate. *Amen.*[38]

Here are simply doublets of single words, but something that in his original prayers and meditations Johnson could carry further. For example:

34. *Lectures on Rhetoric and Belles Lettres* (Dublin, 1783), I, 309, Lecture xiii, "Structure of Sentences—Harmony." Cf. I, 265, 278, 285–6. Cf. Henry Home, Lord Kames, *Elements of Criticism* (New York, 1823), II, 55–6.
35. *Life* I, 40.
36. *Works* I, 543. Cf. *Works* I, 540; XI, 214, *Apophthegms*.
37. *Works* XI, 402–3.
38. *Annotated Book of Common Prayer*, ed. John H. Blunt (New York, 1889), p. 237, "A Prayer that may be said after any of the former [Prayers and Thanksgivings]." The other three which Johnson translates are the Collect for the Seventeenth Sunday after Trinity (p. 316), that for the One-and-Twentieth (p. 319), and that for the Communion (p. 371). Johnson's Latin is a free expansion of the English in which perhaps the exigencies of the verse prevent him from reproducing the doublets with any care.

Almighty God, our heavenly Father, *without whose help labour is useless, without whose light search is vain, invigorate my studies* and *direct my enquiries,* that I may, by *due diligence* and *right discernment* establish *myself* and *others* in thy holy Faith. . . .[39]

The italics are mine. There must certainly be a doubt that Johnson did not bring to the composition of his prayers more than he took from the liturgical models. But it is not altogether idle to notice that such prayers, short compositions aiming at a kind of completeness, should exhibit the formality of parallels, and that Johnson's paragraphs in the *Rambler* are, as we have said, short detached essays in themselves, each achieving in itself a considerable completeness through the emphasis of parallel and antithesis. We may add that the collect, with its frequent allusion to this life and the next life, or to the *desire* to do good and the *accomplishment,*[40] is a fertile ground for antithetic thought. We may almost hear a collect when Johnson reminds us that his "last *Idler* is published in that solemn week which the Christian world has always set apart for the examination of the conscience, the review of life, the extinction of earthly desires, and the renovation of holy purposes." [41]

39. *Misc.* I, 122, *Prayers and Meditations.* Cf. *ante* p. 36, n. 86.
40. See the Easter Collect, *Annotated Book of Common Prayer,* pp. 289–90.
41. *Works* VIII, 410, *Idler* No. 103.
In this connection might be considered also the lapidary inscription, whether in English or in Latin, a form of brief composition which often achieves a certain completeness and emphasis through parallels, usually of two or three elements and of perhaps as many as four members. For Johnson's prose epitaphs, see *Life* I, 241, n. 2; III, 82–3; IV, 54, 393, n. 2; V, 367; *Misc.* I, 236–8.

INDEX

THIS is chiefly an index to authors quoted, cited, or discussed in text and notes. Modern editors and translators have been for the most part omitted, and so also have persons appearing in connections other than literary. Eighteenth-century periodicals are entered in the main alphabet. Books are entered analytically under authors. Pages i–xvi are not indexed.